Man trying to act like God ... only Whitehead ...

p.6 (PR-6) also x, 12-13

W9-CHC-633

[ADD to end of W' paper: In W's spirit we may say: "the test is not finality but progress."

p.7 (M) is a description of facts as they really are. (PR-19)

p.9: Meaning of intuition in W!

p.10 On causality as confirmed by non-sensuous experience

p.16 The subjectivist principle!

p.94 language - & thought! p.95. (see PR-35 + 40)

p.160-161

INTERchangeability of insight & imagination!, p.161!

p.164 Relation of human to non-human experience!

p.168 W. as solitary figure!

p.170 Diff. w/ Hegel on inter-relation of things!

p.171: There is no ultimate structure or order manifest in all experience!

p.174 W's self-criticism on (m)!

(NOTE*: (IF W'S RATIONALISM IS BASED ON REJECTION OF C+D PREMISES + PRIMACY OF MATH. FORM OF DEDUCTION, THEN HE HAS LITTLE IN COMMON W/ GREAT RUN OF RATIONALISTS.)

197: Fruitful application of W's ideas!

Whitehead's Theory of Reality

by A. H. Johnson

DOVER PUBLICATIONS, INC.   NEW YORK

Copyright © 1962 by Dover Publications, Inc.

Copyright © 1952 by The University of Western Ontario.

All rights reserved under Pan American and International Copyright Conventions.

Published in the United Kingdom by Constable and Company Limited, 10 Orange Street, London W. C. 2.

This new Dover edition, first published in 1962, is an unabridged and corrected republication of the work first published by the Beacon Press in 1952, to which has been added a Preface and Supplementary Bibliography especially prepared by the author for this edition.

Copyright material has been quoted in this book by permission of The Macmillan Company (see page v).

Library of Congress Catalog Card Number: 62-6841

Manufactured in the United States of America
Dover Publications, Inc.
180 Varick Street
New York, N. Y. 10014

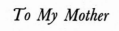

To My Mother

Acknowledgments

The Macmillan Company has kindly given permission to quote from the following books by A. N. Whitehead: *Adventures of Ideas, Modes of Thought, Process and Reality, Religion in the Making, Science and the Modern World, The Aims of Education;* and from S. Alexander's *Space, Time and Deity.* Other quotations have been acknowledged in the Notes (pages 225–54).

I am grateful to the editors of *The Journal of General Psychology* and *Philosophy of Science* for permission to use material from the following articles which appeared in these journals: "The Psychology of Alfred North Whitehead," "A. N. Whitehead's Theory of Intuition" (*The Journal of General Psychology*) ; " 'Truth, Beauty and Goodness' in the Philosophy of A. N. Whitehead," "Whitehead's Theory of Actual Entities: Defence and Criticism" (*Philosophy of Science*).

Financial support, making possible the publication of this book, was provided by two "societies" (to use a Whiteheadian term) which wish to remain anonymous. To them I am very grateful. Thanks are due Miss Mabel Hynd for her cheerful labors in preparing a well-typed manuscript. My wife has greatly aided in this project.

I wish to acknowledge my very great indebtedness to my teachers in philosophy: Professor R. B. Liddy who, at Mount Allison University, first aroused my interest in the philosophy of Alfred North Whitehead; Professors W. B. Lane and John Line of The University of Toronto, Professors Charles Hartshorne and H. N. Wieman of The University of Chicago—who aided and encouraged my continuing study of Whitehead. Above all I profoundly appreciate the immense assistance given by two men who no longer "walk the earth"—Professor Alfred North Whitehead and Dean George Sidney Brett. In the nature of things Professor Whitehead was in a position to render the greatest assistance. In weekly private tutorial sessions, in subsequent correspondence, in a last chat in the fall of 1947, he made luminous his life and philosophy.

This book is dedicated to my mother. Early in life she taught me to disregard the lure of the transitory in order to concentrate on those things which are of enduring worth.

A. H. J.

The University of Western Ontario
London, Canada

Preface to Dover Edition

The original edition of this book is now out of print. I am gratified that Dover Publications, Inc., has decided to reissue it in paperback format.

The only changes in the text are corrections of typographical errors, a few revisions in the Index, and the addition of a Supplementary Bibliography.

The extension of the Bibliography (bringing it up to date) calls attention to the fact that the discussion of Whitehead's philosophy has continued with unabated intensity. Many books and articles dealing with Whitehead's theory of "actual entities" have appeared since 1952.

I wish, on the occasion of the re-appearance of *Whitehead's Theory of Reality*, to emphasize the fact that it is designed to be an *introduction* to this phase of his philosophy. The book can be supplemented by reference to my articles dealing with specific topics, as listed in the Bibliography.

1962   A.H.J.

Preface

The preface of *Adventures of Ideas* contains the following statement: "These three books—*Science and the Modern World, Process and Reality* and *Adventures of Ideas*—are an endeavor to express a way of understanding the nature of things, and to point out how that way of understanding is illustrated by a survey of the mutations of human experience." [1]

This way of understanding the nature of things involves a stress on individuality. It also emphasizes creative interaction between individuals. It is claimed that permanence is as inescapable as change; that value is an ultimate component of the universe; that God is one of the interacting individuals. These basic principles are discussed in impressive technical detail in Whitehead's theory of actual entities. The relevance and importance of these principles in the realms of social philosophy, education, and religion are expressed in effective non-technical language. Whitehead also indicates some important applications in mathematics, physics, and astronomy.

It is the purpose of this book to provide an introductory outline and evaluation of Whitehead's theory of actual entities. In order to concentrate on this, the heart of his philosophy, applications will not be discussed in detail.

It should be noted that this philosophy is not expressed exclusively in the books mentioned above. The same general point of view is found in a more recent study, *Modes of Thought,* and in most of the essays and "papers" available in the volume entitled: *Essays in Science and Philosophy.* It is also apparent in some of his earlier books, for example:

The Aims of Education, Religion in the Making, The Function of Reason, Symbolism.

It is important to realize that *Science and the Modern World, Process and Reality,* and *Adventures of Ideas* are not equally important or effective expositions of Whitehead's theory of actual entities. Whitehead himself states that his position is developed very vaguely in *Science.* It is expounded with much more detail in *Process. Adventures* provides further clarification.

Whitehead finds it very difficult to express his philosophy in brief and succinct form. The full meaning of his basic concepts becomes apparent only after extensive examination of their use. It should be observed that frequently he provides an initial statement (in very compressed form) and later offers a more detailed exposition of the same point. Concentration on a cryptic "early" statement generates confusion.[2]

This book involves a considerable amount of quotation from the writings of Whitehead. Such a procedure seems necessary in order to justify the details of the outline and evaluation. There has been much misunderstanding of Whitehead's position. It seems advisable to focus attention on what he actually says. A vague reference to a page or a group of pages of highly technical language frequently is of little value, or—at best—involves loss of time in locating the relevant statement. In some cases it is impossible to improve on his own statement of a topic.

I have used present-tense verb forms in referring to Professor Whitehead because, despite his recent death, his life and work are still vital factors in the contemporary world. After all, the great philosophers of the distant past are treated in a similar fashion.

Since this is an introduction to Whitehead's theory of actual entities, it concentrates on the main aspects of his mature philosophy. Preliminary formulations of basic concepts are not considered in detail. A few of his more tech-

nical and specialized concepts have been omitted from this
discussion.

The literature of recent philosophy bristles with destructive criticisms of various phases of the work of Alfred North
Whitehead. Many of these are unfair and inaccurate. These
matters have been discussed in detail elsewhere.[3] In writing
this book, I have had these criticisms in mind and have tried
to meet them. However, no extensive reference has been
made to individual critics, it being deemed wiser to carry
on such exercises within the pages of technical journals.
Some objections to Whitehead's philosophy, I think, are well
founded. These are stated in Chapter 9. In general I judge
that the excellences far outweigh the deficiencies.

No man can do justice to the greatness of Alfred North
Whitehead. But, when his insights are overlooked or misunderstood, one who received his assistance cannot remain
silent.

Contents

WHITEHEAD'S THEORY OF REALITY

I

Introduction to the Theory of Actual Entities

Whitehead's Definition of Philosophy

The understanding of Whitehead's theory of actual entities is greatly facilitated by a careful examination of his discussion of the nature and function of philosophy.

He provides numerous definitions of philosophy. One of the best occurs in the course of his remarks to members of the American Philosophical Association: "Philosophy asks the simple question, What is it all about?" [1] A statement in *Adventures of Ideas* involves a more detailed exposition of his point of view:

Philosophy is not a mere collection of noble sentiments. A deluge of such sentiments does more harm than good. . . . It is not—or, at least, should not be—a ferocious debate between irritable professors. It is a survey of possibilities and their comparison with actualities. In philosophy, the fact, the theory, the alternatives, and the ideal, are weighed together. Its gifts are insight and foresight, and a sense of the worth of life, in short, that sense of importance which nerves all civilized effort. Mankind can flourish in the lower stages of life with merely barbaric flashes of thought. But when civilization culminates, the absence of a co-ordinating philosophy of life, spread throughout the community, spells decadence, boredom, and the slackening of effort. [2]

It is to be noted that several very important points are emphasized in this outline of the characteristics of an adequate philosophy: (a) Philosophy should not be regarded as an outpouring of platitudes or a ridiculous scuffle in some technical "back yard." (b) Philosophy should be characterized by a serious facing of facts, possibilities, and ideals. (c) Philosophy should have practical value. It should make possible effective activity in every field of endeavor and, in particular, aid in the achievement of the highest possible levels of living.

In Whitehead's opinion, a serious facing of the total situation obviously involves the refusal to accept, as final and absolute truth, any specialized system of thought which limits itself to a restricted group of data. Thus philosophy is a critic of abstractions. This implies that philosophy attempts to harmonize or synthesize the work of scientists in the various special fields,[3] and supplements the work of the sciences by calling attention to data which have been disregarded. In short, Whitehead is emphasizing the conviction that "philosophy is not one among the sciences with its own little scheme of abstractions which it works away at perfecting and improving." [4]

The philosopher should be engaged in a critical examination of the ideas used in current thought. The meaning of these ideas must be determined with the highest possible degree of accuracy. Further there must be a continuous constructive skepticism as to their ultimate validity.[5]

Whitehead's contention that philosophy has practical value, (a) as a guide to activity in various fields and (b) as the basis of civilized living in general, must be given serious consideration. Is it not true that general ideas of philosophical import function as working hypotheses making possible unification and fruitful direction of effort? For example, a physicist carrying out a specific experiment is implicitly assuming a definite type of cosmological theory. Further, a philosopher, having surveyed the work of various scientists, may note gaps in the structure of human knowledge and then indicate, to those competent to carry it out, the area in which new research should be attempted. However, Whitehead is careful to emphasize that a philosopher should not attempt to dictate what a scientist's results should be, nor replace the scientist as an investigator in his own highly specialized field.[6]

It is interesting to discover that many psychologists regard an adequate philosophy of life as one basic condition for satisfactory living. In this connection it is to be remembered that a philosophy is necessary not merely to guide and unify the diverse activities which are involved in living; it also calls attention to the ideal possibilities which must be realized if a genuine civilization is to be achieved and maintained.[7]

It will be obvious that, in Whitehead's opinion, the old charge that "philosophy bakes no bread" is a base canard. True philosophy, as has been shown in the preceding discussion, is inescapably mated with action. He contends that philosophy can be purified from any taint of ineffectiveness by close associations with religion and with science, natural and social.[8] In general Whitehead is profoundly convinced that ideas—philosophical ideas—are essential factors in shaping our patterns of life.[9]

Whitehead's Purpose

Whitehead's theory of actual entities is a serious attempt to develop a system of thought which will manifest the characteristics which he believes should be found in an adequate philosophy. Thus he proposes

to construct a system of ideas which bring the aesthetic, moral, and religious interests into relation with those concepts of the world which have their origin in natural science. . . . [It] is the endeavour to frame a coherent, logical, necessary system of general ideas in terms of which every element of our experience can be interpreted.[10]

A system of general ideas is *coherent* if its components pre-suppose each other.[11] It is *logical* if it is characterized by logical consistency and a proper regard for the principles of definition and inference. In so far as Whitehead's philosophy is concerned with coherence and logical adequacy, it has a *rational* aspect. But, as he points out, it is also unmistakably *empirical*. The system of general ideas must be able to *interpret* every element in our experience. In other words, it should be applicable to our experience—not merely to some but to all factors in our experience. Such a scheme will be *adequate* and *necessary*.[12]

This then is the comprehensive project which Whitehead undertakes. He does not claim to be completely successful. "Philosophers can never hope finally to formulate these metaphysical first principles." Thus there is no place in Whitehead's philosophy for absolute certainty or the irritability which issues in dogmatism. He remarks, with characteristic wit, that "the besetting sin of philosophers is that, being merely men, they endeavour to survey the universe from the standpoint of gods." [13] The same conviction is expressed with candor and vigor at the beginning of *Process and Reality*.[14]

Whitehead's admirable humility is sometimes expressed in rather extreme form, thereby clouding his real meaning. True, we are finite creatures. A complete understanding of the universe involves an awareness of all its details. This obviously is denied us. However, Whitehead is of the opinion that it is sheer dogmatism to claim that finite facts intrinsically lie beyond the reach of human knowledge.[15]

In view of the limited powers of human understanding, Whitehead suggests that we must expect to find many rival philosophical schemes. Each may possess a partial adequacy because of its emphasis on some phase of the total data. Each will suffer from inadequacies because of its omissions. The only proper procedure in dealing with conflicting systems is to carry on further research in an effort to conciliate the differences. If this approach is taken seriously, one of the main criticisms of philosophy "falls flat." Critics point to conflicting systems and to systems abandoned by the way; this, they say, discredits philosophy. No, replies Whitehead; it is a sign of healthy and normal growth, even as it is in science.[16]

The essential details of Whitehead's philosophical system, and some of its more general practical implications, will be considered in subsequent sections of this book. First, however, it is necessary to examine the method which he uses, a method which involves a *fusion of empiricism and rationalism*.

Method

Whitehead suggests that one should begin by examining a relatively restricted group of data—for example, the field of physics, or psychology, or aesthetics. On such a particular basis a general conceptual scheme should be constructed which, it is hoped, will apply to all phases of experience. He expresses this general point of view in terms of an analogy. He contends that the proper method of discovery of first principles is like the flight of an airplane. The field from which the plane takes off is *particular observation*. It soars into the upper air of *imaginative generalization*. It returns to the ground of *particular observation*.[17] But, to continue the analogy, a successful flight involves landing on a field other than the base from which the plane started. To express the point more literally, the speculative scheme must be tested by reference to data other than those from which it was initially derived. Whitehead's method thus involves a *generalized description* of observed facts.[18] This point must be emphasized. In Whitehead's opinion, metaphysics does not set up a procrustean bed into which experience must be forced even at the expense of drastic surgery; rather, metaphysics is simply a description of the facts as they really are.[19]

This reliance on *both* empiricism and rationalism is care-

fully stressed by Whitehead. He contends that "the elucida-
tion of immediate experience is the sole justification for any
thought." [20] The term "experience" does not seem to have
any special, technical meaning. The types of experience on
which he bases his theory of actual entities will be carefully
noted in subsequent discussion. This will serve to clarify the
meaning which he assigns to this term. However, it should
be realized that, while for the most part he refers to the experience of ordinary individuals, also on occasion he makes use
of the experience of small minorities.[21]

This empiricism, as has been indicated, is balanced by an
emphasis on the importance of the guidance provided by
thought systems during the search for facts. Further, the
rational phase of the method provides for the organization of
the facts so that their meaning may be grasped. Thus Whitehead is a rationalist in the sense that he recognizes the usefulness of reason in dealing with ultimate problems. He has
faith that at the "base of things we shall not find mere arbitrary mystery." [22] That is to say, he is stimulated by the
hope that it will be possible to formulate a conceptual scheme
such that everything will be a specific instance of this general
theory. It is obvious that Whitehead's rationalism is not a
self-satisfied "experience-snubbing" pose. It is an experimental adventure, inescapably linked with the facts of concrete experience. He has not the slightest respect for the type
of rationalism which starts with premises which are reputed
to be clear, distinct, and certain—and then proceeds to de-
duce a complete system of thought.[23]

In view of Whitehead's early concentration on *mathematics*, it is very interesting to observe his comments concerning the method of mathematics and its relations to philosophic method. He contends that these methods should not
be regarded as identical. The primary method of mathematics
is deduction, that of philosophy descriptive generalization.
One of the greatest disasters which has befallen much of tra-

ditional philosophy is excessive devotion to deduction. Philosophers have felt obliged to discover absolutely certain first principles from which a dogmatically inflexible system of thought should be derived. As a result philosophy has degenerated into an instrument of intellectual repression. This is not to deny that deduction has a place in philosophic thought. Its proper function is to assist in the process of verifying generalities.[24]

Whitehead assigns an important function to *insight* or *intuition*. The data used by creative imagination, and the facts by reference to which it is tested, are apprehended by intuition. Several statements make this unmistakably clear. "All knowledge is derived from, and verified by, direct intuitive observation." In justifying his categorial scheme, as outlined in *Process and Reality,* he is even more specific: "The sole appeal is to intuition." [25]

It is well known that Whitehead does not always imply familiar meanings when he uses terms current in philosophic discourse. It is, therefore, necessary to discover as accurately as possible what he means when he uses the term *intuition*. This is a somewhat difficult task, since he does not include it in the list of his carefully defined Categories. By *intuition* Whitehead seems to mean direct and immediate experience of fundamental data, the data necessary for an adequate understanding of the situation. Thus he refers to "the complete concreteness of our intuitive experience" and the lack of "analytic divorce from the total environment." He also stresses the directness of intuition.[26] However, intuition is *not* an awareness of *all* the facts in the universe.

A careful examination of the "samples" of intuition which he provides greatly facilitates one's understanding of this key concept. One type of intuition is so-called non-sensuous perception. In order to make clear the nature of non-sensuous perception, Whitehead first indicates what he considers to be the characteristics of ordinary sense perception. In sense perception we experience data as here, now, immediate, and discrete. These data imply no necessary connection with each other. They are dumb as to their origin or future function. In addition to these, we experience the far more significant data revealed in non-sensuous perception. For example, there is the experience of one's own immediate past. A person who has been angry for several minutes will note that at the present moment his feeling of anger is literally welling up out of the past and swelling on to the future. According to Whitehead, this sort of experience is disregarded in ordinary sense perception. Hence it is necessary to use what he calls *non-sensuous perception,* or, to employ another term, *intuition.*[27] Whitehead points out that since there are many types of data there are, therefore, many types of intuition. There is, for example, *religious intuition,* the perception that our existence is more than a mere succession of bare facts. There is a rightness in things. What is worth while endures.[28] *Moral intuitions* also occur.[29] For example, the notion that "speculative understanding for its own sake is one of the ultimate elements in the good life," is grasped by intuition.[30] According to Whitehead many venerable problems are solved, or shown to be pseudo-problems, by the use of intuition. Can one have experience of one's self? Is the mind influenced by the body? Can one have direct experience of the world of external nature? In Whitehead's opinion the answer to all these questions is "Yes." Further, the widely accepted Humian discussion of causation is relegated to the museum of lost causes. This follows because in our non-sensuous experience of the past we experience the fact of causation.[31] Whitehead contends that one cannot understand adequately the process of social history unless the method of intuition is employed. Consider the early days of the presidency of Franklin D. Roosevelt. A person who approached this situation on the basis of ordinary sense experience and scientific theory would discuss these events in terms of complex patterns of sense data and the rapid movement of atoms. However, this is a completely inadequate description of a vast process of social change.[32]

Whitehead's discussion of intuition indicates that he is *not* a blind, uncritical devotee of this method. He observes that some intuitions, particularly moral intuitions, are not experienced by many people.[33] He stresses the fact that our intuitions are not always clear.[34] He is careful to indicate that what he calls *intuitions* are not to be regarded as merely private psychological experiences. These intuitions may first occur under exceptional circumstances, but their data must be shown to have objective status independent of the exceptional experience of one person.[35]

Sources of Whitehead's Philosophy

In *Science and the Modern World,* Whitehead states that he formulated the outlines (but only the *outlines*) of his theory of actual entities as the result of his studies in mathematics and physics. However, he points out that it is equally possible to reach the same general conclusions if you start from the fundamental notions of psychology and physiology.[36] Thus there seem to be two chief types of data used by Whitehead in constructing his speculative philosophy: (a) the data of natural science (physics and physiology) and mathematics and (b) the data of psychology and other social sciences.

Before proceeding to examine Whitehead's uses of these data, it is essential to remember that we are not dealing with a disembodied observer of facts in abstraction from the total environment. Whitehead's theory of actual entities is the product of a lifetime of rich and vivid experience. In his youth he watched his father, and other clergymen, exerting a pervasive influence on the life of the entire community. Historic remains reminded him of the past and its continuing efficacy in the present. Values, chiefly aesthetic, early occupied his attention. He developed a strong interest in literature. His advanced studies and his early professional career at Cambridge involved a concentration on mathematics and physics. But this keen mind refused to be confined within these narrow limits. He maintained and developed his boyhood interest in literature, history, religion, politics, and art. As an administrator at the University of London, he continued to expand his intellectual horizon, and increasingly interfused theory and practice. At Harvard he exerted a profound influence through the medium of teaching and personal contacts.[37] Whitehead's theory of actual entities stresses change, permanence, the interaction of creative individuals, God, and value. These emphases were not derived *only* from his work in physics, mathematics, and the technical observation of physiological and "psychological" data. The relevance of these principles is inescapably obvious in the details of Whitehead's career. His keenly reflective mind has not failed to note the fact.

An examination of Whitehead's writings in the era before the publication of *Science and the Modern World* serves to indicate the sort of mathematical and physical data which influenced his later theorizing. His first attempts to formulate a philosophy of science are also very significant, in particular because they involve his early studies in epistemology. Further, his characteristic blend of empiricism and rationalism obviously is being developed. However, a detailed examination of these early discussions is not relevant at this point.[38] We are now concerned with his mature philosophical position, the theory of actual entities. This is also unnecessary because scattered through Whitehead's *later* books one finds statements which constitute an effective summary of the more important of those recent developments in natural science and mathematics which he considers of supreme importance. It might be well to remind ourselves of these points before proceeding to examine the *psychological data* which he also (and chiefly) uses in formulating his theory of actual entities.

In modern physical science, independently existing bits of
matter (enduring substances sustaining persistent qualities)
are no longer taken seriously. Energy is now recognized as
basic. Energy is not localized but pervades space and time.
This means that it is impossible to refer, validly, to "self-
contained" existence. Further, this flux of events is such that
there is an organic interrelation of entities which involves
the entire environment. The environment interpenetrates
every center of energy. There are, however, definite patterns
manifest in the flux of events. In understanding the events
of nature, quantities of energy must, of course, be considered. But, the factor of pattern is no less fundamental.[39]

Surveying four centuries of physical science, Whitehead
observes a change from emphasis on space and matter to an
emphasis on patterned process.[40] Yet he is very careful to
point out that the modern emphasis on continuity and
process should not blind one to the fact that the concept
of distinguishable individuality (in this sense, atomicity)
still has a respected place in scientific thought. Thus he
argues that an adequate cosmology must involve both continuity and atomicity.[41] Yet, to repeat, it is not the old-
fashioned atomicity. In modern physics a thing is not confined to one locus. Its influence streams away into the outmost
recesses of the universe.[42] In commenting on the implications
of the quantum theory, Whitehead suggests that if a vibratory theory of existence is taken seriously the field is open
for the introduction of a new philosophy of organism. It will
follow that each primordial element in the universe should
be regarded as an organized system of vibratory streaming
energy. Any "element" requires a temporal duration to become the organization of vibrations which constitute it. It *is*
this system of vibrations. There is no mysterious underlying
sub-stratum.[43]

In discussing the intellectual environment of the nineteenth century, Whitehead emphasizes the importance of the

theory of the "cell," and in general, the concept of *organism*.[44] He observes with approval that recent work in physiology, and in particular biochemistry, lends further credence to the organic approach to nature. Both "disciplines" stress the essential interrelation of part to whole and of entity to environment. For instance, one implication of physiology is the inescapable relationship of mind to the rest of nature.[45]

However, it must be recognized clearly that in formulating his philosophy of organism, Whitehead does not rely exclusively, or even chiefly, on the data of mathematics and of the natural sciences (physics and biology). He states: "The point before us is that this scientific field of thought is now, in the twentieth century, too narrow for the concrete facts which are before it for analysis. This is true even in physics." [46] An analysis more concrete and comprehensive than that of natural science must then be provided. It must be based on psychological data. "If you start from the immediate facts of our psychological experience, as surely an empiricist should begin, you are at once led to the organic conception of nature." [47] He also refers to "the direct inspection of the nature of things as disclosed in our own immediate present experience." [48] As Whitehead aptly points out, it is easier to study a human individual than an individual molecule or electron.[49] It is to be noted that an examination of psychological data reveals the same basic information provided by physics. Also *additional information* is derived from the more concrete data of psychology. These facts will become increasingly evident in the course of this book. Thus the point must be emphasized that the concepts used in the *full development* of Whitehead's theory of actual entities are psychological concepts. This is not to deny that the basic general ideas in Whitehead's theory of reality were developed at a time when he was working in the fields of mathematics and physics. However, the inescapable fact remains that when Whitehead comes to express, as fully as possible, the meaning of these general ideas he employs the data and the language of psychology almost exclusively. The term "psychology" is used, in a very broad sense, to refer not only to perceptions, feelings, volitions and thoughts, but also to value and religious experiences. This point will become increasingly obvious as one examines the complex details of Whitehead's theory of actual entities.

Speaking technically, Whitehead stresses the fact that he is an advocate of the "subjectivist principle" in philosophy. "The subjectivist principle is that the whole universe consists of elements disclosed in the analysis of the experiences of subjects. . . . It follows that the philosophy of organism entirely accepts the subjectivist basis of modern philosophy." [50] Whitehead emphasizes his concentration on what he calls *aesthetic experience* rather than on cognitive experience. The terms *cognitive* and *aesthetic* have rather specialized meaning for Whitehead. This matter will be discussed in the context of his technical treatment of the process by which actual entities come into existence.[51]

2

The Analysis of Actual Entities

Whitehead contends that actual entities [1] "are the final real things of which the world is made up." [2] These actual entities are infinite in number. [3]

A non-technical paragraph in *Modes of Thought* provides one of the most effective introductions to the theory of actual entities. It is an analysis of what is involved in human experience. For example, during the course of a day a person meets other persons and comes in contact with things. He reacts to them in an "affective" fashion. In a real sense these persons and things contribute something to the individual who experiences them. However, what he obtains from his environment depends on his purpose in life. Whitehead's analysis states:

I find myself as essentially a unity of emotions, enjoyments, hopes, fears, regrets, valuations of alternatives, decisions—all of them subjective reactions to the environment as active in my nature. . . . The individual enjoyment is what I am in my role of a natural activity, as I shape the activities of the environment into a new creation, which is myself at this moment; and yet, as being myself, it is a continuation of the antecedent world. If we stress the role of the environment, this process is causation. If we stress the role of my immediate pattern of active enjoyment, this process is self-creation. If we stress the role of the conceptual anticipation of the future whose existence is a necessity in the nature of the present, this process is the teleological aim at some ideal in the future. [4]

A careful examination of the preceding quotation will indicate that Whitehead is making the following claims concerning the nature of a subject: (a) The content of a subject's experience is chiefly, though not exclusively, *affective;* (b) it is a *unity* of its component parts; (c) a subject has its environment active in its nature; (d) it becomes what it is as the result of its *subjective* reactions to the data provided by its environment; (e) a subject selects data from its environment in accordance with a conceived ideal.

According to Whitehead, the characteristics noted in the foregoing analysis are present in *all* actual entities. When he uses the technical term *actual entity,*[5] he is referring to the sort of entity which is ordinarily called a *subject* or *self* (or, more accurately, the momentary experience of a subject or self) . As a matter of fact, both terms, *subject* and *actual entity,* are used as synonyms.[6] Whitehead employs other technical terms to replace those commonly used. It must be emphasized that the following sketch of the meaning of Whitehead's basic terms suffers from extreme generality and brevity. An adequate exposition involves a far more detailed discussion. This is attempted in subsequent sections. However, this initial statement seems necessary in order to provide the general basis for the later discussion.

The process by which an actual entity reacts to its environment is called *prehension.*[7] If the actual entity prehends a "general" idea, or ideal, this is called *conceptual prehension.* Conceptual prehensions constitute the *mental pole* of an actual entity. If an actual entity is reacting to another particular concrete actual entity, this is called *physical prehension.* Physical prehensions constitute the *physical pole* of an actual entity.[8] The term *data* is applied to the contents or materials which are prehended.[9] These data are also called *potentialities.*[10] The term *feeling* is used as a synonym for *positive* prehension (i.e., process of inclusion of data) , either physical or conceptual. Some of the data experienced are also called feelings (for example, particular patches of color, sounds, odors) .[11] An actual entity builds itself up by its prehensions of data. This general process of grasping data into the life of a newly arising actual entity is called *concrescence*.[12] Rejection of data is termed *negative* prehension.[13] When the process has been completed, Whitehead speaks of the attainment of *satisfaction*.[14] The attitude which is taken toward a prehended datum is labeled *subjective form*.[15] This is also called a feeling.[16] The term subjective form is also applied to the entire inner life of an actual entity.[17] As has been noted, an actual entity, in its process of development, is guided by an ideal or "abstract" pattern. These "ideals," regarded as general possibilities, are called *eternal objects*.[18] This teleological aspect of the behavior of an actual entity is termed *subjective aim*.[19] Thus, Whitehead's impressive list of technical verbiage is simply a group of terms which apply to various phases of ordinary human experience. He believes these terms are more adequate than those usually employed. In order to understand Whitehead's discussion of an actual entity, the meaning of these basic technical concepts must be kept clearly in mind. In addition it should be realized that he uses the terms *entity* and *object* with a wider meaning than that involved in the preceding exposition. The term *entity* applies not only to actual entities but also to prehensions, *nexūs* (groups of actual entities), subjective forms, eternal objects, and propositions. These, with the addition of *generic contrasts* [20] (contrasts are syntheses of entities in one prehension), are termed *proper entities*.[21] The term *object* is applied not only to eternal objects but also to propositions, objectified actual entities (i.e., actual entities available for prehension) and nexūs.[22] Thus, to repeat, it must be remembered that when Whitehead uses the term *object* he does not necessarily mean eternal object. When he uses the term *entity* he does not necessarily mean actual entity. It might also be noted that the term *multiplicity* has a technical usage. A multiplicity is a group of entities. Its bond of unity is the fact that each entity possesses at least one common characteristic which no entity outside the group possesses.[23] For example, the group of all eternal objects constitutes a multiplicity. They all manifest "eternal objectiveness." No other entity does.

Let us now consider, in detail, these basic concepts.

Eternal Objects

Eternal objects [24] are synonymously designated "pure potentials for the specific determination of fact," or "forms of definiteness." [25] In an attempt to clarify his meaning Whitehead states: "Any entity whose conceptual recognition does not involve a necessary reference to any definite actual entities of the temporal world is called an 'eternal object.' " [26] In other words, the type of entity, apprehended by reason, which in the past has been called a *universal* or a *Platonic Idea* or an *abstract idea* is given a new label by Whitehead—*eternal object*. The term *form* is also used.[27]

According to Whitehead, eternal objects are either simple or complex. Typical simple eternal objects are those designated by the words whiteness, hardness, sweetness, man, army, drunkenness.[28] A definite finite relationship involving a specific group of eternal objects is itself a *complex eternal object*. It may also be called an *abstract essence*.[29] For example, the components of a complex eternal object might be the simple eternal objects *redness, whiteness,* and *blueness* arranged with the spatio-temporal relatedness to each other of the faces of a regular tetrahedron anywhere at any time. Some complex eternal objects involve a tremendous degree of complexity. A series of eternal objects regarded as successive steps in the direction of increasing complexity is called an *abstractive hierarchy*.[30] Whitehead contends that there are no new eternal objects.[31] He apparently considers them to be infinite in number.[32]

In his discussion of eternal objects Whitehead distinguishes *relational essence* from *individual essence*.[33] Each eternal object is uniquely different from every other eternal object in the sense that it can be distinguished. Good is not Bad. Threeness is not fourness. Thus eternal objects have an individual essence. However, eternal objects also have a relational essence. That is, any eternal object has reference (a) to other eternal objects and also (b) to actuality, though no *necessary* reference to any particular actuality. The relationship of an eternal object to other eternal objects is said to be *internal*. In other words, each eternal object is involved in a general systematic complex of mutual relatedness.[34] Eternal objects are said to be *externally* related to actual entities because a particular eternal object is not necessarily related to a particular actual entity. This does not mean that eternal objects are isolated from actual entities. Whitehead is simply referring, for example, to the obvious fact that the general notion of *redness* is not necessarily involved in any particular chair. Because of their presence in God's primordial nature (see later discussion), eternal objects have a locus in actuality and there is a continuous tendency toward their realization in *some* actual entity (or entities). Thus he states that in the essence of any eternal object there is a *patience* for relationship to actual entities. Yet any eternal object is indeterminate as to particular ingression.[35]

It is to be noted that, in Whitehead's opinion, actual entities and eternal objects are *the* fundamental types of entities. All "other types of entities only express how all entities of the two fundamental types are in community with each other, in the actual world." [36]

Prehensions (General Outline)

"The theory of 'prehensions' embodies a protest against the 'bifurcation' of nature." [37] Actual entities are analyzable into component prehensions, physical and conceptual.[38] This type of analysis is termed *division*.[39] "Every prehension consists of three factors: (a) the 'subject' which is prehending, namely, the actual entity in which that prehension is a concrete element; (b) the 'datum' which is prehended; (c) the 'subjective form' which is *how* that subject prehends that datum." [40]

A *positive prehension* is one in which data are genuinely included in the real internal constitution of a new actual entity. In this process of concrescence the derived data are literally absorbed into the complex life of the new entity. They are essential components. They are no longer external facts to which the entity responds. They are part of its ultimate privacy.[41] For example, when a student (a subject) comes across a theory (datum) which appeals to him as a profound truth, he pounces on it with delight (subjective form) and henceforth it is part of his very being.

A positive prehension may be analyzed into two phases: (a) (i) Concrete specific data from other actual entities are made available by them. This process is called *objectification*. It is also called *expression*.[42] (ii) Eternal objects (abstract in the sense of "general" data) are also available. This process is called *ingression*.[43] These data, concrete and abstract, are termed *initial data*. (b) As the result of a selective process, which involves *elimination, some* of these data are included in the real internal constitution of the prehending actual entity. This process is termed *feeling*.[44] These data are called *objective data*.[45]

A *negative prehension* is one in which data are considered, but then are rejected. That is to say, concrete data or eternal objects are recognized as available data (objectification or ingression occurs) but they are not considered to be suitable and are, therefore, rejected. Thus, feeling does not occur. In this sense negative prehension involves elimination; or, speaking more technically, the data of negative prehensions are held as *inoperative*. This actual process of "blotting out" is also termed *anaesthesis*.[46] Whitehead emphasizes the importance of considering negative prehension with great care. He is concerned to show how necessary it is to realize the significance of avoiding certain facts. For example, the North American continent is what it is today because it was *not* dominated by Spain.[47] Whitehead argues that a negative prehension makes a real contribution to a newly arising actual entity even though the initial data are rejected. The subjective form of the negative prehension becomes part of the new actual entity. In this sense a negative prehension is said to constitute a bond of relationship.[48] For instance, when one stops just in time and avoids a conversational "boner," the feeling of "unsuitability" which was influential in this rejection is a real part of one's experience at the moment. It will be obvious from the preceding discussion of positive prehension, that negative prehension is included within the complex process of positive prehension, in the sense that the transition from initial to objective data is characterized by elimination.

Conceptual Prehension

The process by which an eternal object functions in the growth of a newly arising actual entity is very complex. First of all there is *conceptual prehension*. That is to say, an actual entity apprehends [49] the eternal object (ingression occurs) as a pattern which may be exemplified in the experience of the actual entity. If the pattern is retained as a usable form of definiteness it is, therefore, positively prehended. That is to say, feeling takes place. A conceptual prehension has occurred. It is to be understood that conceptual prehension is not merely the inclusion of the eternal object in the life of a new actual entity. There is always the factor of subjective form or attitude with which the actual entity reacts to the presence of the eternal object. That is to say, a possibility is apprehended with hope or fear, joy or sorrow. Whitehead contends that careful observation will reveal such an emotional factor even in the "calmest moments." [50] In emphasizing this point, conceptual prehensions are also termed appetitions. An appetition is defined as an urge to achieve something which is not, but may be. [51]

The process by which an eternal object is embodied in the life of a new actual entity more completely than by conceptual prehension is called *exemplification* or *illustration* or *realization* or *participation*. [52] This distinction between *exemplification* and *conceptual prehension* is a very important one. It is the difference between the apprehension of the general notion (eternal object) "anger" and the concrete manifestation of this notion as a specific angry feeling. This realization occurs because some actual entity has conceptually prehended the eternal object anger and then decided to exemplify it in its experience.

The preceding discussion provides the basis for the solution of the apparent problem which arises when we find Whitehead stating that *sensa* constitute the lowest category of eternal objects. [53] There are also references to the sensuous apprehension of eternal objects. This seems completely contrary to the previously stated contention that eternal objects are apprehended by "reason" and not by the "senses." This difficulty can be cleared up by noting that Whitehead apparently has been careless in his use of language. What he really means to say is this: The eternal object, as such, is conceptually prehended. A particular exemplification of this eternal object is sensuously apprehended. Thus, instead of referring to the sensuous apprehension of an eternal object, Whitehead should refer, more accurately, to the sensuous apprehension of an exemplification of an eternal object. For example, we rationally apprehend (conceptual prehension) *triplicity*. We sensuously apprehend three specific mice. We rationally apprehend *greenness;* we sensuously apprehend, not the eternal object *greenness,* but its exemplification—the patch of green present before our eyes as a visual sensum. It must be admitted that this point is not very clearly expressed by Whitehead in his publications. However, a careful perusal of his writings will indicate that this is what he means.[54] This point is involved in his discussion of the "dual existence" of eternal objects: (a) in *potential* appetition, (b) in realized fact.[55]

There is, unfortunately, considerable variation in Whitehead's use of the terms *ingression* and *feeling*. It has been observed that in one usage of the term ingression he means that eternal objects are *available* for possible feeling and that feeling means that eternal objects are *included* in the actual entities concerned (i.e., conceptually prehended).[56] However, Whitehead also provides an analysis of ingression which suggests that it involves feeling. An even more divergent analysis also seems to use the wider meaning of ingression, including both availability and feeling, and *in addition* realization or exemplification.[57] Reference is made to three modes of *ingression* of an eternal object into an actual entity: (a) It can be an element in (i.e., exemplified in) the datum of a positive physical prehension. (b) It can be an element in (i.e., exemplified in) the subjective form of some prehension. (c) It can be an element in the datum of some conceptual prehension. Whitehead suggests that this third type of ingression is a restricted ingression, yet that it is a real ingression. The matter is further complicated by Whitehead's remark that in the first two cases unrestricted realization of the eternal object has been achieved. It is thus implied that conceptual prehension—case (c)—is an instance of realization, albeit a restricted realization. Here, obviously, Whitehead is abandoning the usual meaning of realization. That is to say, conceptual prehension is not ordinarily called *realization*.[58] A further confusion is involved in Whitehead's suggestion that an eternal object may ingress as relevant or irrelevant. In other words, the eternal object may be positively or negatively prehended.[59] How the term *ingression* in the wide usage noted above can be applied to negative prehension is difficult to understand.

Whitehead contends that all conceptual prehensions are derived from physical feelings.[60] Physical feelings occur. There is, then, a so-called conceptual registration; that is, there develops a conceptual feeling which has as its datum the eternal object which was exemplified in the actual entity which was physically felt.[61] For example, anger coming from a previous actual entity is absorbed by a newly arising actual entity. (Both, of course, are members of a series of actual entities which constitute a self, in the non-technical sense of the term.[62]) The newly arising actual entity notes that the eternal object *anger* is exemplified in the concrete state of anger, as felt. Thus there is a conceptual prehension of the eternal object *anger* which has been derived from the physical prehension of the concrete anger state. There are also conceptual feelings which do not merely provide a conceptual registration of physical feelings. These latter conceptual feelings have data which are both partially identical with and also partially divergent from the eternal objects exemplified in the basic physical feeling.[63] (How this occurs will be discussed at a later point.)

Whitehead states that in conceptual prehension there is no *necessary* change from initial to objective data.[64]

The realm of eternal objects has a diversity of relevance to any actual entity.[65] The meaning of this statement is clarified by reference to Whitehead's chapter in *Science and the Modern World* entitled "Abstraction." The lowest grade of relevance occurs when an eternal object makes no positive contribution. It is merely there as available content.[66] The problem posed by the relational essence of eternal objects is noted and faced. The problem is this: If any eternal object is internally and inescapably related to all other eternal objects, does it not follow that if one eternal object is exemplified in an actual entity, therefore all others must be exemplified also? Whitehead points out that this would be impossible, because some of the eternal objects related to a given eternal object would be its contraries. He deals with the problem in more technical form (in connection with a discussion of the possibility of finite truths). He states that the relational essence of an eternal object is not *unique* to that object. There is a uniform scheme of relationships among all the eternal objects which fit into the scheme. In order to refer to this systematic pattern of relationship it is not necessary to refer to the individual essences of the component eternal objects. Thus it is possible to refer to the "addition table" without mentioning all the component members individually.[67] Since this systematic pattern of relationship is not uniquely linked to any particular eternal object, therefore it is not necessarily exemplified, in part or in whole, when a particular eternal object is exemplified.

Whitehead distinguishes *pure conceptual prehensions and impure prehensions*. The data of pure conceptual prehensions are eternal objects. The data of impure prehensions are more complex. They are propositions or theories.[68]

One phase of Whitehead's discussion of eternal objects involves a distinction between *objective species* and *subjective species*. Eternal objects which are members of the objective species are the so-called mathematical forms. Eternal objects of the subjective species are those exemplified in the subjective form of an actual entity. The distinction between eternal objects of the objective and subjective species is further clarified by reference to their function in the process of objectification. An objective eternal object may be exemplified in the data provided by an actual entity. A subjective species of eternal object may also be exemplified in the data provided by a deceased actual entity. That is to say, the subjective form of the departed actual entity may constitute part of the available data for a new actual entity. However, while both subjective and objective species of eternal objects may be involved in objectification, no objective eternal object can be exemplified in the subjective form of an actual entity.[69]

In other words, a number might be manifest in a pattern of *some* types of data, but no mathematical factor can be found in the data provided by a subjective form (in the more restricted use of this term) of a previous actual entity. A subjective form involves states such as anger, fear, consciousness. These do not exemplify mathematical principles (objective eternal objects). For example, an emotion of anger is neither square nor round nor any other geometrical shape.

It has been noted that the data used in the process of prehension are of two chief sorts: (a) abstract (general) data (eternal objects), (b) concrete data (concrete components of actual entities). Whitehead applies the technical term *general potentiality* to the multiplicity of eternal objects. *Real potentiality* is the label used in referring to concrete data provided by actual entities. It should be obvious that while general potentiality is the same for all actual entities, real potentiality changes as actual entities rise and pass away.[70] The term *function* [71] is used to refer to the process by which an actual entity provides determination (data) for other actual entities. The fact that all entities (the term *entity* being used in its widest connotation—not merely implying actual entity) are in some sense involved in the concrescence of each newly arising actual entity (i.e., they provide data for physical or conceptual prehension, positive or negative) is what Whitehead calls the *principle of relativity*.[72]

Physical Prehension

Whitehead contends that the data of physical prehensions consist of concrete components of actual entities. This material undergoes a literal transfer. By a process of re-enaction, reproduction, conformation (the terms are synonymous), it becomes a component of another, different, actual entity. "The primitive form of physical experience is emotional—blind emotion—received as felt elsewhere in another occasion and conformally appropriated as a subjective passion." [73] "Feelings are 'vectors'; for they feel what is *there* and transform it into what is *here*." [74] Whitehead bases this doctrine on the observed fact that, for example, when a person is angry, the anger continues; and passing from the past moment of experience (a past actual entity), is absorbed into the present moment of experience (the present actual entity). It is also based on the report of modern physicists that energy from one center flows out and influences other centers.

It is essential to notice the type of relationship which holds between a prehending and a prehended entity. In the case of a physical prehension of actual entity B by actual entity A, data for prehension into A are available only after the internal existence of actual entity B has "evaporated, worn out and satisfied." Thus, the relationship between actual entities is "appropriation of the dead by the living." [75] It is as though one man B gives a pint of blood to another man A, thus making possible the existence of A. But the transfusion can occur only if it has been preceded by the demise of B. This theory is summarized in the statement that actual entities "perpetually perish" subjectively (they are no longer living, concrete, active subjects), but are immortal objectively. Thus, when part of the content of an actual entity is taken in by a new actual entity, the former achieves objective immortality in the latter. [76]

A very important implication of this situation is that direct relationship between actual entities only occurs when they are in a serial order one in the past of the other. The subsequent discussion of contemporary actual entities deals with an aspect of this matter. [77]

The process which occurs in ordinary physical prehension

does *not* involve an *exact* or a *complete* transfer of content from the old to the new actual entity. The preceding actual entity passes on its feeling to be reproduced by the new subject as its own—but the re-enaction is not perfect.[78] Only *some* of the components are transferred in the process of re-enaction. "There are factors in the environment which are eliminated from any function as explicit facts in the new creation. The running stream purifies itself." [79] "The crude notion that one actual entity is added to another *simpliciter* . . . is not what is meant." [80] The experienced anger of a present moment is not completely identical with the experienced anger of the preceding moment. Whitehead expresses the same point in terms of one of his technical analyses. He distinguishes the *responsive* from the *supplemental* phase of feeling. In the responsive phase the data are felt as coming from outside sources. They are not yet absorbed into private immediacy. In the supplemental phase the data are *transformed* into a novel, private unity of aesthetic experience.[81] Thus the transmission of content from actual entity B to actual entity A entails loss, or elimination, for two reasons. *First,* the inner life of actual entity B has terminated. Its former contents no longer glow with living immediacy. Further, certain private factors have disappeared upon the demise of actual entity B. *Secondly,* even the contents actually available are not all used. In the transition from initial (available) data to objective (used) data there is considerable elimination. Further, data are *transformed* by being placed in the context of a new subjective experience.

Unfortunately, Whitehead carelessly uses the term *objective datum* with reference to content present in the responsive phase. This sort of datum is what he elsewhere terms *initial datum.*[82] Indeed, he notes this fact, though in doing so he adds to the confusion by suggesting that an initial datum should be designated *objective content.*[83] Whitehead uses various other terms with reference to data. An objective datum is also called a *perspective*. The term *perspective* is apparently also applicable to *any* type of datum initial or objective.[84]

It must be emphasized that the process of transfer, or re-enaction, is not due entirely to the prehensive activity of the newly arising actual entity. As was pointed out in the first reference to objectification, the actual entities, which in "passing" provide data, have a drive or urge to make contributions to new actual entities. Thus, in this sense, data are not passively available.[85] In other words, each actual entity is concerned not only with "self-formation" but also with "other-formation." [86]

There are several passages in Whitehead's writings which seem to imply a theory of re-enaction different from the one outlined in the preceding paragraphs. He states, for example: "An eternal object when it has ingression through its function of objectifying the actual world, so as to present the datum for prehension, is functioning 'datively.' . . . The eternal objects function by introducing the multiplicity of actual entities as constitutive of the actual entity in question." [87] Such passages as these have led critics to hold that the *only bond* between successive actual entities is the eternal object (or objects) which they prehend in common. However, in considering such statements, it must be remembered that in all instances Whitehead is apparently discussing the transfer of feelings (concrete data). It is, therefore, not to be thought that the eternal objects involved are the only content composing the bridge between actual entities. By virtue of the process of physical prehension, there is a genuine transfer of concrete content. The same eternal object appears (as manifest or exemplified) in two successive actual entities. It is not the eternal object *anger* which is the link; it is the concrete manifestation of anger which is "handed on." Thus, with the important exception of hybrid physical prehension (see next paragraph), the prehensive connection between two actual entities is not due primarily to the fact of the presence of the same eternal object in the two actual entities. Whitehead states: "A 'relation' between occasions is an eternal object *illustrated in* the complex of mutual prehensions by virtue of which those occasions constitute a nexus." [88] The misunderstanding of Whitehead's position in this matter arises because he usually does not distinguish clearly between (a) eternal objects as potential for realization and (b) eternal objects as realized, or exemplified, or illustrated, in the experience of some actual entity. Thus, when he refers to the relational function of eternal objects, he really means (except in the case of hybrid physical prehension) the relational function of realized or exemplified eternal objects. The same comment applies to his synonym for eternal object—*universal*.[89]

Whitehead's discussion of prehension involves a reference not only to physical and conceptual, positive and negative, prehensions. He also considers so-called hybrid physical prehensions. This type of prehension is one in which an actual entity is prehended. Hence it is a physical prehension. However, the contents involved in the process of transfer are derived from the mental pole of the prehended entity. This is not what usually happens in physical prehension. Hence, it is a distinct type. (Ordinarily the contents prehended are derived from the physical pole.[90]) That is to say, actual entity A has a hybrid physical feeling of actual entity B if A has a conceptual feeling involving the same datum as is prehended by a conceptual feeling in B. In other words, there is no transfer of concrete content. The datum involved is a general or abstract entity, an eternal object. Though the datum is the same, the subjective form (how the datum is felt) may be different in the two actual entities.[91]

Hybrid physical prehension makes it possible for an actual entity to have "direct" prehension of non-contiguous actual entities.[92] Whitehead contends that the occurrence of so-called mental telepathy is understandable on the basis of hybrid physical prehension. This experience, of course, is said to involve shared conceptual content without dependence on any physical linkage of a contiguous sort.[93]

Physical prehension, so far, has been discussed in terms of hybrid physical prehension and the more common form of physical prehension which Whitehead calls *simple physical feeling* (i.e., the sort of feeling which occurs when the initial datum is part of the concrete content of a single actual entity). However, physical feeling includes not only the types mentioned but also so-called *transmuted feelings*. Transmuted feelings occur when a nexus of actual entities provides the data.[94] A *nexus* is a group of actual entities joined together by their objectifications in each other.[95] A fairly complex process is involved in transmuted feeling. There are a number of simple physical feelings of *some* of the actual entities composing a nexus. From these simple physical feelings are derived conceptual feelings. That is to say, the eternal objects manifest in the data of the simple physical feelings are apprehended (in their status of ideal possibility) as data for conceptual feelings. There is also the possible case of the same eternal object being manifest in *all* the actual entities under consideration. Hence one and the same conceptual feeling is derived from all these simple physical feelings. In either case, the derived conceptual feeling is integrated with the simple physical feelings. The result is that the prehending subject transmutes the datum of the conceptual feeling into a characteristic of the one nexus containing the actual entities which were physically felt.[96] For example, some, or all, of the component actual entities of a book are green. This greenness is felt. From these physical feelings are derived conceptual feelings of the eternal object *green*. This eternal object is regarded as a characteristic of the entire group of actual entities.

Subjective Form

In discussing *subjective form* [97] ("how a subject prehends a datum"), Whitehead has two different meanings in mind: (a) Many of his illustrations of subjective form indicate that he implies what might be called *attitude* or emotional reaction. For example, he mentions adversion, and aversion, horror, anger, disgust, indignation, enjoyment, as instances of subjective form.[98] (b) However, there are numerous instances when obviously he is referring to the entire inner life of an actual entity, including subjective form in the sense of meaning "a." For instance he states that "the individual immediacy of an occasion [actual entity] is the final unity of subjective form, which is the occasion as an absolute reality." [99] The "private side [of an actual entity] is constituted by the subjective form." [100] Whitehead suggests that subjective form (in this more inclusive sense) has two factors. There are elements in qualitative pattern and also the factor of intensive pattern. For example, consider the experience of a musical note (regarded as a private sensation). It can be analyzed into fundamental tone and overtones. These components manifest a qualitative pattern. Each tone has an intensity. Thus there is a pattern of intensities.[101]

In his list of subjective forms, Whitehead mentions *consciousness*. It might be assumed that any conceptual prehension must have consciousness as its subjective form. This, however, is not the case. Consciousness is *not* present in the experience of most actual entities. In order to understand Whitehead at this point, it must be remembered that he uses the term *consciousness* in a very special and restricted sense. It is not synonymous with "apprehension of." Consciousness "is the feeling of the contrast [102] of theory, as *mere* theory, with fact, as *mere* fact." [103] The prehension of fact or theory does not involve consciousness. The factor of contrast is basic. (See Chap. 5, pp. 83–86.)

Whitehead states that all conceptual prehensions have *valuation* as their subjective form. In the case of a simple conceptual prehension, where only one eternal object is involved, it is merely a matter of approval or disapproval. However, in the instance of a complex conceptual feeling, the subject is faced with several eternal objects. These must be arranged in order of importance with reference to the subjective aim of that subject. On the basis of this standard each eternal object is approved or disapproved in varying degrees. This valuation has two aspects: (a) qualitative—a determination is reached as to how the eternal object is to be utilized; (b) intensive—the importance of its utilization is also determined.[104] Thus it is possible to achieve harmonious unity within an actual entity.[105]

Subjective Aim

The factor of aim or purpose is a basic element in all actual entities. According to Whitehead "the determinate unity of an actual entity is bound together by the final causation towards an ideal. . . . The ideal, itself felt, defines what 'self' shall arise from the datum." The ideal has this power because it is prehended by the subject with the subjective form of "purpose to realize it." [106] For example, a person (in the non-technical sense) who wants to be a scholar selects from the available possible experiences those which further the achievement of that ideal. The actual experiences which result are integrated in terms of the same ideal. Thus, a person becomes a scholar. In general, all actual entities have as their subjective aim the achievement of intensity of individual satisfaction and transcendent creativeness (i.e., the contribution of data to others).[107] The various prehensions which compose an actual entity are interrelated because of the guidance exercised by the subjective aim of the actual entity in question.[108] It is, of course, obvious that the subjective aim is the basis of the self-identity of an actual entity.[109] The continuous control by the subjective aim in a sense provides for the "pre-established harmony" of the component elements of the actual entity. That is to say, they must join in that particular fashion because their inclusive actual entity has that particular subjective aim.[110] *In this sense* there is an "inflexible determinism." [111]

In some discussions of the factor of guidance, or control, Whitehead seems to emphasize subjective form rather than subjective aim. For example: "The process of the concrescence is a progressive integration of feelings controlled by their subjective forms." [112] However, when the total context is examined, one notes that the subjective forms of the various component prehensions of an actual entity are guided in their origination by the subjective aim of the actual entity.[113]

It has been pointed out that all actual entities have as a general subjective aim the achievement of individual satisfaction and the contribution of data to other actual entities. Whitehead states that actual entities, as distinguishable individuals, differ from one another because of differences in subjective form. Data may be the same for many actual entities, but the subjective form is the basis of novelty.[114] However, as in the case of the discussion just preceding, it must be emphasized that the subjective aim has priority over subjective form as an explanatory factor. Thus, the individualizing subjective form is novel because it is directed by a novel subjective aim.

Whitehead claims that the subjective aim does not necessarily remain unchanged during the "epoch" required for the completion of an actual entity. However, despite any modifications, it retains its substantial identity and is the basic unifying factor.[115] For example, an artist in painting a picture has in mind a basic plan. However, the details are modified during the process of the work.

As in the case of all his basic concepts, Whitehead regards his theory of subjective aim as simply a statement of the obvious facts of experience. We are directly conscious of our purposes directing our actions.[116] In a criminal trial, aim or motive is a factor which is considered with great care. The efficient conduct of international relations depends to a considerable extent on an understanding of the aims of the leaders of other nations. Lower animals also manifest this characteristic. A lost dog tries to find his master. An exasperated reader decides to denounce the object of his irritation.

3
The Characteristics of Actual Entities

Causation

Whitehead contends that both *final* and *efficient* causation are manifest within the experience of any actual entity. The objectifications of available actual entities constitute the efficient causes which contribute to the origination of a new actual entity.[1] The actual entity from which these objectifications come is also termed an *efficient cause.* The subjective aim of the newly arising actual entity is its *final cause.*[2] The actual entity which has, or experiences, these data and activities is the *effect.*[3]

The significance of Whitehead's position will be clear when one recalls the traditional difficulties with the problem of causation. Whitehead proposes to bridge the gap between cause and effect by appealing to a simple fact of direct experience. When, for example, anger from a past occasion of experience is carried over into the present, "there is an observed relation of causation between such occasions."[4] There is a directly felt transfer of energy from cause to effect.

It should be obvious that in Whitehead's opinion no one actual entity can be the sole cause of another actual entity.[5] Any actual entity receives data from many actual entities. In any case each actual entity is autonomous.[6]

In his analysis of actual entities Whitehead distinguishes a factor which he terms *physical purpose.*[7] Physical purpose originates when (a) there is a physical feeling; (b) there is a conceptual feeling of the eternal object exemplified in the actual entity physically felt. Physical purpose is the integration of the physical and the conceptual feeling in such a fashion that a decision is reached as to the importance of the physical feeling (or—perhaps more accurately—its data). As a result of this decision, the place of these data in subsequent process is definitely delineated. This is to say that if the subjective form of the conceptual feeling involved in physical purpose is adversion (valuation upward), then the data of the physical feeling involved are retained in the actual entity and transmitted to other actual entities at its demise. If, on the other hand, the subjective form of the conceptual prehension is aversion (valuation downward), then the data of the physical prehension are either eliminated or reduced in importance. The preceding discussion of physical purpose has concentrated on the simpler sort. The more complex species of physical purpose involves not merely the control of physical data exercised on the basis of conceptual valuation; there is also an increase in complexity in the experience of an actual entity possessing the second species of physical purpose. This is due to a process of conceptual reversion guided by the aim at complexity.[8]

It should be noted that when Whitehead states that blind physical purposes reign,[9] he apparently is not using the term *physical purpose* in the technical sense discussed above. He is referring, rather, to the fact that consciousness is negligible in the universe. It is present, as subjective form, in only a relatively small proportion of actual entities. "Blind [i.e., non-conscious] prehensions, physical and mental, are the ultimate bricks of the physical universe." [10]

The Two Poles

This reference to the ultimate bricks of the physical universe serves to emphasize a point briefly mentioned previously. Every actual entity has a physical and a mental pole— i.e., every actual entity is composed of physical and mental activities.[11] Physical prehensions have already been discussed at sufficient length. It is important to discover exactly what Whitehead means by the mental pole of an actual entity. He claims that the basic operations of mentality are conceptual prehensions (so-called pure mental activity). However, in a broader sense, the term mentality is also applied to integrations of conceptual and physical prehensions as in physical purpose and propositional prehensions (so-called impure prehensions).[12] Further, Whitehead seems to be suggesting that by mental he means the subjective side of experience, which is the essential uniqueness of individual reaction to data.[13] Mentality involves the introduction of emphasis, valuation, purpose. In other words, the subjective aim of an actual entity is one phase of its mental pole.[14] Whitehead seems to involve himself in contradiction when he suggests that the mental pole is inescapably one and then refers to the conceptual prehensions of (involved in) a mental pole.[15] Actually Whitehead is trying to indicate that the unified result issues from a plurality of productive processes.

The Autonomy of Actual Entities

The preceding discussion of mentality provides a background which facilitates the understanding of Whitehead's theory that any actual entity is *causa sui* and autonomous in the sense that "it is finally responsible for the decision by which any lure for feeling is admitted to efficiency." [16] In other words, no datum can force itself, or be forced, into the experience of any actual entity. It is to be realized, of course, that an actual entity cannot "conjure up" data which are not available. The only available ideals or patterns of possible behavior are those found in the (vast) realm of eternal objects. No new eternal objects can be created by any actual entity. The only concrete data available are those provided by the actual entities which have just terminated their existence. Since a newly arising actual entity must make use of *these* data, to that extent it is limited by them.[17] Thus there is no such thing as absolute freedom.[18]

All this must be borne in mind when one reads Whitehead's statement: "The freedom inherent in the universe is constituted by this element of self-causation" (of actual entities).[19] On the other hand, Whitehead's final position is that "the concrescence of each individual actual entity is internally determined and is externally free." [20] To repeat—no data can be forced into the life of an actual entity. Its own subjective aim is responsible for the selection of concrete and abstract data and for the use to which these data are put.[21] Whitehead argues that in human experience there is considerable evidence of freedom from the control of external determinations. This is the assumption underlying the imposition of praise and blame and the general notion of human responsibility.[22] He is prepared to admit that the characteristics of high-grade human experience may not be found *with equal intensity* in other types of actual entities. In the actual entities constituting an atom, for example, there is little evidence of initiative or ability to rise above the pressure of the immediate environment. However, he would contend that in all actual entities there is manifest the characteristic of autonomous self-creation.

The suggestion that there are no new eternal objects—no new ideal possibilities—seems, to some students of Whitehead, an intolerable and frigid restriction on novelty and freedom. It apparently involves the possibility that the boredom of repetition may be forced upon the universe. However, the number of eternal objects apparently is infinite. Further there is much complexity of interrelationship between the component members simple and complex (see the chapter on "Abstraction" in *Science and the Modern*

World). By allowing for varying degrees of relevance of these eternal objects, the principle of uniqueness could perhaps be preserved for actual entities even without assuming that the realm of eternal objects is infinite. In any case most people would be very happy to have at least some experiences repeated.

Contemporaries

A general discussion of the problem of freedom involves a reference to Whitehead's controversial theory of the "complete contemporary freedom" of actual entities. The situation in which complete contemporary freedom arises is that in which two actual entities do not immediately prehend each other. There seems to be a difficulty here in view of Whitehead's claim that all actual entities prehend each other.[23] However, a careful consideration of the details of his metaphysics indicates that this doctrine of complete contemporary freedom does not involve him in hopeless contradiction and confusion. It will be remembered that if actual entity B is to be objectified in actual entity A, B must be past with reference to A, past and gone (as an actual entity); otherwise no data would be available for physical prehension (as will be noted, God is an exception). It is, therefore, impossible for two ordinary actual entities which are contemporary—i.e., each in the process of self-creation at the same time—to provide data for each other. The fact of the matter is that they have not reached the stage in the career of an actual entity when it makes data available.[24] It should be observed that when Whitehead refers to the "mutual immanence" of contemporaries he makes it clear that speaking literally this means "causal independence." [25] It is interesting to realize that contemporaries do enjoy a linkage, albeit a rather tenuous one. This indirect linkage (so-called) occurs when two contemporaries have developed from a common past and tend toward a common future.[26] Whitehead is well aware of the bearing of the theory of multiple space-time systems on this discussion.[27]

Each actual entity is essentially *social,* since it receives data from an environment composed of other actual entities. An actual entity is also social in that it provides data for other actual entities.[28] In an attempt to stress the co-operative nature of actual entities, Whitehead suggests that "an actual entity is to be conceived both as a subject presiding over its own immediacy of becoming, and a superject which is the atomic [29] creature exercising its function of objective immortality." [30] It is more accurate to refer to an actual entity as *subject-superject* rather than a subject. The subject builds itself up by prehension of data. However, the superject phase is essential. Data are provided for other actual entities. Whitehead's statement that an actual entity is both subject and superject *at the same time* is not in accordance with his actual point of view, which is that the superject stage is reached (i.e., data are available for other actual entities) when the subject has *finished* its career.[31]

Process

Implied in the meaning of both terms, *subject* and *superject,* is the basic notion that process is inescapable. There is unending creative advance into novelty. Actual entities "become" and then "perish." [32] Whitehead takes a page from Heraclitus' book and remarks that no subject ever experiences twice.[33] It is important to realize that despite this emphasis on process [34] Whitehead contends that an actual entity never moves. Change in position is explained by reference to groups of actual entities.[35] Change is also dealt with in terms of the exemplifications of eternal objects in the creative world of actual entities. Thus, in a technical sense, actual entities do not change. They are what they are.[36] In other words, there is "change" in the sense that an eternal object is now exemplified in an actual entity whereas previously it was not exemplified in any actual entity. Further, a society may have certain characteristics for "a time" but later no longer have them.

Whitehead's theory of actual entities involves him, as he recognizes, in an apparently paradoxical position. It is the difficulty that although actual entities are the only real things in the universe, yet any actual entity "is always in the process of becoming and perishing and never really is." [37] That is to say, it never really is if by existence is meant static endurance. [38] In other words, an actual entity is either constructing itself by taking in data, and is thus not yet a complete actual entity; or, having reached completion, it immediately ceases to exist as a self-creating entity and its content becomes available for inclusion in some subsequent actual entity. Thus when Whitehead refers to an actual entity he is not referring to anything which endures, static and unchanging. He is designating either (a) an entity which is in process of self-creation, or (b) an entity which has just achieved completeness and is in process of going out of existence so as to provide data for another actual entity. Strictly speaking, in this situation a reference to the preceding entity is a reference to an entity which no longer exists. All that remains is some of the content which once belonged to this past entity. It should be noted, in addition, that (c) it is possible to refer to future actual entities. This statement means that present actual entities provide data which will have some influence on future actual entities. In this tenuous sense, future actual entities are immanent in the present. Further, one present fact is that the nature of things is such that there is a tendency toward the future. Whitehead makes it clear that the future is not yet actual, and hence it is not literally true to say that a future actual entity (in final form) is in the present. [39] This point is given technical exposition in terms of a distinction between *objective reality* and *formal reality*. The future lacks formal reality because it is not yet included, as such, in the inner life of an actual entity.[40] In this apparently peculiar theory, Whitehead is trying to do justice to a very obvious fact— the fact that, in a sense, the future does exert a very important influence on the present. For example, agreements of any sort, ambitions, anxieties—even railway timetables—indicate that the future is something for the present.[41]

Time

Another apparent paradox is involved in Whitehead's claim that actual entities are both "in time" and "out of time." "Every actual entity is 'in time' so far as its physical pole is concerned, and is 'out of time' so far as its mental pole is concerned." [42] In other words, he is pointing out that actual entities have physical prehensions of other actual entities, and these other actual entities are in the past. Further, each actual entity makes a contribution to future actual entities. Thus in these senses any actual entity is in time. This seems to be involved in the statement that "each temporal succession is temporal because it is incomplete." [43] Another phase of the meaning of the term *time,* in Whitehead's usage, is brought out in his discussion of the contention that a past actual entity is not present, in all its living intensity, in a newly arising actual entity. The past fades. Speaking technically, objectification involves elimination. Thus "time is a 'perpetual perishing.' " [44] However, since an actual entity has conceptual prehensions, it is out of time in the sense that it is prehending eternal objects which are, of course, timeless. (Here only ordinary actual entities are being discussed. As will be shown later, God is an exception.)

Although Whitehead claims that an actual entity is in time (in the sense just specified) , he contends that the process by which an actual entity builds itself up is not a temporal process. That is to say, the genetic process by which an actual entity creates itself is not in physical time.[45] Physical time involves division—distinction between present, past, and future actual entities. On the other hand, the self-creative process of any actual entity is so thoroughly unified by its subjective aim that this division cannot be made. However, according to this "epochal" theory of time, each actual entity is the experience of a certain quantum of physical time.[46] It is said to have temporal extension or duration,[47] and to involve a specious present during which the complicated, successive, creative process takes place.[48] In a sense, temporalization is not another continuous process. It is an atomic succession of actual entities, the inner life of each being timeless (in Whitehead's technical sense) i.e., a "seamless whole." [49] Whitehead also states that an actual entity, "in its character of concrete satisfaction, is divisible into prehensions which concern its first temporal half and into prehensions which concern its second temporal half." [50] In short, no temporal distinction may be applied properly to any actual entity *if* you consider its process of origination. From this point of view it is one indivisible process. This is the so-called genetic approach. However, Whitehead apparently admits that if you consider the completed actual entity you can discern that the process involves phases, one following after the other. By using this analytic or "coordinate" method of approach, temporal distinctions may be made with reference to an actual entity.

Space

Whitehead points out that since an actual entity in its process of concretion takes in data from actual entities at different spatial positions,[51] the region constituted by these contributing actual entities is included in the newly arising actual entity. Hence actual entities have a spatial aspect. Only the physical pole of an actual entity is, in this sense, spatial. The mental pole is non-spatial.[52] It must be reiterated that in making temporal and spatial distinctions we are proceeding by co-ordinate rather than by genetic analysis. The genetic approach stresses the fact of creative growth. From this point of view, spatial and temporal distinctions cannot be made legitimately in the seamless texture of experience. The co-ordinate approach stresses the fact of satisfaction or final completion which occurs only after the inner creative process of the actual entity has died out. In this approach such distinctions are permissible.[53]

According to Whitehead, so-called "empty space" is composed of actual entities which manifest no important or obvious degree of novelty.[54] Spatio-temporal relations of events are internal relations. That is to say, apart from the spatio-temporal relationships of the events, those events would not exist.[55] But it should be obvious from the preceding discussion that space-time cannot be regarded as a self-subsistent entity. Space and time are relations between actual entities. They have absolutely no independent status.[56] Whitehead emphasizes that since there are many different lines of development within the universe—i.e., many different sequences of events—there are many space-time systems. Each of these linear series is one space-time system.[57]

The Interfusion of Actual Entities

One of Whitehead's basic contentions is that "if we allow for degrees of relevance, and for negligible relevance, we must say that every actual entity is present in every other actual entity." [58] This is not true of eternal objects. Any actual entity (God excepted) prehends only part of the vast realm of eternal objects.[59] The term *relevance* means not only positive relevance but also "the zero of relevance" involved in a negative prehension.[60] This must be remembered when reading Whitehead's statements that every entity in the universe, of whatever sort, contributes data to every other entity.[61, 62] After all, even in his analysis of positive prehension, Whitehead includes, as one of its components, a process of partial rejection of available data due to negative prehension.[63]

The phrase *actual world* has a technical meaning which is rather difficult to grasp. There are many different actual worlds. The term *actual world* apparently means the actual entities available for prehension at any particular time (or— more accurately—space-time). There are many actual worlds because of the continual emergence of new actual entities. In other words, the actual entities available at T-1 are different from those available at T-2. In this sense the actual world is always "relative." [64] Whitehead seems to have a somewhat different notion in mind when he suggests that an actual entity selects the actual world from which it originates. In this sense there is an indeterminacy concerning the actual world which is to condition the newly arising entity.[65] In view of the uniqueness of each actual entity, Whitehead states that no two actual entities can have identical actual worlds.[66] In any case, though actual worlds may differ, the realm of eternal objects remains the same for all actual entities.

In dealing with the possible influence of actual entities in the distant past upon actual entities in the present, Whitehead suggests that each actual world (a nexus of actual entities) is objectively immortal in the actual entity which arises from it. When in its turn this actual entity (AE-1) is objectified in a newly arising actual entity (AE-2), the nexus of actual entities from which AE-1 arose is present, in a sense, in AE-2 through the mediation of AE-1. Previous discussion of the relation of future actual entities to present ones is the basis of the contention that future actual entities constitute part of the actual world of a newly arising actual entity. Finally, in the tenuous sense indicated in previous discussion, present (contemporary) actual entities are in the actual world of a newly arising actual entity.

Whitehead's Subjectivism

"The feeler (subject) is the unity emergent from its own feelings." "*How* an actual entity becomes constitutes *what* that actual entity is." [67] In short, there is no initial self which exists before the process of feeling takes place.[68] This, then, is the exact antithesis of the position of Kant and all "substance" philosophers. For Kant, the world is derived from the subject; for the philosophy of organism, the subject develops from the world.[69] This type of exposition seems to contradict other statements made by Whitehead. For example, he refers to the "subject" which is prehending. He claims that a feeling cannot be abstracted from the actual entity experiencing it.[70] In Whitehead's opinion these two apparently contradictory points of view are seen to be consistent when one bears in mind the relationship of a subject to its feelings. He seems to have two explanations of this relationship, which in the last analysis can be fused together: (a) The subject is the final end or goal which the feelings (prehensions) strive to attain.[71] (b) The other type of relationship between a subject and its feelings is that the subject is simply the integrated totality of the feelings which together achieve the unity.[72] Whitehead fuses these two usages of the term by stating: "The word 'subject' [73] means the entity constituted by the process of feeling, and including this process. The feeler is the unity emergent from its own feelings." [74]

It will be obvious from the preceding discussion why Whitehead contends that self-realization is the ultimate fact concerning actual entities.[75] These "selves" have a triple character. They function as recipient, patient, and agent.[76]

Since Whitehead contends that actual entities are subjects, he obviously accepts the subjectivistic basis of modern philosophy. "Nothing is to be received into the philosophical scheme which is not discoverable as an element in subjective experience." [77] He contends that it is a "reformed subjectivism—reformed in the sense that organic interaction between subjects is adequately emphasized. Thus the defects of traditional subjectivism are overcome.[78] (For a detailed consideration of the extent of Whitehead's reform see Chapter 7, pp. 130–32.)

This subjectivism may seem a far cry from the position sketched in *Science and the Modern World*. Here he discusses prehensions in terms of volumes and stand-points. (A standpoint is a region of space-time, a volume of space through a duration of time.) Yet, as pointed out, Whitehead in this book recognizes the limitations of an analysis based on mathematics and physics. In order to express his basic insights he turned to the more adequate approach in terms of the data of psychology.[79, 80] This subjectivism does not deny the "objectivistic philosophy" which Whitehead defended in *Science and the Modern World*.[81] The objective world, independent of the experience of human beings, is retained. However, the inner nature of these objective facts is now given detailed interpretation.

The process by which an actual entity achieves selfhood is a *very complex one*. A vast multitude of prehensions constitute an actual entity. These prehensions occur at different periods within the duration required for the development of the actual entity.[82] These many component prehensions are integrated because of the unity of the subject, a unity achieved by its controlling subjective aim. In this process of concretion, potentiality is transformed into actuality. In a genuine sense, data from other actual entities are absorbed into the inner life of the new actual entity.[83] In the self-creation of an actual entity, novel prehensions, nexūs, subjective forms, propositions, multiplicities, and contrasts appear. However, as has been noted, there are no new eternal objects.[84]

The term *satisfaction* (as has been indicated briefly) refers to (a) the *completion* of the process of concentration.[85] It is the superject aspect of the actual entity (the subject-superject). The inner life of the entity has evaporated. (b) The providing of data for the use of new actual entities is also the satisfaction stage of an actual entity. The satisfaction is the so-called *objective* constitution of an actual entity in contrast with its *formal* constitution—i.e., its inner life as a process of concrescence.[86] There can be no duplication of an objective datum in the satisfaction of an actual entity.[87] Further, diverse elements in the objective datum cannot have identity of function in the satisfaction.[88] It must be observed that the usage of the term *satisfaction,* discussed above, is sometimes replaced by a usage which involves a more restricted meaning. The terms *satisfaction* and *decision* are both required to refer to the two phases of an actual entity's experience, which were previously covered by the one label *satisfaction.* Thus, in this latter analysis, satisfaction is defined as the completion of an actual entity and decision is defined as the providing of data for the use of other actual entities.[89] This discussion of satisfaction and decision is part of a four-stage analysis of an actual entity. This analysis stresses datum, process, satisfaction, and decision.[90] An alternate analysis (provided in *Modes of Thought*) refers to data, form, transition, issue.[91] The meaning of the term *data* is clear. The term *form* is a synonym for eternal object (either as potential or as realized). The inner life, the concrescence, of the actual entity is called "process." This process has a form of transition (or form of process or composition). By *form of transition* Whitehead apparently means what he usually calls subjective aim, although he may possibly mean subjective form. The term *issue* means data available for other actual entities. It is interesting to observe that starting with a four-term analysis (data, form, transition, issue), Whitehead concludes his discussion with a three-term analysis: data, process, issue.[92]

Societies of Actual Entities

The preceding discussion apparently has little relevance to the physical objects of everyday experience. Also, certain phases of ordinary mental experience seem to be disregarded. Specifically, there is Whitehead's claim that actual entities incessantly rise and pass away (God being the only exception; see Chapter 4). The question occurs as to whether he can do justice to the evident permanence of observed physical objects and the apparent continuity of personality. His theory of "society" is concerned with these problems.

Societies arise because of the fundamental characteristic of all actual entities: the immanence of one in others by means of a process of prehension. When the actual entities in any group are interrelated in this most general sense, these actual entities constitute a *nexus*.[93] A *society* arises as the result of a more specific, intimate sort of relationship characterized by "social order." A group of actual entities constitute a society when they all manifest a common eternal object and this "common element of form" is derived from other members of the social group of actual entities.[94] Thus actual entities rise and pass away, but societies endure, at least for a time.[95] On the basis of Whitehead's general position, it is obvious that a society must involve antecedents and subsequents,[96] or, in other words, temporal contiguity. Thus a contemporary group of actual entities could not form a complete society since, as such, they could have no direct interrelations.

The meaning of *change* (as well as the meaning of *endurance*) is explained by Whitehead's theory of society. When in addition to common elements in a group of actual entities (whereby it is constituted a society), there are also diversities, the fact that there are these diversities is the fact of change.[97]

When there is a continuous succession of actual entities, one after the other—the common characteristic being present because a preceding actual entity is objectified in the immediately succeeding actual entity—such a strand of actual entities (single file as it were) is called a *personal* society.[98] (It is also termed an *enduring object*.[99]) A man defined as an enduring percipient is an example of a personal society. It is, of course, evident that there are other types of social organization manifest in the more complex interrelations of actual entities. A complex society analyzable into various series or strands of personal societies is called a *corpuscular society*.[100] For example, an animal body is not a society of the simple personal sort—one linear sequence of entities. It is composed of many entities, co-ordinated in a very complex fashion. At any moment an animal body is composed of a vast group of contemporary actual entities, each a member of a different personal society, corpuscular society, or general nexus.

In general, Whitehead contends that the universe is analyzable into societies of societies of societies. For example, an army is a society of regiments, regiments are societies of men, men are societies of cells, and cells are societies of protons.[101] Thus there are *structured societies* containing within them *subordinate societies*.[102] It is evident that the complex, structured society provides a suitable environment for the subordinate societies harbored within it. In some cases the general environment is sufficient to maintain a society. In other cases a more specialized society is required.[103] It should be noted that Whitehead tends to use the term *society* in *Process and Reality* and *Adventures of Ideas,* whereas in *Science and the Modern World* he employs the term *organism*.[104]

It is very important to grasp Whitehead's contention that the characteristics of a society are, *without exception,* the characteristics of at least some of its component actual entities. That is to say, *no* new characteristics emerge in the social organization which are not present in the component members.[105]

If it be objected that Whitehead has not really accounted for complex social organization, his reply can only be that in the last analysis we do *discover* societies in varying degrees of complexity. All the details of Whitehead's system are reputed to be descriptions—descriptive generalities which have been seen to be applicable to vast ranges of experience.

Turning now to more specific applications of Whitehead's theory of society, it is relevant to observe that the difference between a *living* society (an organism) and a *lifeless* society (an inanimate object) is explained in terms of whether or not there is a novelty of experience which does not involve mutual thwarting. More specifically, a living society is one in which novelty of experience is directed successfully to secure a proposed goal despite varying environmental factors. On the other hand a non-living society loses novelty because of mutual thwarting by its components. The various novelties cancel each other out. As the result there is a dead level of uniformity. Whitehead is prepared to admit that there is no absolute gap between living and non-living societies.[106]

The technical difficulty arises that "life" cannot be the defining characteristic of a society since it is a denial of repetition, and a society involves repetition.[107] Whitehead's attempt to meet this difficulty, which he notes, is not particularly impressive. Further, there is a variation in his usage of the term *life*. In one context he states that no simple occasion can be termed *living*.[108] In another context, life is assigned to single occasions as well as to societies.[109] For example, the three distinctive characteristics of life mentioned in *Modes of Thought*—(a) self-enjoyment, (b) creative activity, (c) aim—are obviously found in individual subjects.[110]

An attempt to differentiate *life* from *mentality* is also found in *Modes of Thought*. Whitehead contends that mentality is characterized by conceptual experience and is one of the *ingredients of life*. A more clear-cut distinction is embodied in the claim that mentality is the contemplation of ideal alternatives. Life, on the other hand, is defined as the enjoyment of concrete emotional data derived from the past and directed toward the future. However, in stating that "life lies below the grade of mentality" which is found in conceptual experience, Whitehead seems to blur or erase the distinction which he has apparently attempted to make.[111] In any case, as has been pointed out above, he had distinguished the living from the non-living by assigning to *life* the characteristic of novelty—indeed of conceptual novelty.[112] There is the further difficulty that *each* actual entity (even the components of non-living entities) is essentially bi-polar: *mental* and physical.[113]

A differentiation of the mental (in the ordinary, non-technical sense of the term) from the merely vital in a fashion more consistent with his general analysis is also offered. It is suggested that the difference is a matter of degree of complexity of novel experience.[114] In the component "subjects" of the animal body there is not the same degree of initiative, creativity, and complexity of experience found in the actual entities composing the human mind.[115] It has been customary, at least since Aristotle, to attempt to show that men differ from lower animals. Whitehead's basis of distinction is stated thus: We share with some lower animals purposes, hope, aesthetic insight, technological attainment, social organization, affectionate feeling. However, only men are concerned with the understanding of individual facts as illustrations of general principles. This interest in science and philosophy is the characteristic which really distinguishes men from lower animals. More specifically there is the pursuit of ideals, ideals which stretch beyond any immediate realization.[116] Another method of differentiating higher levels of existence from lower requires reference to the *degree of control* exercised by dominant centers. For instance the difference between an animal and a vegetable is explained in terms of the degree of control exercised by centers of experience within the composite society which constitutes the animal or vegetable. Generally an animal has one or more centers of dominance. A vegetable is a democracy of component subjects. However, Whitehead is willing to admit that a vegetable shows some traces of dominance and the constituent elements of an animal show some signs of democratic independence.[117] The nature of the "dominance" exercised by the personal society, or any other society, merits careful consideration. The personal society (or more accurately the component actual entities) cannot *force* any line of activity on the members of the complex society in which it finds itself. It can only provide data and trust that these data will be taken into the being of the other component actual entities of the complex society.[118]

In summary, it may be noted that Whitehead analyzes nature into four main types of societies of subjects, as follows: (a) *Non-living.* There is no impressive distinctiveness about the activity of the component subjects. Whatever degree of individuality there is lacks obviousness. The general effect is uniformity. (b) *Vegetable.* Here we also find uniformity but there is some element of diversification also. More accurately, there are individual parts distinguishable. However, there is a co-ordination of different activities in order to achieve the goal of survival. (c) *Animal.* There is at least one central agency obviously providing guidance, yet dependent for support upon its related entities. Mere survival is not the only goal. Some concern for importance, or value, is also shown. (d) *Human.* This higher grade of animal life involves more emphasis on novelty, width, and depth of experience, particularly value experience.[119]

Mathematical Applications

Part IV of *Process and Reality* is an attempt to improve Whitehead's previous discussion of various phases of mathematics. In these earlier studies the notion of *whole and part* was taken as fundamental. The concept of *extensiveness* was obtained as a derivate. On this basis a point could not be defined without including a reference to duration. This approach tended to disregard the extensive relations of actual entities mutually external to each other. Whitehead now proposes to start with *extensive connection* and define whole and part in terms of this notion. This makes it possible to define basic mathematical concepts without reference to measurement or duration.[120] Without going into technicalities, it may be observed that a point is now defined in terms of relationship (extensive connection) between the actual entities composing a nexus. "A point is a nexus of actual entities with a certain 'form.' "[121] Straight lines, triangles, planes, tetrahedrons, three-dimensional flat spaces, are all defined in terms of relations of points.[122] This procedure frees geometry from entanglement in particular physical fact. If, on the other hand, straight lines—for example—could only be defined in terms of measurement, that would inescapably require the activity of particular actual entities. Further, Whitehead contends that "unless the notion of straightness has a definite meaning in reference to the extensive relations, this whole procedure in practical measurement is meaningless."[123] Whitehead's thoroughgoing interest in *process* is shown in his suggestion that simple mathematical statements such as $3 \times 2 = 6$ should not be regarded as tautologies. Such statements record the form of a process and refer to the completion of a process.[124]

The Extensive Continuum

Whitehead's concept of *extensive continuum* merits careful consideration. "This extensive continuum is one relational complex in which all potential objectifications find their niche." More specifically, "an extensive continuum is a complex of entities united by the various allied relationships. . . . It is not a fact prior to the world; it is the first determination of order;—that is, of real potentiality—arising out of the general character of the world."[125] In other words, Whitehead is referring to the fact that when a new actual entity arises it has available a group of data arranged in a specific fashion because the data are provided by a group of actual entities in various co-operative relationships. Thus, the extensive continuum is not an underlying or all-inclusive entity. The term refers to the fact that data are available in a definite complex fashion.[126] It must be admitted that Whitehead apparently has a different and contradictory meaning for the term *extensive continuum*. On occasion he refers to something apart from actual entities. Linking this meaning of the concept of Plato's "receptacle" theory, Whitehead states that he is thinking of the "essential unity of the Universe conceived as an actuality, and yet in abstraction from the 'life and motion' in which all actualities must partake." [127] He also refers to the systematic structure of the extensive continuum "apart from the particular actualities into which it is atomized." [128]

4
God

This chapter is concerned with an actual entity which differs in a significant fashion from all other actual entities. This uniquely different actual entity is called *God*. With characteristic humility Whitehead states that his discussion of God is not based on absolute certainty. At best, human concepts give only a glimpse of the nature of God.[1] He indicates that he is attempting to express some of the religious and moral insights which occur in the course of human experience. Just because this type of experience is relatively rare, we are not, therefore, justified in disregarding it.[2]

The fact that Whitehead's most comprehensive and systematic discussion of the nature of God is found in a brief section at the end of *Process and Reality,* and in a short chapter in *Science and the Modern World,* should not mislead one into thinking that God is relatively unimportant in this cosmological scheme. As a matter of fact, God performs many essential functions.

Before proceeding to an examination of the creative interaction between God and other actual entities, one point must be clarified. It is this: According to Whitehead, "God is not to be treated as an exception to all metaphysical principles. . . . He is their chief exemplification." [3] Like any other actual entity, God has both mental and physical poles. These poles are referred to as the *primordial* and *consequent* natures of God. The *primordial* nature of God is a unity of conceptual prehensions which together bring within God's experience all eternal objects. The *consequent* nature of God is constituted by his physical prehensions of other actual entities.[4] God also has a *superject* nature in that he provides specific, concrete, data to be used in the self-creative process of other actual entities.

In discussing God, Whitehead concentrates first on the primordial nature. He then considers the consequent nature and finally refers very briefly to the superject nature. It is unfortunate that, on occasion, he carelessly refers to these components of the actual entity God as though they were, each, distinct actualities. For example, we find him using the phrases *non-temporal actuality, conceptual actuality,* and even *primordial actual entity.*[5] It will be obvious from his total discussion that these phrases are not to be taken literally. (See Appendix B, pp. 214, 218.)

The Primordial Nature of God

In their process of self-creation, actual entities require the lure of ideal possibilities to stimulate them and at the same time offer a pattern for the guidance of their ongoing process of development. It has been previously noted that eternal objects fulfill this function. However, unless eternal objects are organized and interrelated they will provide little practical guidance. For example, the eternal objects *fire* and *burn* are far more effective in the experience of a subject if they are conceptually prehended as related, than if they were prehended as part of an incoherent conglomeration. In order to account for the experienced patterned relationship of eternal objects, Whitehead claims that it is necessary to refer to an agency which is responsible for the arranging. Thus, he argues that all real togetherness must be togetherness within the experience of some actuality.[6] He contends that the eternal objects have "subsistence" in an entity which he terms God.[7] Not only does God (primordial nature) arrange the eternal objects; he also makes them available for use by other actual entities.[8] This is God's function as the *principle of concretion*.[9] This phase of God's activity is one of the basic facts of the universe, or as Whitehead calls it, "the ultimate irrationality"—the fact that must be accepted without demanding "reasons why." [10] The objection which is frequently raised with reference to Whitehead's phrase *ultimate irrationality* seems hardly justified. After all, are there not some ultimate facts which are the starting point used in explaining other—less ultimate—facts?

God's purpose, in so far as his primordial nature is concerned, is the achievement of depth of satisfaction. He is indifferent alike to preservation or novelty. In other words, he is not concerned whether an occasion is old or new as long as depth of satisfaction is achieved.[11] God, in his primordial nature, desires that the eternal objects be received as data by other actual entities. Thus, Whitehead suggests that in God there is a "yearning after concrete fact—no particular facts, but after *some* actuality." [12] As a result of this yearning, any actual entity finds available in God data for its conceptual aim.[13] It may seem that if, as Whitehead contends, the constituent activities of an actual entity are the outcome of the subjective aim of the subject, and this is initially derived from God, then it would follow that actual entities are not really autonomous or self-creative. This interpretation overlooks the fact that while God provides a *possible* pattern (eternal object) which *may* serve (when exemplified in the actual entity) as the subjective aim, each actual entity is entirely responsible for the *selection* and *use* of this pattern. In this sense each actual entity is self-creative.[14] "Thus an originality [an actual entity] in the temporal world is conditioned, though not determined, by an initial subjective aim [involving an eternal object which constitutes a goal] supplied by the ground of all order and of all originality [God]." [15] This point is brought out even more clearly when Whitehead states that the conceptual aim is derived "with indeterminations awaiting" the decisions of the newly rising actual entity.[16] The contention that God (in his primordial nature) is "unmoved by love for this particular or that particular" has given rise to considerable misunderstanding of Whitehead's theory of the relation of God to other actual entities. There is a similar statement to the effect that God's primordial nature is not directly related to a particular course of history.[17] However, an examination of the context of these statements indicates that Whitehead is merely saying that when God is having conceptual prehensions of eternal objects, he is not dealing with specific actual entities. If some particular actual entity has a conceptual prehension of one of the eternal objects in God's primordial nature and then realizes it, at that point God is related to the other actual entity as a specific entity but not until then. However, as has been noted before, he does not force any actual entity, or group of actual entities, to come into existence. In this sense he is not involved in a *given* (one, and only one specific) course of history. What the course of history actually is depends on the autonomous decisions of all actual entities involved in that history. Since God provides some of the data used by other actual entities, in this sense, he is inescapably involved in the process of history.[18]

Whitehead's statement that every eternal object is included in the conceptual feelings of God [19] may seem to indicate that eternal objects are simply aspects of one actual entity, God. The erroneous nature of this interpretation should be evident from a careful examination of his theory of eternal objects. It is true that eternal objects do not "dwell apart," in absolute abstraction, from actual entities. As potentialities they are related to all actual entities. That is to say, they are envisaged by God and hence made available for the use of all other actual entities. But they are not merely *aspects* (adjectival qualities) of actual entities. Eternal objects are distinct *components* of actual entities. Any actual entity is a creative grouping of these components (and others). In any case, Whitehead clearly indicates his answer to the specific problem: What is the relative status of eternal objects and God? He states: "He [God] does not create eternal objects; for *his nature requires them* in the same degree that they require him." [20] This, Whitehead suggests, is an illustration of his specification that a speculative system should manifest coherence—i.e., its ultimate notions require each other.

There are two obvious questions which arise with reference to Whitehead's theory of God. These are: (a) Why apply the term *God* to the type of actual entity so designated? (b) How do you know that such an actual entity, possessing these characteristics, exists? In answer to these questions, he replies that the fact we find eternal objects available and organized for the use of all ordinary actual entities indicates that God does exist as an organizer and as a co-operating member of the active environment of actual entities. In short, as Whitehead himself expresses the matter, the general character of things requires that there be such an entity.[21] As further proof of the existence of God and justification for his use of the term *God,* Whitehead claims to have a direct prehension of this timeless source of all order. There is a feeling of the refreshment and companionship which characterizes religious experience.[22]

In discussing the primordial nature of God, Whitehead provides additional comment concerning his Category of Conceptual Reversion. He points out that, as it stands, it does not explain how, and in what sense, an unrealized eternal object can be more or less proximate to a realized eternal object. This deficiency can be overcome by reference to God's primordial nature. The process of apprehending relevant alternatives—i.e., the prehending of proximate novelties— occurs because of hybrid physical prehension of God. That is to say, the actual entity God (hence the prehension is physical) is prehended through the medium of data derived from his conceptual feelings (hence hybrid physical feeling). These data, the complex patterns of eternal objects, when apprehended, provide for the experience of proximate novelties. When one has once noted this implication of hybrid physical prehension of God, the category of reversion can be eliminated as a necessary explanatory principle.[23]

The Consequent Nature of God

Whitehead's discussion of the consequent nature of God is woefully condensed, being confined almost exclusively to the last few pages of *Process and Reality*. The task of interpretation is not rendered any easier by the snatches of glorious literature which are packed into this short space. The somewhat extensive usage of conventional religious terms is not an unmixed blessing. Yet through it all there shines a basic insight which perhaps could not have been expressed more adequately.

Whitehead's consideration of the consequent nature of God is a manifestation of his attempt to show that God is like any other actual entity, having not only conceptual prehensions (primordial nature) but also physical prehensions of other actual entities. God's consequent nature is the physical prehension of available actualities.[24] God's consequent nature is not complete. It depends upon the continuous emergence of new actual entities.[25] As new actual entities appear, he absorbs new content which they provide. Yet, in one sense, the consequent nature of God does manifest the characteristic of *completeness*. The meaning of this apparently contradictory contention must be carefully examined.

Ordinary actual entities rise and pass away—droplets of experience, creatures of short duration. They create themselves and then pass on, leaving dead fragments as data for the possible use of newly arising actual entities. In this sense the temporal process is a perpetual perishing.[26] In striking contrast to the short and simple annals, the brief and transitory existence of ordinary actual entities is the experience of the uniquely different actual entity, God. Whitehead contends that God's consequent nature is characterized by "everlastingness." He means that God is an entity which does not perish. God's content never becomes available for other actual entities as the result of a process by which God passes out of existence. The contents of his nature are not lost to him by being objectified in some other actuality at his demise. God grows by taking in new content, but the content already present is retained in all its vividness. In this fashion Whitehead attempts to offer support for the insight of religion that there are things which must not be allowed to perish in the ongoing process of life. Thus it may be said (concentrating on his consequent nature) that God is temporal in the sense that development occurs within his being. But God is non-temporal in the sense that he never perishes. Further, God is non-temporal in that his primordial nature (the envisagement of eternal objects) is not characterized by process.[27]

It is very important to understand thoroughly the process whereby data from other actual entities are absorbed into the consequent nature of God. In the first place the transfer involves *some loss of content*. Further, objectification cannot occur without the literal death of the actual entity which obtains objective immortality in the other. The state of objective immortality is fundamentally different from the process of self-creation during which the actual entity is alive and enjoys its own content. As a matter of fact, Whitehead specifically states: "Each novel actuality in the temporal world contributes *such elements as it can* to a realization in God." [28] It is true that he says that God exercises "a tender care that nothing be lost," but it is essential to note that he adds a very important qualifying clause—"that can be saved." [29] The implication is clear in both quotations. Everything in ordinary actual entities is *not* used by God—and thus saved. Other statements support this interpretation. For example: "Each actuality in the temporal world has its reception into God's nature. The corresponding element in God's nature is not temporal actuality." [30] When Whitehead claims that God's consequent nature is characterized by creative advance and the retention of mutual immediacy, he is not referring to the preservation of the inner life of ordinary actual entities.[31] Rather, he is discussing the preservation of God's inner life. Similarly Whitehead, in analyzing the experiences of God, refers to "the phase of perfected actuality, in which the many are one everlastingly, without the qualification of any loss either of individual identity or of completeness of unity." [32] Here again, apparently, he is not suggesting that actual entities are preserved completely, with undiminished reality, in God. Rather, he seems to be saying that the elements contributed by actual entities (at their demise) to God retain their identity within God's experience. These *accepted elements* are not drastically changed by God. This point is given specific illustration in his contention that good and evil are taken into the experience of God with undiminished distinctiveness. All the "opposites" (including good and evil) are there.[33] (See Appendix B, pp. 217–18.)

It is true that Whitehead refers to the "overcoming of evil by good" and the "transmutation of evil into good." However, a careful examination of the context in which these statements occur indicates that he is not attempting to deny the reality and existence of evil. On the contrary, Whitehead is pointing out that evil is a stepping stone to good. It is overcome in the sense that it stimulates the development of its opposite. Evil is also overcome, but not eliminated, in the sense that it is placed in the context of a wider experience and is a distinct element in that total experience. When data are absorbed into God's experience, "every fact is what it is, a fact of pleasure, of joy, of pain, or of suffering." [34] Because God is so clearly aware of the reality of evil, he experiences a deep sense of tragedy. He also feels sympathy for the sufferings of other actual entities.[35] Further, as he envisages varying elements in his experience, he shows to other actual entities how positive values may issue from suffering.[36] However, God does not merely save what he can of positive value. He does not merely make the best of real evil. God's discernment leads him to appreciate what is ordinarily considered "mere wreckage." [37, 38]

Whitehead, in conversation, remarked that the ideas expressed in the last chapter of *Adventures of Ideas* entitled "Peace" really involve his theory of God. The state of mind termed "peace" would be difficult, or impossible, to attain unless there were in the universe a being like Whitehead's God. When he discusses the "unity of adventure," he seems to be referring to God in his entirety or—perhaps—to God's consequent nature only. The "eros" factor appears to be very similar to (or identical with) God's primordial nature.[39] One would judge that Whitehead's discussion in *Modes of Thought* of the "intuition of holiness" also involves a reference to God's conceptual nature.[40]

In his essay on "Immortality," Whitehead makes use of the concept of the *World of Value*. Its basic characteristic is "unification." As the exposition proceeds, he indicates that this is closely linked with (or involved in) God's primordial and consequent natures. God provides a persuasion toward *ideal* co-ordination and also achieves actual co-ordination of many diverse data in his own being.[41]

Whitehead uses the concept *Deity*. In language reminiscent of Alexander he states that, in so far as we entertain, realize, or fall below *ideals*, we are experiencing a factor of "Deity" in the universe.[42]

It would appear that Whitehead is guilty of unpardonable verbal juggling when he contends that the consequent nature of God is just as much a multiplicity as it is a unity.[43] However, this statement is not as contradictory as it seems at first glance. In the last sections of *Process and Reality,* he is considering the *final opposites,* among which are *God* and the *World.* Whitehead claims that these opposed elements stand in mutual requirement. The universe, upon analysis, reveals these two factors, both basic elements in the creative process, each making a contribution to the being of the other. The essential element in God's nature is the permanent *unity* of vision (the conceptual prehension of eternal objects) , seeking physical multiplicity (interaction with concrete actual entities via positive prehension) . The essential element in the World (of actual entities) is the volatile *multiplicity* of finite actual entities seeking a perfected unity. God's consequent nature is the prehension of many (other) actual entities. *In this sense* God is many. It must not be forgotten, of course, that these many prehensions of the many actual entities make possible the "absorption" (in the previously noted very technical sense of the term) of this multiplicity into God's *unity,* i.e., unified experience.

In his examination of the consequent nature of God, Whitehead occasionally slips into forms of expression which do not accurately convey his meaning (as expressed more carefully elsewhere) . For example, when he states that God as consequent is "fully actual," he is overlooking the fact that it is the *complete* actual entity God, having both a physical pole (consequent nature) and a mental pole (primordial nature) , which is fully actual. This same general type of criticism also applies to the suggestion that the consequent nature of God is conscious.[44] As a matter of fact, it is Whitehead's considered opinion that God is conscious because he has both mental and physical poles and hence is able to apprehend facts and confront them with alternative theories. (This contrast, it will be recalled, is what he means by consciousness.) In short, the mere fact that God possesses a physical pole does not guarantee that he is conscious. (See Appendix B, p. 218.)

The Superject Nature of God

Whitehead makes very brief reference to the superject nature of God. This is the phase of God's nature whereby his concrete experiences, involved in his consequent nature, are made available to newly arising, ordinary, actual entities. (This, suggests Whitehead, is a further illustration of the principle of universal relativity.[45]) However, it has been noted that God does not provide concrete data for the use of other actual entities in the same fashion as ordinary actual entities. Ordinary actual entities must "die" in order to provide concrete data. God never dies. Whitehead simply does not explain how God is able to provide concrete data—i.e., data for physical prehension. The provision of data for conceptual prehension (abstract data or eternal objects) does not present the same difficulty, since one eternal object may be shared by many actual entities. Whitehead's lack of clarity at this crucial point makes it difficult to interpret his statement that "the objectification of God in a temporal subject is affected by the hybrid feelings with God's conceptual feelings as data." [46] Granted, this is one way of experiencing God. But, if one takes God's superject nature seriously, then there must be a transfer of *concrete* content (ordinary physical feeling) as well as *abstract* content (the data of hybrid feeling). Indeed Whitehead refers to God's "specific satisfaction qualifying the transcendent creativity [self-creative activity] in the various temporal instances [i.e., ordinary actual entities]." [47]

It may seem plausible to regard God's consequent nature as a "society." This would enable Whitehead to avoid the apparent difficulty that, whereas ordinary actual entities have a brief duration, and then disappear, God is unique in that he has unending duration. Further, if God has unending duration, how can he provide concrete data for the use of other actual entities, in the usual fashion? This is a particularly serious problem in view of Whitehead's contention that God is not to be regarded as an "exception."

However, a careful examination of Whitehead's metaphysics indicates that he regards the consequent nature of God as *one* ongoing phase of the experience of *one* actual entity. It is the continuing prehension by God of other actual entities. *If* God were a "society," each member of which exemplified the distinctively divine primordial nature and then passed on, providing data for another, similar, actual entity, this whole series being called God; then one of the most essential characteristics of God would be lost—the retention of immediacy. If God were a society, there would be an inescapable loss of divine content since the linkage between members of a society is the process of transfer of content, and this involves elimination. In any case, Whitehead has not formulated his theory of the consequent nature of God in terms of the concept "society."

Creativity

Creativity (one phase of the Category of the Ultimate) is a Whiteheadian concept which is readily misunderstood. It would, on occasion, appear that he regards creativity as the *ultimate reality*—more fundamental than actual entities, even the actual entity God. A passage in *Science and the Modern World* seems to support this interpretation: "In the analogy with Spinoza, his one substance is for me the one underlying activity of realization individualizing itself in an interlocking plurality of modes. Thus, concrete fact is process." [48] However, a careful examination of all phases of Whitehead's discussion of this concept indicates unmistakably that he does not regard *creativity* as more ultimate than actual entities. (The preceding quotation is a sample of his occasional carelessness in exposition.) Actual entities retain their status as the final real things of which the universe is

made. In the early pages of *Process and Reality,* where Whitehead attempts to indicate the meaning of his basic categories,
he states that *creativity* is a universal characterizing ultimate
matter of fact.[49] Thus, in Whitehead's broadly Platonic language, creativity is an *Idea* (eternal object) which is exemplified in particular actual entities. More specifically, the
creative process whereby one actual entity appropriates data
provided by other actual entities, and so constitutes itself, is
an exemplification of the eternal object *creativity.* "Creativity is not an external agency with its own ulterior purposes.
[It is not an actual entity.] All actual entities share with God
this characteristic of self-causation." [50]

The preceding discussion should serve to indicate answers
to several critical questions which are suggested by Whitehead's position. There is, for example, the problem of how
he can claim consistently that: (a) Creativity is a universal
(an eternal object) ; (b) apart from God any eternal object
is indistinguishable from nonentity; (c) God is a creature of
creativity.[51] This apparent confusion, or contradiction, is overcome if it is understood that the term *creativity* refers to an
eternal object and *also* to the exemplification of that eternal
object. Since God's primordial nature envisages the eternal
object creativity, the object is included in an actuality. In this
sense the eternal object creativity is saved from being a "nonentity." In stating that God is a creature of creativity, Whitehead is merely indicating that God is the "creature" or
"outcome" of his own self-directed process of self-creation.
Whitehead also terms God an "accident of creativity." Here
he is using the word "accident" in a highly technical sense. It
is a synonym for choice or decision. More accurately, he is suggesting that God is the result of a series of decisions or choices
made in the course of his self-creative activity.[52] Whitehead
also seems to involve himself in difficulty when he suggests that
creativity is very similar to Aristotelian matter.[53] Aristotelian
matter is a passive, receptive, sub-stratum. These character-

istics are definitely not assigned to creativity. How then can creativity be similar to Aristotelian matter? The answer to this question seems to be that the only point they have in common—though this is an essential one in Whitehead's opinion—is the feature that each is without any specific *concrete* character of its own. Is it not true that an eternal object (e.g., *creativity*) is abstract, awaiting exemplification in some particular, specific, actual entity? Also, *creativity* is a common, general characteristic of all (otherwise different) actual entities; similarity *matter* in Aristotle's philosophy. A further confusion is likely to arise unless one notes, rather carefully, another slightly different usage of the term *creativity*. Whitehead sometimes states that "God and the actual world jointly constitute the character of the creativity for the initial phase of the novel concrescence." [54] By *character of creativity* he apparently means the data provided by God and the world of ordinary actual entities.

The preceding discussion should clarify the meaning of Whitehead's Category of the Ultimate. He states: " 'Creativity,' 'many,' 'one' are the ultimate notions involved in the meaning of the synonymous terms 'thing,' 'being,' 'entity.' " [55] These three notions, or eternal objects, are ultimate in that every actual entity exemplifies them. (All other eternal objects *may* remain unexemplified in the experience of a particular actual entity.) That is to say, every actual entity must, as such, exemplify *creativity*. It must prehend data from the *many* actual entities in its actual world and unify these data by a self-creative process into *one* new actual entity, namely itself. "The novel entity is at once the togetherness of the 'many' which it finds, and also it is one among the disjunctive 'many' which it leaves. . . . The many become one, and are increased by one. In their natures, entities are disjunctively 'many' [i.e., there are many component prehensions] in process of [creative] passage into conjunctive unity." [56] This statement is not completely unambiguous. It should be realized that the many which become one are not the same many to which the new one is added. Also the new entity is not a literally complete togetherness of the many which it finds.[57] (See Appendix B, pp. 216, 219–23.)

Origin of the Universe

Questions concerning the temporal origin of the universe and the relative importance of its various components have involved much learned discussion. Whitehead suggests that in all probability there was no "first day" of creation. The self-creative process of actual entities is occurring *now*. It did in the past, and it is likely to continue in the future. Whitehead seems to believe that, as far as we can tell, the metaphysical situation has always been as it is now—actual entities, both ordinary ones and God (possessing all his natures, primordial, consequent and superject) interacting creatively. The fact that God's consequent and superject natures are mentioned last in *Process and Reality* does not mean that they are comparatively recent additions. He is *not* suggesting that for a long time God's primordial nature was deprived of his consequent and superject natures, and that they only arose after some ordinary actual entities had created themselves. Thus, God "is not *before* all creation, but *with* all creation." [58]

Whitehead handles the problem of priority of status, in the universe, in an interesting fashion. He does not regard God as pre-eminently real and assign dependent reality or non-reality to other entities.[59] Rather, he stresses the notion that God and other actual entities are mutually dependent. Without each other they are not themselves.[60] As has been reiterated, God cannot bestow reality on any actual entity. Each actual entity is its own self-creative agent. God provides data for any actual entity (newly arising), and any actual entity provides data for God. However, God is unique in the sense that he provides for the organization and relevance of eternal objects and he "saves" some data by absorbing them in his enduring life. Further he does not derive his conceptual data from any other actual entity. Finally, God, unlike other actual entities, does not perish.[61]

5

Whitehead's Philosophy of Mind

This chapter deals with a number of related topics which, for want of a better term, may be called "philosophy of mind." Chief among these are: the nature of the self, the relation between body and mind, immortality, epistemology, language.

In indicating the scope of "mental" investigation, Whitehead writes in a fashion strikingly reminiscent of William James. He contends that *all* types of experience must be investigated. Nothing can be omitted. This refusal to be restricted to one area of experience is an outstanding characteristic of Whitehead's approach.[1]

In examining human experience various methods may be used: (a) introspection; (b) a more penetrating and hence more satisfactory method, which Whitehead terms "intuition"; (c) a consideration of the vast store of evidence provided by language, social institutions, and action; (d) the scientific method of experiment.[2]

As the result of his own careful observations, and having made use of the work of others as preserved by language, social institutions, and actions, Whitehead has reached the conclusion that "the subject-object relation is the fundamental structural pattern of experience."[3]

The Subject

Whitehead's point of view concerning the nature of the "experiencing subject" is clearly expressed in the following statement:

I find myself as essentially a unity of emotions, enjoyments, hopes, fears, regrets, valuations of alternatives, decisions—all of them subjective reactions to the environment as active in my nature. . . . The individual enjoyment is what I am in my role of a natural activity, as I shape the activities of the environment into a new creation, which is myself at this moment; and yet, as being myself, it is a continuation of the antecedent world. If we stress the role of the environment, this process is causation. If we stress the role of my immediate pattern of active enjoyment, this process is self-creation. If we stress the role of the conceptual anticipation of the future whose existence is a necessity in the nature of the present, this process is the teleological aim at some ideal in the future.[4]

As has been noted, Whitehead makes important use of this observation in formulating his theory of actual entities. His discussion of the experiencing subject is expressed in the technical language of this metaphysical theory. It will be recalled that he reaches the conclusion that any actual entity (subject) endures for only a relatively brief duration. It is composed of various prehensions. When these achieve unity, the subject, as such, ceases to exist. However, part of its content may be included as a datum in a succeeding subject. For example, if a person were angry a few seconds ago and the anger carried over into the present, Whitehead would explain it by saying that the subject which had been angry a few seconds ago had gone out of existence but part of its content, the anger, has objective immortality. That is, it has been included in the life of a new subject. These two subjects are part of a linear succession. They constitute what he terms either a *personal society* or a *living person,* or a *society of presiding occasions,* or a *society of percipient occasions.*[5] Thus he is contending that what used to be called a "soul" and later was termed a "self" or "mind" is really an interrelated series of subjects, or a society (in Whitehead's technical usage). The terms *self-identity* and *enduring personality* thus refer to the serial repetition of a common quality by a process of inheritance. Whitehead claims that this retention of common quality is not absolute. As long as there is an identity of primary character there may be secondary changes.[6]

The Relation Between Body and Mind

In Whitehead's opinion a mind is very closely related to its body. It seems to him that the venerable body-mind problem is a tremendous fraud. In supporting this position he simply calls attention to the very obvious experience (which everyone has) of unity with the body. In ordinary human experience the question of the intercommunication of mind and body simply does not arise. It would be regarded as perfectly silly for a person to announce, with a sense of achievement: "Here am I and I have brought my body with me." If the devotee of traditional metaphysics objects that this is too easy a solution, Whitehead's reply would be that metaphysics must be based on ordinary human experience. By all means let there be accurate analysis, but by the same token one must avoid the lure of artificial problems.

Not only does Whitehead stress the obvious interrelationship between a subject and its body; he also emphasizes the fact that the entire body is efficacious in experience, and that the body is the mind's link with the external world. Indeed, it is very difficult to tell where the body ends and the external world begins.[7] He provides a large number of specific illustrations to justify his contention that the human individual is a unity composed of distinguishable aspects, body and mind.[8]

As a result of this consideration of the relationship between body and mind, the preceding discussion of personal identity must be supplemented to include a reference to the function of the body and the external world, as a foundation for personal identity. They provide an element of stability which makes possible the endurance of mental processes manifesting continuity of characteristics.[9]

Immortality

Whitehead claims that every subject (actual entity) has "objective immortality" in those succeeding subjects which have prehended it. But the wider problem remains: What is the ultimate fate of that personal society which for a man's lifetime is intimately associated with that complex society of societies which constitutes the body? Whitehead offers a very tentative answer. He suggests the possibility of a union with the everlasting nature of God. In such a case, of course, the soul would be freed of dependence on the body.[10] Just what this position involves is difficult to ascertain. However, in Part V of *Process and Reality*, where the topic is discussed, he seems to reject personal immortality in the usual sense. We find him stating that in God, as receptive of the content of other actual entities, "there is no loss, no obstruction." God exercises a "tender care that nothing be lost." Yet Whitehead goes on to speak, in qualifying fashion, of "tenderness which loses nothing that can be saved." [11] There is, of course, the basic principle underlying all objectification—that what is preserved is not the "departed" actual entity as such. Its unique individuality must fade out before some of its contents are absorbed by a new entity.[12]

Perception

According to Whitehead there are two types of perception: (a) perception in the mode of *causal efficacy;* (b) perception in the mode of *presentational immediacy*. When a person is prehending *vague* data, felt as coming into the experience of the subject from the past, through the mediation of the body [in a subject's experience there is also a vague feeling of "ongoing" toward the future]—this is perception in the mode of causal efficacy.[13] Perception in the mode of presentational immediacy involves an experience of clear-cut sense data definitely located, and with emphasis on the present and a minimum of reference to past or to future.[14] In Whitehead's opinion there is a very close relation between these two modes of perception. The data of presentational immediacy are derived from the data of causal efficacy. There is, however, a significant change in the characteristics of these data. In presentational immediacy what (in causal efficacy) was vague in quality and function becomes clear and distinct.[15] For example, a subject vaguely experiences pain as derived from the body. This is perception in the mode of causal efficacy. When this pain is clearly apprehended as localized, this is perception in the mode of presentational immediacy. It should be obvious that presentational immediacy is a type of experience found only in organisms of a fairly high grade.[16]

It is very important to note Whitehead's contention that the clear data of presentational immediacy are the bases of all exact measurements. Further, they exhibit that complex of systematic mathematical relations which participate in all the nexus (groups of actual entities) of our cosmic epoch.[17] Some contemporary epistemologists refer to the projection of sense data. Whitehead deals with this topic in the context of his discussion of presentational immediacy. He suggests that the process of projection depends on the condition of the body. A state of "strain" determines where the data of presentational immediacy are "experienced as being." For example, the degree of strain determines the relative apparent distance of the data in front of the observer.[18] These "strain" feelings are called "geometrical" because they are directional and dimensional.[19]

Despite his recognition of the importance of experience in the mode of presentational immediacy—for instance, the fact that it provides the data to which mathematical calculations apply—Whitehead offers very vigorous criticisms of this essentially abstract approach to the complex environment. In presentational immediacy (or, to speak non-technically, in ordinary sense experience), there is a tendency to assign excessive importance to clear-cut, apparently unrelated bits of sense data. This is the basis of Whitehead's vigorous and recurrent criticism of Hume.[20] For Hume, sense data are here, now, immediate, and discrete. The superficiality of this analysis is obvious if one gives serious consideration to what happens when the phrase *United States* is uttered. True, there are the two distinguishable sounds, as Hume pointed out. But, in addition, there is a less obvious but more important feeling of a strong tendency for the sound *United* to be followed by the sound *States*. Within the specious present of a moment of experience there is a felt transition from the prior to the subsequent.[21] Indeed, as has been noted, Whitehead contends that this experience of causal tendency occurs not only in a specious present but also in the experience of the past welling up into the present. Thus, Whitehead does justice to the relationship of causal efficacy which was disregarded by Hume.[22] Referring to this so-called "non-sensuous" perception of the immediate past, Whitehead proceeds to show the bankruptcy of Hume's theory of association of ideas. Using the same example, he cites the case of a man uttering the word *United*. As a loyal citizen of the United States, he would, if the association of ideas were a valid explanatory principle, go on to say *States*. Instead, in this case, the complete phrase was *United Fruit Company*. In his immediate past was a tendency which gave rise to the word *Fruit* rather than the word *States*. He was unfamiliar with the United Fruit Company (this is assumed). He, therefore, had no association connecting the words composing the name. On the other hand, as a patriot, he had a very strong associative link between United and States. Thus, the principle of association does not account for what hap-

pened in this case.[23] Whitehead also pokes fun at Hume's
attempt to account for a common physical world. Hume experiences a complex of sense impressions and then conjec-
tures a world. This, says Whitehead, is sheer nonsense. He
remarks that a young man does not begin by meeting a
complex of sense data and then proceed to conjecture a
charming young lady as dancing partner. We may analyze
our experience in terms of discrete sense data, but we thereby
perform an artificial reduction which omits essential factors.
It is Whitehead's contention that we experience clearly the
impact of other agents. We do not need to postulate them
on the basis of shaky indirect evidence.[24] As a further criticism of Hume, Whitehead claims that his theory of discrete
sense data makes it impossible to account for memory and
induction because, for Hume, there is nothing in the present fact which inherently refers either to the past or to the
future.[25]

In summary, it may be noted, Whitehead constantly
stresses the point that ordinary sense perception—that is to
say, perception in the mode of presentational immediacy—
is a very inadequate method of observing the external world
in its entirety. This type of perception overlooks the essentially dynamic nature of the universe. In general only what
is clear and obvious is observed. This procedure blinds one
to the less apparent fact of the genuine interconnection of
observed data. The inadequacies of clear sense data should
be obvious from the fact that many of them are controllable
at will. Some can be eliminated completely and yet the person can still function effectively. Whitehead's remarks concerning the deficiencies of presentational immediacy are applicable to the method of *introspection* since it concentrates
on the data of presentational immediacy.[26]

In a less technical discussion of perception, Whitehead
emphasizes the point that observation is carried on most
effectively when there is *interest* in the observed objects.

Indeed, he goes so far as to suggest that without interest there is no observation at all.[27] In dealing with the perception of other persons, he suggests that mental telepathy is quite possible. The technical foundations of this point of view are stated in Whitehead's theory of hybrid physical prehension.[28]

Whitehead rejects "representative theories" of perception because in his opinion they are contrary to the facts of experience. As he once remarked: "When you are confronted with a complex pattern of sense data, you don't say, with due solemnity, 'I'll bet my boots there is a world at the back of this.' " In other words, a person uncorrupted by metaphysics and epistemology admits direct awareness of an external world. The experience of memory, and the more general awareness of the derivation of data from past experiences, also refute the notion of representative perception. Speaking technically, the transfer of feeling does not involve a mere representation. It is a literal presence.[29]

It must be pointed out that Whitehead's *direct contact* with the external world is of a rather special sort. It is a direct contact with an external world (of actual entities) which has gone out of existence. An act of faith (an assumption) is involved in Whitehead's epistemology. It is the faith that the components of the objects in the contemporary world are essentially the same as their past components. The contemporary components are not, as such, objectified (present) in the prehending subject. This is so because, since the contemporary actual entities have not yet reached completion (satisfaction), they are not yet ready to provide content for the use of new actual entities. There are further difficulties. The actual world, external to the experiencing self, includes the body of the experiencer. The body may be responsible for experiences which seem to be due to the (more) external world of tables and chairs.[30] The problem of "time-lag" in perception is also noted. His treatment of the problem of perceiving a star is not particularly clear.[31] Despite these admitted difficulties, Whitehead does not feel inclined to accept the usual forms of epistemological dualism.[32] He refuses to agree that sensa are alien to external nature and present only because of the productive powers of a high-grade precipient organism. "The experience of the simplest grade of actual entity is to be conceived as the *unoriginative* response to the datum with its simple content of *sensa*." [33]

Whitehead suggests that there are at least three tests of the validity of perception: (a) force and vivacity; (b) a careful check on the origin of the experienced data; (c) the conformation of the future to expectations.[34] He admits that these are not infallible.

In addition to recording the usual sources of erroneous perception (discussed above), Whitehead calls attention to other causes. This involves the use of some of his technical terms. For example, it may happen that the data provided by causal efficacy are so vague, quite apart from bodily distortion, that it is easy to misinterpret them. Further, transmutation [35] may occur. Also distortion may be produced in the course of presentational immediacy, in that the data received through causal efficacy are subject to intensifications and inhibitions.[36]

It should be clearly understood that in Whitehead's opinion no error is involved in abnormal bodily activity, causal efficacy, or presentational immediacy, *as such*. Thus, in referring to presentational immediacy, he points out that the image of a colored chair seen in a mirror is just as much a presentation of color present in the world as is our direct vision of the chair.[37] Erroneous perception occurs only when a mistake is made in *symbolic reference*—that is to say, when it is *incorrectly assumed* that the data experienced in presentational immediacy characterizes the society (e.g., a physical object) experienced in the mode of causal efficacy. For example: Through the mediation of the body, a subject becomes vaguely aware of the existence of an external object possessing certain qualities—for instance "greyness." By the process of presentational immediacy this greyness is clearly apprehended. There is no doubt about it.[38] The greyness is referred by the subject to a specific area. It is assumed (the term is Whitehead's) that this grey quality, as experienced, applies to the external physical object (for example, a stone). When this assumption is incorrect, error arises.[39]

Consciousness (Two Meanings)

The preceding discussion of causal efficacy and presentational immediacy forms a background for some of Whitehead's comments concerning consciousness. For instance, it is obvious that in Whitehead's opinion the data of consciousness are not the most important data. Hence, the tradition which overemphasizes clarity and distinctness is subject to constant criticism by him.[40] Here Whitehead is employing the term *consciousness* in its ordinary meaning. However, he also introduces a specialized and highly technical usage.

This specialized use of the term *consciousness* is based on the claim that consciousness presupposes experience.[41] Consciousness is a quality which emerges. It is the result of relationship between a fact and a supposition about that fact.[42]

Propositions

In order to understand fully Whitehead's comments concerning consciousness, it is necessary to examine his discussion of propositions. A theory, or *proposition,* has as its subject an actual entity or a nexus of actual entities. The predicate of a proposition is an eternal object or a group of eternal objects. The proposition is the *possibility* of *that* predicate applying in that assigned way to *those* logical subjects.[43] It should be obvious that the logical subjects involved are impartially related. That is to say, any one proposition is not the exclusive possession of any one percipient subject.[44]

It is important to note that Whitehead makes a clear distinction between a *judgment* and a *proposition*. A judgment is a complex comparative feeling. It is concerned with the contrast between an objectified nexus of actual entities and a proposition whose logical subjects makes up that nexus.[45]

It will be realized that since the logical subject of a proposition is an actual entity, or a group of actual entities, there is an obvious restriction placed on the number and nature of such logical subjects available for use in propositions. Thus no person can apprehend a proposition if the specific logical subjects of that proposition are not available for prehension. For example, the proposition "Caesar crossed the Rubicon" could not have been thought by Hannibal. Obviously, then, new propositions appear with the passing of time.[46] That is to say, new actual entities become available as logical subjects. However, the propositional experience of a person is not as restricted as it may at first appear. It might be argued that there can be no propositions about hypothetical entities, since only *actual* entities can serve as the logical subjects of propositions. Similarly, it could be contended that there can be no propositions about future entities since they also are not actual. Further, it would seem that there can be no universal propositions, since an attempt to refer to past and future would involve propositions which would have non-actual subjects. Such propositions would be impossible. These objections lose potency when one notes exactly what is involved in Whitehead's position. He contends that the logical subject must be in the *actual world* of the person prehending it. By *actual world* he apparently means not only the present but also the past and the future (in so far as it is definite).[47] For example, in a general discussion of freedom Whitehead makes this comment: "Some actual entities may be *either* in the settled past, *or* in the contemporary nexus, *or* even left to the undecided future." [48] Concerning universal propositions, Whitehead states that the only difference between a particular proposition and a universal proposition is the degree of generalization. If this is stated, the problem of referring to a universal proposition is solved.[49] With reference to propositions about hypothetical entities, it may be observed: (a) Future entities are in a sense hypothetical, i.e., they are not actual, yet they can be referred to, since they are in a sense present in the experience of the prehending subject. (b) The hypothetical element is also introduced in that the eternal object (predicate) *may* apply to the logical subject.

Whitehead seems to involve himself in the apparently conflicting claims that: (a) propositions only exist as entertained in experience; (b) a proposition is a datum for feeling, awaiting a subject feeling it. The apparent contradiction may perhaps be cleared up by assuming that Whitehead's meaning is: A proposition prehended in the experience of one actual entity A serves as a lure for feeling and thus contributes to the rise of another actual entity B. Thus a proposition existent in A is awaiting its use by actual entity B.[50] Or Whitehead may be contending that a newly arising actual entity uses a proposition to guide its process of self-creation. The proposition, of course, would exist in the experience of the actual entity in question.

Consciousness (*Technical Usage*)

Returning to the more general discussion of consciousness, it will be remembered that consciousness is that quality which emerges, as a result of the conjunction of a fact and a supposition (theory or proposition) about that fact. This conjunction must take the form of a contrast, or as Whitehead terms it *affirmation-negation*.[51] Consciousness is a feeling. It is a feeling of the contrast of theory, as *mere* theory, with fact as *mere* fact.[52] For example, a person experiences a stone. A proposition is formulated about the stone: "The stone is grey." The stone, as experienced, is a fact. The proposition about the stone is an assumption concerning a possible quality of the stone. In this situation there is a contrast between a fact, the existence of which is affirmed, and a possibility which is, in a rather technical sense, the negation of (the affirmation of) the fact. It is to be noted that consciousness is more fully present in cases where the contrast is most obvious. This would occur, for instance, in a situation where a person experienced a stone and observed that the stone was *not* grey. In Whitehead's opinion, the highest form of consciousness is that in which one experiences a contrast between a possibility to be realized in the future, and present facts which as yet fall far below the ideal possibilities involved in the expectation.[53]

It is obvious that by restricting the use of the term *consciousness* to cases where there is a contrast between fact and a theory about the fact, Whitehead is denying that many experiences, ordinarily called conscious, really are such. For example, he states that when a person experiences a proposition, he is not conscious, unless the proposition is contrasted with facts, as indicated above. Thus he contends that propositions are not primarily for belief, but for feeling at the level of unconsciousness.[54] He also claims that it is possible to experience a concept (eternal object) without being conscious. Indeed, any type of *feeling* does not require consciousness.[55] It follows, then, that perception in the modes of causal efficacy and presentational immediacy occur unconsciously.[56] This is equally true of their mixture in instances of symbolic reference. Thus, in his own particular fashion, Whitehead claims that a very considerable portion of a person's experience is unconscious. To this extent he agrees with Freud. However, this is as far as the agreement goes.

Memory and Imagination

Whitehead's theory of the interrelation of actual entities leads him to claim a direct intuition (experience) of *memory*. That is to say, a past actual entity provides data for a present actual entity. The data received into the life of the present actual entity are experienced as coming from the past. This, then, is the basis of memory.[57]

Imagination is also discussed, briefly, by Whitehead. He notes that novelty of conceptual prehension is the basis of imagination. The self-determination which characterizes the activity of subjects is ultimately a matter of creative imagination. He also stresses the importance of past experience as a source for the material which undergoes imaginative reconstruction. This past experience is most conveniently preserved in verbal form.[58] Finally, Whitehead does not greatly fear the possible extravagances involved in imagination. As he once remarked: "Imagination is up the right street even if it sometimes stops at the wrong door."

Thinking

Whitehead regards thought as one of the routine activities of a normal human being. It is not assigned a status of exalted superiority.[59] Thought is closely related to bodily activity. Indeed, he argues that there is a very intimate relation between thinking and manual dexterity. He suggests that aristocracies suffer from brain lethargy because they are never forced to develop complex manual skills. The dexterity required in the sporting activities of members of the "upper class" is of a restricted and somewhat gross type in most instances.[60] As may be gathered from the preceding comments, certain phases of Whitehead's discussion of thinking are strikingly similar to the point of view popularized by John Dewey. The following quotations substantiate this judgment: "From the moment of birth we are immersed in action . . . We have, therefore, in various spheres of experience to adopt those ideas which seem to work within those spheres." [61] Like Dewey, Whitehead is very critical of all attempts to claim completeness and finality for knowledge.[62] After all we are finite creatures. Speaking technically, it is obvious that *all* the interconnected actual entities of an actual world cannot be fully prehended by any actual entity.

The foregoing outline of Whitehead's position tends to obscure one very important phase of his general point of view. It has been noted that he stresses the practical aspect of thinking. This, however, is not the whole story. There is the theoretical type of reason which deals with the realm beyond the concerns of the animal body. These two types of reason are best exemplified by Plato, who shared reason with the gods, and Ulysses, who shared it with the foxes.[63]

Whitehead believes that both types of reason are present in men and that there must be due cognizance of the possibility of their mutual interaction. He provides impressive illustrations of the fruitful co-operation which has been achieved between speculative and practical reason. He points out, for example, that the apparently fantastic speculative deviations from Euclidian geometry produced during the late nineteenth century turned out to be of great value in expressing modern scientific knowledge.[64]

With characteristic playful irony Whitehead remarks: "It has been said that 'men are rational.' This is palpably false: they are only intermittently rational—merely liable to rationality. . . . The intellect of Socrates is intermittent: he occasionally sleeps and he can be drugged or stunned." [65] *Pure* thought is impossible. It is aroused by some present situation. It has effects. Thoughts can disturb the whole being of a man.[66]

In dealing with "creative thought," he notes the danger involved. The attendant novelty may be productive of anarchy or, at least, error. However, Whitehead has sufficient confidence in human mentality to claim that the power of sane judgment is likely to be generated. It will then serve as a corrective. In examining the bases of creative thinking, it is suggested that the range of thinking becomes enlarged when an individual is able to travel in safety and thus break through the limited horizon of one social structure.[67] Further, he proceeds to debunk the ancient nonsense that "Necessity is the mother of invention." Under the pressure of necessity, there is a strong temptation to be satisfied with shoddy substitutes for accurate thinking. Great ideas are more likely to occur under pleasant conditions. The task to which one is driven is not apt to be done well.[68] Whitehead is also aware of the importance of mechanical improvements in scientific instruments. For example, more effective instruments help reveal new facts which may arouse and stimulate creative thought. It is, of course, obvious that the words of others serve to arouse thought processes.[69]

Creativity is unmistakably involved in the process of *inductive thinking*. Whitehead's discussion of inductive reasoning stresses the point that it is based on an assumption or presupposition. It is assumed that what is discovered in the future will have some close analogy to what is found in the present.[70] There seem to be grounds for at least a limited trust in induction [71] because the dominant facts in a situation *tend* to be repeated in the future. However, the only proper procedure is to limit the scope of induction to the prediction of some of the characteristics of some particular future. This restriction is necessary because the characteristics of one era of actual entities may not be the characteristics of another era. Thus, induction should not attempt to deal in unlimited generalities.[72] Whitehead's confidence in the possibility of induction is derived ultimately from his belief that the future has a sort of "existence" in the present.[73] However, it is there "according to the mode of anticipation." In apparent contrast, he proceeds to postulate a

very different sort of link between present and future, a
link which *determines* the nature of the future. Whitehead
states that the future is in the present "with such general
determinations as it lies in the nature of the particular present to impose on the particular future which must succeed
it." [74] Either this is a careless expression, or a contradiction.
In any case its obvious meaning is contrary to one of Whitehead's basic concepts. No present actual entity can impose
data on a future actual entity. The future actual entity is
autonomous. Because of this one cannot have absolute confidence in the uniformity of nature. What has been true of
the present need not be true of the future.

Whitehead tries to correct an undue emphasis on induction (in the ordinary sense of proceeding from particulars
to general). He stresses the fact that *deduction* plays an important part in adequate scientific thinking. The applications of general principles to particular situations must be
elaborated by deduction. Otherwise one engages in barren
intellectual gymnastics. [75]

Whitehead provides a brief discussion of sampling *procedure* with reference to the problem of statistical probability.
He argues that "random sampling" does not really escape
the difficulties involved in an infinite ground—first, because
no notion of ratio can apply to infinites; secondly, because
no sampling is random. In reality it has followed a complex
method. He suggests that his theory of the primordial nature
of God provides the basis for a non-statistical approach to
probability. [76] That is to say, the interwoven complex of
eternal objects constitutes a frame of reference whereby,
given the realization of one eternal object, the probability
of another eternal object being realized can be inferred.

In his discussion of knowledge Whitehead makes a useful
distinction between *wisdom* and *intelligence*. Intelligence
has as its goal the achievement of a neat, simple system. It
pays the price of the omission of much relevant data. Wis-

dom takes a wider view. It is concerned with the conflicting complexities of things. Thus it tries to correct the "too simple" systematization of intelligence.[77] Wisdom involves the application of knowledge to human problems, specifically to the achievement of values.[78]

On the basis of the preceding discussion, it is easy to understand why Whitehead contends that *vagueness* and *clarity* should be regarded as essential factors to be considered in any discussion of knowledge. Clarity, as has been noted above, is achieved at the expense of a disregarding of the vague background of facts which a seeker after wisdom cannot afford to overlook. In developing this general theme Whitehead suggests that any attempt to understand a complicated intellectual product must involve a genetic approach. This is so because such an approach takes into consideration essential facts of interconnection.[79] He states that the search for knowledge may be attempted logically or aesthetically. In a word, the method of logic is abstract, that of aesthetics is concrete.[80] Because the greater concreteness of aesthetic experience provides the basis of a more comprehensive and adequate analysis, Whitehead states: "Logic, conceived as an adequate analysis of the advance of thought, is a fake. It is a superb instrument, but it requires a background of common sense." [81] He illustrates this contention by pointing out that the apparent logical clarity and exactness of "one and one make two" is a gross deception.

Those who disregard these basic facts concerning knowledge fall into serious errors:

(a) In order to obtain a clear-cut and final solution to a complex problem, vast areas of relevant fact are disregarded. These minds make the serious error of assuming that their interests and skills delimit the entire field of knowledge. They consider that what falls outside their range is nonsense.[82] Many scientists think in this fashion. The scientific devotion to exact measurement is very commendable—where relevant. But the skeleton fingers of statistics cannot grasp all the complexities of life.[83] Many scientists crave simplicity with feverish urgency. The claim that the human intellect is an instrument capable of functioning, with absolute clarity, for extended periods of time, is one of the myths of the twentieth century. As a matter of fact there are many data which, at the moment, cannot be stated with anything approximating clarity.[84]

These comments should not be misinterpreted. They are not a thoroughgoing disparagement of logic in particular and clarity in general. Rather it is an attempt to correct the overzealous enthusiasm of some contemporary scientists and philosophers. No one is more aware of the value of abstract thinking and clarity of thought than the co-author of *Principia Mathematica*.

(b) There is also a second type of error. It is assumed that ideas handed down from the past provide an adequate solution for present problems. This is a very grave mistake. The meaning of ancient ideas can never be fully grasped. Their context is now missing. In any case, new facts may be available which demand the abandonment, or at least the revision, of traditional ideas. Yet one should not disregard the wisdom of the past. Critically used, it is of great value.

As has been noted, Whitehead claims that, in the last analysis, genuine knowledge is obtained by a method which he terms *intuition*.[85] Thus he contends that understanding is not based on inference but rather on self-evidence. Various passages in Whitehead's writings clarify his meaning. For example, in his discussion of causal efficacy and presentational immediacy, there is involved the claim that one can intuit, via causal efficacy, data which are disregarded by presentational immediacy. In short, intuition enables us to grasp the massive interconnectedness of things and the vague data which are not in the clear focus of "awareness." It reveals the facts as they *are* rather than as they *appear* to superficial observation.[86]

As a result of his emphasis on intuition, Whitehead has some very critical comments to make concerning proof, as it is frequently conceived. In Whitehead's opinion, the demand for proof is a symptom of lack of understanding and half-heartedness. A mind freed from prejudice can derive from immediate experience information sufficient to deal with many basic human problems. Those who demand the support of some complicated artificial system of thought indicate their second-rateness. Self-evidence renders disreputable the nagging whine for proof.[87] However, in one sense of the term, Whitehead recognizes the value of proof. That is, he is well aware of the necessity of supporting statements by a careful appeal to (direct) experience.

Whitehead recognizes that in the process of proof, in the latter sense of the term, what is regarded as evidence depends on the theory which happens to control the observation of the person who is looking for evidence. For example, if with Hume you assume that there is no direct evidence for the interconnectedness of things, then you are unable to find any such evidence, even though it is actually there.[88] The deficiencies of special methods of observation, experimental, deductive, inductive, introspective (all are partial and hence inadequate), leads Whitehead to make the apparently paradoxical statement that speculative reason is in its essence untrammeled by method.[89] This preceding statement is perhaps not intended to be accepted with strict literalness. It is possible that Whitehead merely means that speculative reason will rise superior to the restricted or partial methods by means of the intuitive method. Yet even by employing the method of intuition we can never hope to grasp the entire complexity of the universe. Hence the goal of speculative reason (such a complete understanding) can never be achieved fully. After all, any actual entity

subjects some of its available data to the process of negative prehension. Even in the case of the truths which we are
able to grasp there is a further difficulty. We have to express
these truths in the context of a universe of discourse which
is inadequate and may have to be changed.[90]

Language

Whitehead's discussion of the use of words, and in particular their relation to thinking, merits careful attention.
He, of course, notes that words are symbols. The meaning
of a word is the abstract idea or particular concrete datum
to which the word refers or which it arouses. For example,
the word *tree* refers to the object *tree*. It may also arouse
certain abstract ideas, images, and emotions.[91] In this connection it is necessary to realize that Whitehead is among
those who recognize the importance of the emotional aspect
of meaning. He points out that an American and an English-
man, both reading,

> this little world,
> this precious stone set in a silver sea,

will derive very different meaning from these same words.
The denotative meaning will be the same (if both have
taken a course in Shakespeare), but the emotive meanings
are likely to be vastly different. Whitehead also emphasizes
the *practical* importance of the emotive phase of meaning.
Emotionally charged words frequently have served as ce-
ment, binding together diverse peoples into a unified nation.[92] He is well aware of the fact that symbol and meaning
are interchangeable in the sense that the word *forest* (as
symbol) may have as its meaning a group of actual trees.
It is also possible that the actual forest may serve as a symbol to refer to the word, which is now the referent (meaning). He suggests, further, that there are instances when
aesthetic data are more effective symbols than words. This

is particularly true in the religious sphere.[93] The importance of symbols in facilitating adjustment to distant objects and in making possible preparation for future events—in general, the "labor-saving" aspect of the use of symbols—is continually emphasized by Whitehead.[94]

According to Whitehead, the importance of language is such that, in a sense, language is responsible for human mentality. If it were not for the subtleties and abstractive function of language, the "soul of man" could not have reached its present high stage of development.[95] This sounds very much like a liberal type of Behaviorism. However, Whitehead endeavors to distinguish his position from that of Behaviorism. He argues that if language is the same as thought, then translation from one language to another is impossible. This follows because, if Behaviorism is accepted, a sentence in English would be one thought and a sentence in Spanish (supposedly expressing the same thought), since it is a different sentence, would, therefore, be a different thought. A second criticism is that when a person tries to find a word with which to express an idea, he illustrates a state of affairs which according to a Behaviorist cannot occur—because, for them, ideas are words (or, to be more accurate, symbolic activities). However, despite his contention that language is not to be identified with thought, Whitehead is anxious to show that language is of very great assistance in the process of retaining, recalling, and communicating thought.[96] His enthusiasm concerning these matters is not carried beyond reasonable limits. It is emphasized that language has been developed in the course of dealing with practical problems. It provides a useful, though not very accurate, method for referring to obvious facts. In this connection, Whitehead reminds us that one set of words may symbolize a large number of different propositions.[97] Further, language is very inadequate in dealing with intangible situations which involve vast subtleties of meaning.[98] He goes on to point out that there are many ideas which cannot be expressed by the language at present available. However, he stresses the fact that the apprehension of the meaning of a proposition is not dependent upon its accurate verbal expression. For example, the notion of irrational number had been used in mathematics for over two thousand years before it received accurate definition in the last quarter of the nineteenth century.[99] There is a further difficulty involved in the use of words. Whitehead quotes, with approval, J. S. Mill's comments concerning Greek slavery to words:

They [the Greeks] had great difficulty in distinguishing between things which their language confounded, or in putting mentally together things which it distinguished; and could hardly combine the objects in nature, into any classes but those which were made for them by the popular phrases of their own country; or at least could not help fancying those classes to be natural, and all others arbitrary and artificial.[100]

6

Whitehead's Theory of Value

One of the distinctive characteristics of Whitehead's philosophy is his contention that "value is inherent in actuality."[1] In other words, value is not an artificial construct. Rather, the word *value* denotes "the intrinsic reality of an event."[2]

Whitehead's discussion of value is concerned chiefly with Truth, Beauty, Goodness, Peace—and their opposites.[3] His work in this field is for the most part expressed in the technical terminology of the theory of actual entities. However, there are numerous non-technical clarifications.

His general theory of value embodies the contention that the process of *realization,* by which an actual entity achieves complete selfhood, is in itself the attainment of value.[4] More specifically: (a) Value results from *limitation.*[5] This follows from Whitehead's theory that an actual entity constitutes itself by selecting some data and rejecting other data— hence limitation.[6] Further, (b) value originates because of the *immanence of infinitude* in a finite entity.[7] That is to say, value is present when an actual entity (a finite) creates itself by absorbing data from the infinite environment of other actual entities. (c) The fundamental character of value is *co-ordination.*[8] In other words, the data used by the newly arising actual entity are co-ordinated in accordance with its subjective aim. It is to be noted that an actual entity can enjoy its own value.[9]

In view of the prominent place which "interest" theories

of value occupy in modern axiology, it is relevant to observe
Whitehead's opinion concerning this position. He claims
that a definition of value (importance) in terms of interest
is inadequate. He suggests that value *arouses* interest. Hence
value is not the *resultant* of interest.[10] In more technical
fashion, he argues that value involves (a) co-ordination and
(b) individuality of details. "Interest" seems to concentrate
unduly on the latter aspect.[11]

Whitehead's discussion of value-in-general is complicated
by an analysis which he provides in his essay on "Immortality." In his earlier studies, as has just been noted, he emphasizes the point that value is inherent in actuality. However, in this later essay he seems to stress a contrast between
"the world of fact" and "the world of value." Thus he
states: "The basic elements in the World of Fact are finite
activities; the basic character of the World of Value is its
timeless coordination of the infinitude of possibility for
realization." [12] In other words, Whitehead seemingly is iden-
tifying value with eternal objects and not with the concrete
reality of actual entities. However, this apparent digression
from his usual value theory is seen, on careful examination,
to be more apparent than real. He emphasizes that the world
of value (in its abstract phase) requires, for its *completion,*
finite activity.[13] More specifically, he contends that the qualities of immortality and self-endurance, which characterize
the world of value (considered as an abstraction), are reproduced in the world of fact by the personal identity which
is manifest by some societies of actual entities.[14, 15] Thus, it
would seem that Whitehead is not offering two distinct theories of value. Rather, he is pointing out that there are
value ideals (abstract possibilities—eternal objects) which
when realized, or exemplified, constitute *actual values.*

In describing the process by which actual entities come
into being, Whitehead uses the term *valuation.* He employs
this concept in at least three rather technical senses: (a) He

refers to the Category of Conceptual Valuation. This is simply a matter of noting that an experienced actual entity, or nexus of entities, exemplifies a specific eternal object.[16] (b) Whitehead uses the term *conceptual valuation* in another sense. He refers to the function performed by the "primordial nature" of God.[17] Conceptual valuation, in this sense, means simply arrangement in varying degrees of relevance. (c) There is a third meaning for valuation—which is more in accord with ordinary usage. Whitehead states that the subjective form of a conceptual feeling (i.e., the type of prehension which feels an eternal object) involves valuation.[18] In other words, the *decision* as to what contribution an eternal object shall make to the development of an actual entity is the *valuation* of that eternal object by that actual entity.[19] Obviously, valuation, in this sense, is the basis of purpose.[20]

Whitehead's consideration of the relation of God to value is worthy of at least brief reference. In one of his earlier books he states that the purpose of God is to facilitate the attainment of value in the world of actual entities.[21] In discussing valuation, it was noted that God organizes and makes relevant all eternal objects. In so far as these constitute value ideals, he is concerned with value. In this connection, Whitehead refers to God as "the poet of the world," who patiently strives to arouse actual entities by a vision of Truth, Beauty, and Goodness.[22] Thus God (in his primordial nature) serves as a lure to which actual entities respond in various ways and hence achieve varying degrees and types of value. In describing the so-called consequent nature of God, Whitehead claims that God is able to preserve and *unify* some of the values achieved by other actual entities.[23]

The preceding examination of Whitehead's discussion of value-in-general serves as a background for consideration of his treatment of Truth, Beauty, Goodness, Peace—and their "negatives."

Truth

Whitehead defines truth as the conformation of *appearance* to *reality*.[24, 25] In order to understand what is meant by this definition, it is necessary to discover the meaning of *appearance, reality,* and *conformation.* The concrete data which actual entities prehend from other actual entities constitute *reality* (in Whitehead's special, technical use of the term), and the novel use which the new actual entity makes of these data, in accordance with its own subjective aim, constitutes what Whitehead calls *appearance.*[26]

A consideration of three types of *conformation* of appearance to reality, will perhaps serve to clarify further Whitehead's use of these basic terms.

(a) One type of conformation (truth relation) is illustrated in the case of a relation which is sometimes found between propositions and objects. A proposition[27] is true when the thing to which it refers does, as a matter of fact, possess the quality assigned to it, as specified in the predicate of the proposition. Or there is a truth relation when the experienced sense data do, as a matter of fact, qualify objects which they seem to qualify.[28]

(b) According to Whitehead, the type of truth relation illustrated in the cases of a true proposition and a true sense perception, considered above, is not the only type of truth relation.[29] Thus, in cases where a person's sensory experience is normal, in a normal environment, the truth relation is said to occur. He apparently means to say that this type of truth relation is not concerned exclusively with an accurate report of external events. Rather the data may be chiefly of internal origin.[30]

(c) There is a third type of truth relation which is even. more vague and indirect than the type "a" considered above. This is so-called symbolic truth.[31] The relation in this instance is vague because there is no obvious causal relation between appearance and reality. Words (in most cases) have no inherent relation to their meanings (referents). Similarly the symbols used in art and religious ceremonial function on the basis of a conventional linkage. These latter symbols chiefly convey, or arouse, emotion rather than indicate objective meaning (i.e., indicate literal facts).[32]

Whitehead's claim that the truth relation is "the conformation of Appearance to Reality" obviously indicates a species of the *correspondence theory of truth*.[33] He uses the term *coherence* also, but he really means what is ordinarily implied by the correspondence theory.[34] He notes that his theory of truth is in a sense—but not in an ultimate sense—pragmatic. It is pragmatic in that it stresses consequences—indeed, in some cases, practical consequences. However, the pragmatist is like Hamlet, continually postponing a final decision. Whitehead contends that intuition (immediate experience) in at least some instances removes the need for this tentativeness.[35]

Apart from his very technical treatment of truth, Whitehead makes a number of penetrating comments of general interest. He remarks, for example, that there are two attitudes toward truth. One regards truth as "a dodge usually necessary for a happy life." On the other hand, truthfulness may be regarded as "an element in one's own self-respect." [36] It is also shown that in some cases truth may involve deception. For example, the smile of a hypocrite is deceptive. That of a philanthropist may be truthful. Both of them are truly smiling. With characteristic emphasis on the importance of avoiding misplaced concreteness (reliance on abstraction), Whitehead suggests that a partial grasp of the truth is a distortion of the truth.[37]

Whitehead is very anxious that our interest in "truth" be placed in its proper perspective. For instance, it should be recognized that actually very few propositions are entirely true or false. In practice we may know that a proposition

expresses an important truth but that it is subject to limitations and qualifications which may be unknown at the present moment. For example, Galileo was convinced that the
earth moves and that the sun is fixed. The Inquisition contended that the former is fixed and the latter moves. The
Newtonian astronomers, postulating an absolute theory of
space, argued that both the sun and the earth move. However, any one of these three statements is equally true, provided you have fixed your sense of *rest* and *motion* in the
way implied by the statement which is accepted. In short,
his position seems to be that truth and falsehood, in some
areas, vary—depending upon initial assumptions.[38]

In the course of his discussion of truth, Whitehead remarks, with characteristic sanity, that "a clash of doctrines
is not a disaster—it is an opportunity." [39] It is not accurate
to conclude that when theories are in opposition one must
be true, the other false—the false to be completely rejected.
Rather the clash may lead to the discovery of additional
truth. He illustrates this point by reference to the work on
nitrogen done by Lord Rayleigh and Sir William Ramsay.
These men, having obtained nitrogen by different processes,
noticed a slight difference in the atomic weight—depending
on the method used. This discrepancy was not regarded
as a calamity to be "hushed up" or a situation in which one
result was right and the other wrong. Rather it gave rise
to a search for possible explanations. The discovery of argon
resulted from this project. Further the fruitful concept of
isotope was developed.[40] In any case a false statement is not
merely wrong: "Error is the price which we pay for progress." [41]

Perhaps his most striking comment on truth is the "shock-
ing" remark that "it is more important that a proposition be
interesting than that it be true." [42] This seemingly arrant
disregard for the value of truth is set in its proper perspective when one observes the context in which Whitehead

makes this comment. He contends that a proposition should serve as a lure.[43] If this fact is borne in mind, the implications of the preceding statement can be grasped more adequately. After all, some of the most compelling propositions cannot be definitely classified as true or false. In his class on "The Function of Reason," he once remarked: "You don't go through Shakespeare or a detective story and at the end of each sentence say: True or False?" Thus Whitehead seems, on occasion, to take the apparently extreme position that even though a proposition, if taken literally, may be false, it still can perform an important function. *If* this be a correct interpretation, he is simply stressing the value of an occasional vacation from the world of reality by entry into the world of "make believe." There is a further point. Sometimes value ideals are expressed in statements which are not literally true. Yet these statements are very important as stimuli which facilitate the realization of these ideals. For example, we say that our nation is a democracy. Actually the statement is not completely true. However, the fact that we make the statement may arouse us to at least attempt a closer approximation to the ideal of democracy. Finally, it is interesting to note Whitehead's suggestion that there are occasions when a myth has an important part to play in the expression of truth. Here, obviously, he is in agreement with Plato.[44] In any case, it must be observed—in fairness to Whitehead—that, having said, "It is more important that a proposition be interesting than that it be true," he proceeds to emphasize that a true proposition is more apt to be interesting than a false one.[45] Towards the end of his main discussion of truth, he offers a vigorous comment concerning its fundamental importance: "But after all, it is the blunt truth that we want. The final contentment of our aims requires something more than vulgar substitutes, or subtle evasions, however delicate. . . . Apart from blunt truth, our lives sink decadently amid the perfume of hints and suggestions." [46] Yet even so it must be remembered that it is not necessarily good to know the truth. Sometimes truth may be used to beget evil.[47] It should also be noted that the successful pursuit of truth involves a thoroughgoing morality, the fundamental honesty which earnestly seeks to apprehend all the available facts.[48]

Whitehead is of the opinion that, in a genuine sense, there is a universality of truth. This is because of the universality of interrelations between actual entities. This relativity, in other words, is universally true. Further, any actual entity imposes a universal obligation in the sense that it is there as a datum which all other actual entities must deal with, either positively or negatively. Finally, it must be remembered that "truth" is one of the *eternal objects*.[49]

Beauty

Beauty is the mutual adaptation of the several factors in an occasion of experience.[50] In this definition Whitehead is referring to beauty as concrete and actualized. He is indicating the state of affairs which must be present in an actual entity if beauty is to be achieved.[51] Whitehead also thinks of beauty as an ideal potential—an eternal object.[52] Thus he states: "Beauty is a quality which finds its exemplification in actual occasions: or put conversely, it is a quality in which such occasions can severally participate." [53]

He discusses, in considerable detail, the conditions which must be present in an actual entity to make possible the achievement of beauty—i.e., the exemplification of the eternal object *beauty*. As has been noted above, there must be "adaptation" of the several factors in the entity. There are two main types of adaptation: (a) The first is characterized by the lack of mutual interference among the various prehensions; [54] this type of adaptation characterizes a *minor* form of beauty. (b) There is also the *major* form of beauty; here also there is absence of mutual interference. In addition there are striking contrasts of content.[55] This set of conditions results in an increased intensity and issues in a higher form of beauty. There is a *harmony of patterned contrasts* in which the various distinct elements contribute to the total effect and also are enhanced by the totality of which they form a part. Whitehead provides an excellent illustration of what he means by a reference to the Cathedral at Chartres. The sculptured figures on the famous porch of the Cathedral both have *individual* importance and effectively function as details in the *whole*. Each has its individual beauty. All contribute to the beauty of the whole.[56]

It should be realized that Whitehead is willing to admit that the achievement of major beauty does not always involve *harmonious* patterned contrast. There are cases where the perfection of harmony ranks below imperfection or discord because the eternal object *beauty* is more completely exemplified in the latter than in the former. This is so where the perfection is deadening. Granted that there is frustration involved in the experience of discord. But this may be the lesser of two evils, because it contributes to a greater good. As an alternative, the relapse into monotony or complete somnolence is far worse.[57, 58]

The preceding reference to *pattern* indicates Whitehead's recognition of the importance of this factor as a requisite for the achievement of beauty. Pattern is involved in both the minor and major forms of beauty. The absence of mutual inhibition occurs when a certain pattern is followed (minor beauty). "Patterned contrast" is a condition for major beauty. Whitehead has expressed this general point on numerous occasions. He notes, for example, that Greek statues express the dependence of beauty on regularity of geometrical forms.[59] There is also the more general comment: "I suggest that Symbolic Logic, that is to say, the symbolic examination of pattern with the use of real variables, will become the foundation of aesthetics." [60] It is to be emphasized that

Whitehead *does not* claim that a reference to pattern constitutes a *complete* explanation of the presence of beauty. For
example, in evaluating a picture, geometrical form is not
the only factor to be considered. Color is also very important.[61]

Whitehead claims that there is an infinity of grades of
beauty. He admits that we can conceive only a finite segment
of this infinite series. Further, he does not deal very exten-
sively with the problem of how to distinguish degrees of
beauty. For example, he suggests that it is obvious that in
comparison with the enjoyment of a color, the experience
of a picture—if it is a good picture—involves a higher grade
of value.[62]

It is interesting to discover, that, in Whitehead's opinion,
beauty (as actualized) exists even though no percipient organism appreciates it. He considers, for example, a flower
blooming in some isolated area far from the haunts of men.
It can possess a rich and subtle beauty even though it has
never been fully perceived by the animals which are dimly
aware of its presence.[63]

Whitehead suggests that a work of art performs many
useful functions in the realm of value. Art, at its best, is the
expression of both beauty and truth.[64] If values are already
present in a situation, then art consists in arranging the facts
so that attention may be directed to the enshrined values.
Men require something which will absorb them for a time;
from art is derived both transient and permanent refreshment.[65] Further, a work of art is a reminder of the power
of human creativity, a creativity limited in scope but genuine
nevertheless. When one sees a fragment of nature shaped by
human hands in accordance with value ideals, one is stimulated to rise and do likewise.[66] More specifically, Whitehead
contends that appreciation of art not only stimulates the be-
holder, but also exerts a disciplining influence. One who truly
appreciates the beauty of a great painting will find it diffi-

cult indeed to stoop to ugliness in any realm of experience.[67] Finally, the highly valued quality of Peace (see the discussion in the final section of this chapter) can be achieved through the medium of art. A great work of art provides for the enjoyment of emotions and the reliving of activities which once occurred under stress, and faded much too soon. In aesthetic experience the past can be relived at one's leisure, free from stress and strain.[68]

Good

Prominent among the entities which human intelligence can conceive in abstraction from exemplification is the ideal Good. When the ideal (eternal object) Good is realized (exemplified) in the experience of an actual entity, good is present as achieved value. Whitehead emphasizes the point that while the ideal is never completely realized, considerable progress can be made in that direction.[69]

A number of conditions are necessary before the achievement of goodness can occur. There must be *infusion, stability,* and *modification* of patterns.[70] With reference to the obvious and immediate question, "What sort of pattern?" Whitehead's reply is vague—perhaps necessarily so. In general terms, he suggests that it is the sort of pattern which makes possible the union of *harmony, intensity,* and *vividness.*[71]

In the last analysis, the type of pattern of behavior which makes possible the achievement of goodness is the sort of pattern which exemplifies the eternal object *good.* "In itself a pattern is neither good nor bad." [72] Whitehead apparently assumes that people who have had a conceptual prehension of the eternal object *good* will be able to select or identify the specific patterns which make possible its exemplification.[73]

It is to be understood that, just as with beauty, so in the case of goodness, a certain amount of *disorder* is desirable —as well as order. "The right chaos, and the right vagueness, are jointly required for any effective harmony. . . . Thus

chaos is not to be identified with evil." [74] This, of course, is
strikingly contrary to the usual assumption that clarity and
order are the basis of goodness whereas vagueness and disorder are productive of evil. As has been stated, in more
general terms, modification of pattern is a necessary condition for the achievement of positive value. This point of view
is based on Whitehead's profound conviction concerning the
fundamental importance of "adventure." Without the spirit
of adventure, there can be no progress or productive excitement in life. Mere conformation to the traditional techniques
produces degradation and an accompanying inability to deal
with novel situations and to become aware of the ill defined
and the relatively unknown. [75] For example, there is Whitehead's stinging reference to "static goodness." Those afflicted
by this blight of the spirit are so satisfied with their narrow
and selfish pseudo-perfection that they are incapable of real
moral feeling. Their degree of degeneration is not much
different from that of a man reduced to the level of a hog.
The differentiation between this type of "goodness" and stark
evil is difficult to find. [76]

In connection with this general point, there is an apparent
criticism. It would seem that Whitehead first suggests that
beauty and goodness are characterized by harmonious unity
and then contradicts himself by claiming that discord and
disorder sometimes are necessary for the achievement of a
higher type of beauty and goodness. [77] It is to be reiterated
that the apparent difficulty, and contradiction, is cleared up
when it is remembered that the eternal object *good* or the
eternal object *beauty*, may, in some instances be best exemplified in cases where there is not too much order.

Evil

Whitehead's analysis of *evil* involves a reference to at least
four major types. (a) There is the evil of *triviality*. It arises
when the situation requires a deep experience but a merely

superficial one results. For example, a lecturer may have an opportunity to make a profound and provocative remark, but he misses his chance and indulges in some banal common-place. (b) There is the evil which is characterized by *deprivation due to conflict*. The conflict may arise on the level of (i) concepts (eternal objects) ; or (ii) actualities; or (iii) in the relationship of concept and actuality. For instance if a person accepts one of two contradictory ideas and rejects the other, he suffers loss—in this sense, evil. A conflict between two actualities (or groups of actualities)—for instance between persons—obviously involves loss of mutual support. Finally, the conflict of concept with actuality is a form of evil because here again something is lost. The complete achievement of an ideal possibility is thwarted by the resistance of the restraining actuality.[78] (c) There is a third type of evil which occurs when conceptual experience is carried on without sufficient reference to the necessities of ordinary social activity. The abstract thinker who cuts himself off from his fellow men and their problems is, in a sense, evil. (d) Finally, there is a type of evil which is not too obviously included in any of the others (unless it is "b"). Its characteristics are a reliance on brute force and a lack of coherent purpose.[79] It should be clear from the preceding that the basic characteristic of all types of evil is obstruction, and hence loss—*unnecessary loss*.[80]

In discussing evil, Whitehead states that a fact of so-called evil, since it is an *achievement,* is—in one sense of the term —good. However, in so far as this fact interferes with the attainment of things greater than itself, it loses this tenuous type of goodness.[81] He also makes the much more obvious suggestion that something which is in itself evil may be a means to a greater good.[82]

It is contended that evil is essentially unstable. Evil leads to its own elimination, either by (a) destruction, or (b) degradation, or (c) elevation. For example: (a) A disease may be so intense that the organism dies; hence evil has destroyed itself. (b) A pig as such is not evil. When a man is degraded to the animal level, with accompanying loss of distinctive human characteristics, he is no more evil than the pig—that is to say, not at all.[83] Whitehead qualifies his statement by admitting that such a man would be considered evil if comparison were made with what he might have been. (c) Pain (evil) may lead to an attitude whereby it is disregarded.

In Whitehead's opinion, *good* and *evil*, in the last analysis, are ultimate components of the universe. Specific goods and specific evils may fade from experience, but goodness and badness are inescapable elements in all experience.[84] Whitehead has no respect for the type of absolute idealism which claims that all is harmony and so avoids a serious facing of the fact of conflict.[85] It is true that Whitehead refers to a harmony of opposites. He accepts these opposites as component facts in the universe. On the other hand, absolute idealism only pretends to come to grips with the realm of negative values—pain, evil, frustration.

Whitehead claims that an experience of evil is present in God. It is true that he refers to the overcoming of evil by good and the transmutation of evil into good.[86] However, when one examines what he means by these phrases, it becomes clear that they are *not* to be interpreted as suggesting that evil is eliminated, *its reality denied*. The following statements of his position are worthy of careful examination. "Every fact is what it is, a fact of pleasure, of joy, or pain, or of suffering. In its union with God that fact is not a total loss, but on its finer side is an *element* to be woven immortally into the rhythm of mortal things." [87] "All the 'opposites' [good and evil included] are elements in the nature of things, *and are incorrigibly there*." [88]

Morals

In addition to this general discussion of the nature of good and evil, Whitehead provides a number of more specific comments. For example, he emphasizes the "relativity" of specific moral codes. He notes that the details of these codes are relative to changing environmental conditions. He points out that the meaning of crucial terms is shifting and ambiguous. For instance, the notions of ownership, family, marriage, God, are continually undergoing changes. Sometimes these variations are drastic. Conduct which is satisfactory in one situation, may, in others, be completely degrading.[89]

It is important to realize, however, that this "relativity" is not ultimate. "Our intuitions of righteousness disclose an absoluteness in the nature of things." [90] In short, Whitehead is stating that there are no detailed moral codes applicable to all men everywhere. The details of moral codes must change in order to meet changing conditions. However, while behavior systems may vary, there are universal principles underlying them. Any adequate moral code must be the expression of a certain spirit and attitude. Basically it must be the expression of an ultimate ideal.[91] This is the ideal of the *good*.[92]

By implication, Whitehead's approach to the problem of accounting for moral obligation would involve the position that moral obligation is self-imposed by an actual entity. That is to say, if an actual entity has a subjective aim such that the eternal object *good* (in the moral sense) is set as the guiding principle in the experience of the actual entity, then there will be an overwhelming urge (obligation) to achieve that ideal to the fullest possible degree. The more fundamental question, "Why does that actual entity have that subjective aim?" is not answered by Whitehead. It seems to be one of the "ultimate irrationalities" (factors which cannot be explained in terms of anything else) which crop up in a philosophy which is a "descriptive generalization" (rather than a complete answer to all questions.) [93]

Whitehead is willing to admit that in certain situations moral considerations are possibly irrelevant. Take, for example, the enjoyment of the opera *Carmen*. Strictly from the point of view of morals some of the events in the opera are open to serious objections. However, in the midst of deep enjoyment of the spectacle, "morals vanish and beauty remains." [94]

There is an Aristotelian tinge to Whitehead's ethics. He suggests that lack of awareness of available knowledge exposes a person to condemnation.[95] He goes further and contends, in pragmatic vein, that barren knowledge is evil.[96]

Whitehead has little to say concerning the place of pleasure in a moral life. It is a stimulus to normal, healthy living. Pleasure is not to be regarded as an infallible guide, particularly immediate joys. Rather one should seek to follow natural lines of development and accept gratefully the usual accompaniment of pleasure.[97]

However, he refers, with keen appreciation, to the immense service to democratic liberalism performed by Utilitarianism in providing a practical program of reform. Nevertheless, he points out that the Utilitarians were sadly mistaken in assuming that they had established a solid basis for morals, legislation, and religion, without reference to ultimate metaphysical principles. He emphasizes the possibility of a skeptical attack (on the Utilitarian position) on the basis of the ruthless implications of evolution. Some of the technical difficulties involved in using the principle of "The Greatest Happiness of the Greatest Number" are listed. How can there be an accurate addition of happiness? How can there be an accurate measurement of the qualitative differences, or a comparison of the different endurances of varying states of happiness? Finally, Whitehead contends that Utilitarianism gives *no reason* why one should cultivate universal benevolence.[98]

Which Is the Supreme Value?

There are statements in which Whitehead seems to assign to *beauty* the supreme position in the hierarchy of value. For example:

Beauty is a wider, and more fundamental, notion than Truth. . . . Apart from Beauty, Truth is neither good, nor bad. . . . The real world is good when it is beautiful. . . . The teleology of the Universe is directed to the production of Beauty. . . . Thus Beauty is left as the one aim which by its very nature is self-justifying.[99]

An examination of the contexts from which these quotations are taken, and other phases of Whitehead's discussion of truth, beauty, and goodness, reveals that this interpretation is based on a failure to take into consideration some crucial facts.

To begin with, when Whitehead employs the term *beauty*, he frequently uses it in a very wide sense. In some cases it is synonymous with value-in-general. Thus, he refers to beauty as both (a) moral and (b) aesthetic.[100] More specifically, he mentions (i) intellectual beauty (a somewhat broader notion than that of truth, yet inclusive of it); (ii) sensible (the so-called aesthetic) beauty; and finally (iii) moral beauty. It is very important to note Whitehead's admission that intellectual and moral "beauty," so-called, are "beautiful by *stretch of metaphor*." [101]

Whitehead also uses the term *beauty* in the more ordinary, restricted sense as a member of the value trinity: Truth, Beauty, and Goodness. However, even when the term is used in this restricted fashion, he seems to assign priority to beauty. It must be admitted that it is difficult, in some cases, to determine whether Whitehead is employing the wide or the restricted meaning of beauty.

The statement that "Beauty is a *wider,* and more funda-mental notion than Truth," can be understood against the background of Whitehead's contention that while truth is concerned with the relation of appearance to reality, beauty is concerned with this, *and in addition,* relations between realities and relations between appearances.[102]

It is very important to understand that when Whitehead states, "Thus Beauty is left as the one aim which by its very nature is self-justifying," he is discussing truth and beauty. *He is not referring to good, at all,* in this instance. White-head's claim that truth is not self-justifying seems to mean that truth will only *attract attention* if it is coupled with some other type of value.[103]

Yet, despite this apparent disparagement of truth in com-parison with beauty, Whitehead claims that "the general importance of Truth for the promotion of Beauty is over-whelming." [104] He means that the harmony involved in the truth relation constitutes a factor which conditions the achievement of beauty. As an aid in the production of beauty, the truth relationship becomes of sufficient impor-tance to be subject to a moral evaluation. Yet, "apart from Beauty, Truth is neither good, nor bad." [105]

There is an apparent overemphasis on beauty and dis-paragement of good in the statement: "With the point of view here adopted, Goodness must be denied a place among the aims of art." [106] However, this does not mean that in general beauty is more important than goodness. By defini-tion ("the point of view here adopted"), art is concerned with the adaptation of appearance and reality. This is the field of beauty and truth. Good and evil are concerned with the real world. In other words, these qualities do not fall within the sphere of art. However, it must be admitted that according to Whitehead, "The real world is good when it is beautiful." This statement definitely seems to assign priority to beauty. In all fairness this remark should not be examined out of the context of his complete discussion. Even as it stands, in isolation, it is open to another interpretation. Whitehead did not say: The real world is good *because* it is beautiful. The word used was "when."

In his last discussion of the "World of Value" he obviously assigns at least equality of status to moral and aesthetic value. He refers to ideals of perfection, moral and aesthetic.[107]

Just as Whitehead uses the term *beauty* in two senses, so also he uses the term *good*. Thus, the term *good*, on occasion, is apparently identified with positive value *in general*. On other occasions it has a restricted meaning, on the basis of which it is distinguished from the other traditional values: beauty and truth. In discussing excellence (value) Whitehead claims that ultimately you cannot answer the question: In what does value consist? " 'The Good' is an ultimate qualification not to be analyzed in terms of any things more final than itself." [108] In this instance beauty is mentioned as a species of value, or "the Good." Further, he states: "All *value* is the gift of finitude which is the necessary condition for activity. Also activity means the organization of patterns of assemblage, and mathematics is the study of pattern. Here we find the essential clue which relates mathematics to the study of the *good*, and the study of the *bad*." [109] Also in discussing the value of a picture, Whitehead, at least on one occasion, did not use the terms *beauty* and *ugliness;* rather he employed the terms *good* and *horrible*.[110] Thus, apparently, in some of his examinations of values, Whitehead uses the term *good* rather than the term *beauty* as a synonym for value.

As was noted above, the term *good* is also employed by Whitehead in its usual, restricted meaning. Employing the term *good* in this sense, and also the term *beauty* in its restricted meaning, Whitehead seems to assign moral goodness priority over aesthetic beauty. He states that the devotees of "art for art's sake" should recognize the necessity, on occasion, of banning some art for the sake of moral interests.[111]

Economic Values

Whitehead is well aware of the fact that certain values ordinarily cannot be achieved unless environmental conditions are satisfactory. For example, if a man lives in a thor-oughly regimented social environment, the values which depend on individualized creative experience are denied him.[112] More specifically, if a man is immersed in the complexities of modern industrial life, many areas of higher value experience are beyond his reach.[113] Without adequate stimulation and opportunities for value enjoyment, men are reduced to robots.[114]

Thus in all this discussion of "higher" values, Whitehead has not lost sight of economic values. Food, clothing, and shelter must be available. However, his fundamental point is that the necessities of bodily life provide for only a moderate enjoyment. The higher value experiences—those which make life supremely worth while—depend on a foundation of economic values but rise far above them.[115]

He shows, with great skill, that the thwarting of value achievement is due not only to factors in the physical, economic, and social environment. There is also the intellectual environment which may create or change the other types of environment. For example, the philosophy which assumes that matter is valueless regards art as a frivolity and issues in the industrial defacement of a beautiful countryside. If it is assumed that each man should concentrate on his own private world of experience, this belief issues in a lack of public morals.[116]

Peace

In his discussion of the distinguishing characteristics of *civilization*, Whitehead lists *truth, beauty* (and by implication *goodness*), *art, adventure,* and *peace.* As has been noted, art serves as means of achieving truth and beauty. Adventure (novel experience) is the search for new perfections.[117] Its contributions to aesthetic and moral experience have been mentioned. A careful reading of Whitehead's discussion of peace seems to justify the conclusion that he regards it as one of the supreme intrinsic values worthy to be ranked with the familiar value trinity: Truth, Beauty, Goodness.

Peace is a "quality of mind, steady in its reliance that fine action is treasured in the nature of things." [118] It is an attitude which develops in those who look behind the pressure of immediate events to underlying factors. One sees oneself as a unit in a complex social organization of co-operating members. You come to realize that what is of value in your life will be preserved, and that there are elements of value in the lives of others.[119] Peace is based on the recognition of the fact that though evil is inescapably real yet one must strive to achieve unrealized ideals. The tragic fact of evil does not produce hopeless despair. Rather, it stimulates earthly mortals to strive toward a "fineness beyond the faded level of surrounding fact." [120]

The fruits of this state of mind are many and excellent. Tenderness and a lack of egoism are perhaps the most obvious. Peace, since it is destructive of ruthless and narrow selfishness, involves a relaxation of mutually inhibiting tensions. This is not the relaxation of anaesthesia. Rather, creative activities are strengthened and widened in scope. It should be obvious that this peaceful state of mind arises when one becomes aware of the functioning of God—in particular his consequent nature.[121]

Whitehead's discussion of value is generated by his sense of the basic importance of values. In the first place, they are fundamental components of the universe. Secondly, they constitute a most powerful dynamic once their presence is noted and they are given a decisive place in the experience of a person:

The ultimate motive power, alike in science, in morality, and in religion, is the sense of value, the sense of importance. It takes the various forms of wonder, of curiosity, of reverence, or worship, of tumultuous desire for merging personality in something beyond itself. This sense of value imposes on life incredible labours, and apart from it life sinks back into the passivity of its lower types.[122]

7
Whitehead's Relation to Other Philosophers

In the preface of *Science and the Modern World* Whitehead states: "There has been no occasion to make detailed reference to Lloyd Morgan's *Emergent Evolution* or to S. Alexander's *Space, Time and Deity*. It will be obvious to readers that I have found them very suggestive. I am especially indebted to Alexander's great work." [1] Specific acknowledgments are more numerous in *Process and Reality*. Frequent references are made to Plato, Aristotle, Descartes, Locke, Hume, Kant. Locke is regarded as particularly important as an unconscious forerunner of the philosophy of organism. [2] Whitehead remarks that among his contemporaries his obligations to the English and American realists are obvious—in particular to Professor T. P. Nunn, of the University of London. [3] Further, he acknowledges indebtedness to Bergson, James, Dewey, and Bradley.

An attempt to understand the philosophy of Whitehead is greatly facilitated by an examination of his references to these philosophers. It is, however, very important to realize that it is completely unfair to judge Whitehead's philosophy on the basis of some *superficial* similarity between his position and that of one of the great thinkers of the past or present. As will be shown in subsequent discussion, in most cases the similarities are more apparent than real. Most emphatically Whitehead is not just another Plato, or Bradley, or Alexander, or Bergson. He has achieved a unique synthesis of knowledge available to the twentieth-century mind. The numerous points of agreement and disagreement serve to bring into more meaningful focus the complexities of his theory of actual entities. The present chapter will undertake this project.[4] Attention will be concentrated on fundamentals. Alexander will be taken as representative of "emergent evolution"; little reference will be made to Lloyd Morgan. Only Alexander's metaphysics will be discussed. Some phases of the epistemology he shares with Nunn will be dealt with in discussing the latter. An examination of some similarities and differences between Whitehead and Dewey has already been attempted in the chapter on Whitehead's philosophy of mind.

In addition to those mentioned above, Whitehead compares his position with some phases of the philosophies of Bacon, Berkeley, Spinoza, Leibnitz, Hegel, and positivism. These relationships will also be discussed briefly.

Plato

One of the finest evaluations of Plato's work is provided by Whitehead's comment that he "gave an unrivalled display of the human mind in action, with its ferment of vague obviousness, of hypothetical formulation, of renewed insight, of discovery of relevant detail, or partial understanding, of final conclusion, with its disclosure of deeper problems as yet unsolved." [5] Whitehead suggests that all philosophy is an attempt to develop a coherent system out of the basic notions which were formulated by the Master of the Academy. The notions are: Ideas, Physical Elements, the Psyche, Eros, Harmony, Mathematical Relations.[6] In Whitehead's theory of actual entities, there is a *physical* pole and a mental pole (*psyche*). There is an *eros* (the urge to achieve an *ideal*). The preceding discussion of value has indicated his emphasis on the importance of *harmony*. Whitehead's extensive work in mathematics and science has shown his agreement with Plato concerning the importance of *mathematical relations*. Both are interested in the search for the "forms in the facts." Both believe that things which are temporal exist because of their relationships with what is eternal.[7] The things which are eternal are termed "Ideas" by Plato, "eternal objects" by Whitehead. He indicates that Plato's theory of the receptacle is very similar to his theory of the extensive continuum. The doctrine of the receptacle is an assertion of "a real communication between ultimate realities." [8]

However, there are basic disagreements. Whitehead dislikes the term "Idea" because of its subjectivistic connotation in modern philosophy. Further, he declines to restrict himself to Plato's list of these eternal elements (number, geometrical relations, moral characteristics, and qualitative disclosures of the higher sense perceptions). Finally, he opposes violently the Platonic tendency to apply to the eternal realm of forms such rhetorical, question-begging phrases as *self-sustaining, completely real, certain*.[9] He contends that the claim to be certain is a delusion suffered by dogmatists. In Whitehead's opinion, no entity is self-subsistent. Every eternal object is a potentiality available for the use of some actual entity. In any case the presence of the realm of eternal objects in God's primordial nature renders them inescapably a part of the world of actuality. Also the word *real* is relative. When you refer to something as unreal, you are merely considering an entity to which "something" does not belong.[10]

There are two famous statements in the *Sophist* which seem to indicate a close kinship between Plato and Whitehead: "Anything which possesses any sort of power to affect another or to be affected by another, has real existence. . . . Can we ever be made to believe that motion and life and soul and mind are not present with absolute being?" [11] While these passages may suggest Whitehead's theory of actual entities, they are relatively isolated fragments and do *not* constitute part of a comprehensive attempt to show that all actual entities are centers of feeling. Plato's chief concern (during the period under discussion) in dealing with concrete particulars seemed to be to deny that they are mere imitations of Ideas. Rather he is trying to show that Ideas are really present in them. In other words, particular things are real. That apparently was as far as he cared to go. At any rate, when Plato came to define the ultimate components of physical things (in the *Timaeus*), he referred to geometrical forms being imposed on "empty space," by an artisan-creator. There is no envisagement of self-creative centers of feeling. Whitehead deals with Plato's "deficiencies" in his customary "friendly" fashion, by suggesting that occasionally Plato "wavers." [12] Plato's doctrine of the soul, a divine product, enjoying rebirth, is very different from Whitehead's enduring personality—a linear society of selves, each enjoying only a brief duration of existence. Thus, despite the apparent similarities in the two passages from the *Sophist*, the differences which distinguish Whitehead's work from that of Plato are more fundamental.

Plato conceived God (in the *Timaeus*) as an artisan—building, with the assistance of intermediaries, a good world, as much like himself as possible. On the other hand, Whitehead's God is effective as a "lure," by reason of his effective presentation of eternal objects as available data. (Whitehead claims to find evidence of this point of view in Plato, but he remarks that Plato failed to make serious use of this basic insight.[13]) Also, God provides concrete data in his superject function. But in any case Whitehead's God does not exercise the sort of initiative which characterizes Plato's God. There is a further important distinction between the positions of Plato and Whitehead with reference to God. According to Plato, God "looks to" the Ideas, arranged and interrelated, ready for use. Whitehead contends that it is God's primordial function to take an otherwise chaotic, useless "mass" of eternal objects within his conceptual envisagement and thereby establish their relational essence. He makes them available for use by other actual entities. The Ideas are, for Plato, God-external data to be used as required. Whitehead's eternal objects are essential components of God's nature.

Thus it is true that Whitehead stands in the "Platonic tradition," if that term is so defined as to be elastic enough. In so far as he is in the European intellectual environment, to that extent there are Platonic elements in Whitehead's thought. More specifically, he suggests that *if* Plato's point of view were revised in accordance with subsequent developments in science, religion, art, and social experience, the result would be a philosophy of organism. However, despite this the fact remains that between the actual positions of Plato and Whitehead there are, as has been outlined, many basic differences.[14]

Aristotle

Whitehead's references to the philosophy of Aristotle embody both commendation and destructive criticism. On the positive side, he fully appreciates Aristotle's status in the realm of philosophy. "If we are to accord to anyone the position of the greatest metaphysician, having regard to genius of insight, to general equipment in knowledge, and to the stimulus of his metaphysical ancestry, we must choose Aristotle." [15] He suggests that the famous discussion of the "Unmoved Mover," with a little editing, is a satisfactory statement of the primordial nature of God as it functions with respect to ordinary actual entities.[16] He praises the general Aristotelian contention that "apart from things that are actual, there is nothing—nothing either in fact or in efficacy." [17] According to Whitehead, Aristotle provides a masterly analysis of the notion of generation.[18] He also merits praise for his opposition to the Platonic dualism. It is stated that Aristotle introduced into sciences (astronomy excepted) an awareness of the importance of checking theory by direct, detailed observation of facts.[19] Not only did Aristotle observe detailed facts; he also provided a useful classification. The basic principle involved in this system of classification is "function." This, of course, is quite in accord with the spirit of modern science. Hence, he provided a foundation for a structure of knowledge free from the contamination of superstition and blank mystery.[20] However, Whitehead later remarks that at the end of a long career this analysis lost its utility. It became an obstructive nuisance and is now an archeological curiosity.[21]

Thus, one of Whitehead's main objections to Aristotle is that this interest in classification was carried too far. It resulted in a disregard of measurement.[22] After all, the question "How much?" is a basic one. CO will kill you; CO_2 will merely make your head ache.[23] Further it is Whitehead's opinion that Aristotle's system of classification attempts to make clear-cut distinctions which are not really justified by the facts.[24] Also the Aristotelian logic is a relatively inadequate and superficial weapon to use in the search for knowledge. By its very nature it disregards some very important matters. In addition to the quantitative relations examined in mathematics, there are also the complex possibilities of multiple relationship within a system.[25]

Whitehead's main objection to Aristotle is that his logic has given rise to a metaphysics which conceives each thing as complete in itself, having no essential relations to anything else.[26] Further, these real things are regarded as static.[27] It is interesting to observe that although Aristotle's logic, in Whitehead's opinion, had a bad effect on subsequent thinkers, it is suggested that Aristotle himself was not misled by it, in his own metaphysical speculations.[28] Thus in discussing the dominance of the Aristotelian "subject-predicate" mode of thought, Whitehead facetiously remarks that probably Aristotle was not an Aristotelian.[29]

Bacon

In an initial sketch of his position, Whitehead quotes, with evident approval, a selection from Francis Bacon's *Natural History*. Herein it is suggested that there is a type of perception more subtle than sensation. This perception (this taking account of) is concerned with objects both at a distance and in direct contact. This theory, as Whitehead points out, involves the notion that matter is not to be regarded as inert. Bacon expresses it thus: "When one body is applied to another, there is a kind of election to embrace . . . or expell." [30] Whitehead, of course, is in accord with Bacon's interest in "stubborn facts" and inductive procedure. He regrets Bacon's lack of appreciation of mathematics. [31]

Spinoza

Some of Whitehead's references to Spinoza have had the unfortunate result of leading many of his readers to conclude that, like Spinoza, he is a monist. It must be admitted that a few of Whitehead's earlier comments seem to justify this interpretation. For example, he states: "In the analogy with Spinoza, his one substance is for me the underlying activity of realization individualizing itself in an interlocked plurality of modes." [32] He refers to the "general activity" being individualized by imposed conditions. This general activity is "Spinoza's one infinite substance." One of its *attributes* is its individualization into a multiplicity of modes. The realm of eternal objects constitutes another attribute. [33]

The apparent Spinozistic monism of these passages is either abandoned or shown to be a careless expression of a non-Spinozistic position—in a series of comments which appear in *Process and Reality*:

The philosophy of organism is closely allied to Spinoza's scheme of thought. But it differs by the abandonment of the subject-predicate forms of thought . . . morphological description is replaced by description of dynamic process. Also Spinoza's 'modes' now become the sheer actualities; . . . analysis . . . does not lead us to the discovery of any higher grade of reality.[34]

More specifically Whitehead sets himself in opposition to the claim of some monists that the Absolute or God has a "final, 'eminent' reality." As has been noted, in Whitehead's opinion God and other actual entities are equally real. The "underlying activity" mentioned in *Science and the Modern World* now appears as the common characteristic of all actual entities. *It* is not the ultimate reality. " 'Actual entities' . . . are the final real things of which the world is made up." [35] On several occasions Whitehead specifically states that his philosophy of organism is pluralistic in contrast with Spinoza's monism.[36]

Despite his criticism of Spinoza, Whitehead notes with approval the phase of his definition of substance which stresses the characteristic *causa sui*. Whitehead finds this quality in all actual entities.[37]

Locke

Whitehead discovers great similarity to his own "ontological principle" in Locke's reference to the *real internal constitution* of things.[38] Further, this also involves a fluency of process which is the Whiteheadian concrescence.[39] It is suggested that Locke's discussion of *ideas* indicates his awareness of several important phases of the philosophy of organism. In one usage of the term Locke seems to mean the entity which Whitehead prefers to call *eternal object*. In another usage he implies what Whitehead terms *objectified actual entities*.[40] Whitehead admits that Locke has two distinct approaches to *ideas*. In the first two books of his *Essay* he regards ideas as mere qualifications of the substrate mind. In Book III he introduces a new approach which, as has been indicated above, is supposedly very similar to the theory of actual entities.[41] Thus Whitehead contends that very fruit-ful suggestions concerning an organic theory of nature are to be found in Locke.[42] In the early pages of *Process and Reality*, he remarks that the philosophy of organism starts with a generalization of Locke's theory of mental opera-tion.[43] This point is developed at great length. He claims, for example, that when Locke refers to "simple ideas con-veyed in by the sense, *as they are found in exterior things*," he is asserting what Whitehead terms the vector quality of primary feelings.[44] That is to say that Locke is emphasizing the phase of the philosophy of organism which contends that a new actual entity arises by prehending other actual enti-ties. Locke's exposition of the notion of "power" emphasizes the same thing.[45] Here also Whitehead finds, by implication, his own doctrines of relativity, the relational character of eternal objects, and the composite nature of an actual en-tity. He notes, with great approval, Locke's theory that "time is a perpetual perishing." [46] However, despite these apparent similarities, Whitehead is careful to state: "I am certainly not maintaining that Locke grasped explicitly the implica-tions of his words." [47] This canny comment follows shortly after an enthusiastic outburst in which Whitehead states that Locke outlined the main doctrines of the philosophy of organism.[48]

There are several major criticisms of Locke. Whitehead re-grets that Locke restricted ideas to the realm of conscious-ness.[49] He states that Locke overlooks the fact that a doc-trine of internal relations makes it impossible to attribute change to an actual entity.[50] He is also deficient in that he does not appreciate the relative status of feelings and sensa-tions. Locke attributes an invalid priority to sensations.[51] In so far as Locke conceives the mind as a blank tablet pas-sively reacting to the impact of external stimulation, he is guilty of disregarding a basic fact of process. Further, his primary substances are left essentially unconnected. Here then is an example of the unfortunate influence of Aristotle's logic.[52]

Berkeley

In the Whiteheadian "orders of the day," Bishop Berkeley receives honorable mention for the analysis of perception found in *Principles of Human Knowledge*. One of the main conclusions of Euphranor's argument is accepted by Whitehead as an important insight. It is the contention that there is an experience *here* of things which have a reference to *somewhere else*.[53] Thus Whitehead suggests that Berkeley is implying a relationship which he prefers to designate by the term *prehension*. He hastens to point out that he rejects Berkeley's extreme idealistic position. Further, Berkeley's *mind substance* becomes for Whitehead a society of prehensive unifications (actual entities). Finally Whitehead does not account for the unity, or the present existence, of nature by referring to the all-inclusive mind of God.[54]

Hume

As has been noted in the preceding examination of Whitehead's philosophy of mind, Hume is held in very low repute. In general he is denounced as a pseudo-empiricist. Hume's famous conclusion concerning causation is opposed vigorously. Whitehead contends that a person can have an impression of causality. When a bright light is presented as a stimulus, a person blinks. The subject then reports that "he feels that the experiences of the *eye* in the matter of the flash are causal of the blink. . . . It is the feeling of causality which enables the man to distinguish the priority of the flash." [55] In discussing one's experience of anger, Whitehead notes that it surges from past moments of experience into the present moment of experience. "There is an observed relation of causation." [56] Hume's well-known suggestion that causation can be explained in terms of a habit,

based on the repetition of experiences, is rejected by Whitehead. He contends that Hume, on the basis of his system,
has no right to mention either repetition or habit, since
neither are impressions.[57] There is a further topic. The causal
relation, from Hume's point of view, can hold only in the
case of clear and familiar data. Yet, Whitehead aptly remarks, in the dim consciousness of semi-wakefulness there
is a sense of the causal impact of the environment. Further,
when one walks in darkness through strange territory, there
is an experience of the causal presence of the unfamiliar
and the unknown.[58]

Whitehead charges Hume with radical inconsistency. He
pretends to limit himself to impressions and derived ideas;
yet he slips from his technical ivory tower into the world
of common sense. He refers to subjects (souls) apprehending physical objects.[59] Hume errs also in attributing individual independence to his impressions. Here again is the
venerable fallacy of ultimate elements lacking any essential
interconnection.[60] Like Locke, Hume assigns undue priority
to sense at the expense of feeling.[61]

Yet, in the midst of denunciation, Whitehead admits that
Hume did, after all, unwittingly emphasize process. This is
implied in his discussion of the development of ideas from
impressions.[62] He is even able to find a suggestion of his doctrine of subjective form in one phase of Hume's position.[63]
The preceding discussion must be remembered when one
reads Whitehead's eulogistic comment that the philosophy
of organism "accepts Hume's doctrine that nothing is to
be received into the philosophical scheme which is not discoverable as an element in subjective experience." [64]

Descartes

Whitehead observes, with approval, Descartes' pluralism
and his apparent recognition of the ontological principle:
"When we perceive any attribute, we, therefore, conclude

that some existing thing . . . is necessarily present." [65] It is also remarked that Descartes uses the term *feeling* in an almost Whiteheadian sense.

When he proceeds to destructive criticism, Whitehead's discussion of the philosophy of Descartes provides a very valuable statement of the differences between the philosophy of organism and the philosophy of substance (subject)-attribute (quality, predicate) which Descartes helped to establish in modern thought.[66] It is emphasized that the essential disagreement has to do with the relation between the experiencing subject and the external world. For Descartes the experiencing subject (a substance) has no necessary relation with the external world. In the opinion of Whitehead the experiencing subject (actual entity) is what it is because it is experiencing the "so-called" external world. The substance-quality pattern of thought is the basis of Descartes' dualism. For this reason Whitehead rejects it.[67] Yet, despite this serious disagreement, Whitehead states that he regards Descartes' formulation of the subjectivistic principle as the greatest philosophical discovery since Plato and Aristotle.[68] However, having made this acknowledgment, Whitehead proceeds to denounce the "substance" taint which corrupts Descartes' use of this principle. "Descartes in his own philosophy conceives the thinker as creating the occasional thought. The philosophy of organism inverts the order, and conceives the thought as a constituent operation in the creation of the occasional thinker." [69] It will, of course, be obvious that Whitehead is unalterably opposed to the Cartesian dualism of "thinking substance" and "extended substance," with reference to the body-mind "problem," [70] and to the Cartesian doctrine of imposed (by God) law.[71]

Leibnitz

Whitehead terms his actual entities *monadic creatures*.[72] In introducing the term *appetition* he makes reference to

Leibnitz's *Monology*.[73] One of the early formulations of his organic philosophy, in terms of volumes of space, includes the suggestion that it would be possible to use Leibnitzian language and state that every volume mirrors every other volume in space.[74] Leibnitz is commended for his advocacy of a subjectivistic approach to philosophy.[75] Further he has the good sense to realize that the final reality may be regarded as an organizing activity whereby data are fused into a unity.[76] On the other hand, Whitehead observes, with sorrow, that Leibnitz unsuccessfully attempts to fuse two contradictory points of view: (a) the organic; (b) the substance-attribute.[77] His monads, despite their internal development, have no windows. He also deplores the fact that Leibnitz attributes change to his monads.[78] The one exceptional monad, God, does have contact with others, but this destroys the consistency of the system. No reason can be given why the supreme monad, God, escapes the common fate of isolation.[79]

Kant

As in the case of most philosophers, Whitehead accords Kant both praise and blame. He is commended for his recognition that an act of experience is a constructive functioning. What was vaguely implied in Locke and Hume is stated clearly by the great Kant.[80] Whitehead also approves Kant's contention that occasions of experience provide the forms of connectedness.[81] Further, he is pleased to note Kant's emphasis on feeling in the "Transcendental Aesthetic."

Whitehead disapproves the importance which Kant assigns to "thought" in the rest of *The Critique of Pure Reason*.[82] He goes on to argue that the general relational element in experience does not produce the ordered world, but is derived from it.[83] Thus it is not "pure" in Kant's sense of the term. The fundamental difference between the philosophy of organism and Kant's philosophy is unmistakable.

Kant weaves an "objective" world upon the loom of subjectivity. The "phenomena" are what they are because of the subjective agency applying the forms and categories to the "raw material of sense." On the other hand, Whitehead states that the inner life of subjectivity evolves as the result of relationships to an objective world available for use. In other words, for Kant the subject is the decisive factor at the beginning of the process. For Whitehead the subject is not fully there till the process is finished.[84] In criticism of Kant's position, Whitehead states that in the world of apparent objectivity there is no experient. That is to say, it is not composed of experiencing actual entities. Kant's temporal world is dead and phantasmal. He suggests that Kant, a mathematical physicist (who had not, like Whitehead, gone on to an organic philosophy), was corrupted by his field of specialization and thus accepted an abstract phenomenal world.[85]

Hegel

Whitehead's references to Hegel, to put it mildly, are not excessive. He admits that his philosophy has similarities to the position of the Hegelian school.[86] However, this matter can be best investigated in the subsequent discussion of F. H. Bradley. It can be argued that there is a fairly specific similarity between Whitehead's and Hegel's doctrines of cause.[87] In facetious fashion he pleads guilty to having read *one* page of Hegel. More seriously, he admits that in conversation with McTaggart and Lord Haldane he derived considerable insight into the point of view formulated by Hegel. This was supplemented by the reading of critical studies of Hegelian philosophy.[88]

Bergson

Whitehead assigns Bergson to an honorable place in the philosophical hierarchy because of his introduction of the organic implications of physiological science. There is, of course, a general similarity between Bergson's emphasis on continuous process and that of Whitehead. This was noted by the latter early in his career.[89] On the basis of an examination of the mental experience of a human being, both stress the point that there is no underlying ego. Unification of mental states occurs because of mutual interaction. In general "there are no things, there are only actions."[90] Like Whitehead, Bergson emphasizes the impact of the past and "tendency" toward the future. There is also the suggestion that we create ourselves continually.[91] Like Bergson, Whitehead declines to regard extension as an ultimate self-existent characteristic of reality.[92] God's consequent nature is similar to Bergson's God who has nothing of the already made. "He is unceasing life, action, freedom."[93] Whitehead suggests that Bergson's is the most characteristic philosophy of this era. Its basic importance lies in its attack on the "materialism" which has developed on the foundation of Newtonian physics.[94]

However, despite these valuable features, Whitehead finds himself in opposition to Bergson at several points. He regrets Bergson's tendency to contend that spatialization is a distortion inescapably involved in the use of the intellect.[95] In the first place, "spatialization is a real factor in the physical constitution of every actual occasion."[96] Further, he refuses to accept the familiar Bergsonian dichotomy—"intelligence and instinct are turned in opposite directions, the former towards inert matter, the latter towards life."[97] Whitehead is convinced that there *can* be an intellectual approach to "vital" data and to process.[98] However, in so far as thinking —indeed, consciousness in general—involves selection of some data from the total available data, there is bound to be some distortion. That is to say, a complete "picture" has not been presented. It must be admitted that on occasion Bergson seems to "take the sting out of" his criticism of the conceptual approach to facts. He refers to the possibility of developing "fluid concepts, capable of following reality in all its sinuosities and of adopting the very movement of the inward life of things." [99]

Be that as it may, there are other apparent points of difference. Bergson contends that there is "an *original impetus of life* . . . [which] is the fundamental cause of variations." It is "one single immense wave." [100] This, of course, is completely foreign to the genuine pluralism of Whitehead's system and the autonomous individuality which he finds in actual entities. In particular, Whitehead does not agree with Bergson that things are created by being "cut out" of the stream of consciousness by the understanding. [101] Nor would he accept the alternate suggestion that matter is an inverse movement to that of life. Bergson's contention that possibilities are continually being created, [102] while in accord with one phase of Whitehead's philosophy, is contrary to his doctrine of eternal objects (they are permanent possibilities). The suggestion that nature has predestined man to a social life and thus must use language—hence subject-predicate forms of thought [103]—is entirely contrary to Whitehead's advocacy of the freedom of actual entities and the advisability of abandoning subject-predicate forms of thought. Bergson also leaves himself open to Whiteheadian criticism by making use of the concept *faculty*. [104] Bergson's rather vehement denial that intuition is instinct or feeling, and the claim that it is reflection, [105] seems to refute Whitehead's suggestion that his concept *feeling* is like Bergson's *intuition*. [106] Bergson clarified this point in showing that, after material has been collected with reference to a problem, then intuition unifies and understands it. [107] However, Whitehead's interpretation seems justified on the basis of some of Bergson's comments. For example, he states that intuition is a type of insight which involves contact—indeed coincidence. [108] He also refers to it as "the simple and indivisible feeling." [109] Nevertheless,

Whitehead does seem to err in contending that Bergson's intuition is like his "physical purpose." [110] Physical purpose involves conceptual prehension, while Bergson's intuition, in at least one of its interpretations, apparently requires the complete absence of a conceptual factor.

Bradley

The drastic differentiations which distinguish the philosophy of Whitehead from that of Bradley merit careful attention. This is important in view of Whitehead's statement: "Though throughout the main body of the work I am in sharp disagreement with Bradley, the final outcome is after all not so greatly different." [111] As a matter of fact, these differentiations are so fundamental that the aptness of the last phrase of the quotation is open to serious question. Indeed in a later discussion Whitehead states: "There are, of course, grave differences between my own doctrine and that of Bradley." [112] In the first place, Whitehead suggests that the idealistic school has been too much divorced from the scientific outlook. Having admitted that science provides an adequate description of the facts of nature, the Absolutists proceed to suggest that nature is merely an idea in the Absolute Mind.[113] Thus the idealistic philosophy has failed to face the facts of nature with genuine seriousness.

Bradley bases his philosophy on the "rational principle" that the real must be self consistent and all inclusive. If there *were* a plurality of reals (so-called), the mere fact of plurality would invalidate the claim that any one (or all) of these particulars is real. This follows from the principle that a part, since it is not the whole (all inclusive), cannot be real. In any case, it is Bradley's opinion that reality must be one, since "plurality taken as real, contradicts itself. Plurality implies relations . . . it unwillingly asserts always a superior unity." [114] Bradley argues further, in support of his point of view, that "if, seeking for reality, we go to experience, what we certainly do *not* find is a subject or an object. . . . What we discover rather is a whole in which distinctions can be made, but in which divisions do not exist." [115] On the basis of arguments such as these, the common-sense world of relatively autonomous, separate, distinct persons and things which we find about us, is distilled by the subtle alchemy of Bradley's thought into a timeless unity of feeling. Our familiar world is branded as mere "appearance" and baptized with the corrosive waters of disappearance.[116] According to Bradley, time and change are illusions. Familiar value distinctions are not founded in reality. Such distinctions imply incompleteness. Reality is complete. "We can hardly say that the Absolute consists of finite things, when the things, as such, are there transmuted and have lost their individual natures." [117]

It is true that Whitehead derives from Bradley a hint (or shares a theory) as to how the internal unity of an actual entity may be explained—i.e., as an inclusive whole of feeling. Here, however, all essential similarity stops. Bradley postulates *one* whole of experience, timelessly dissolving all apparent particulars into its real unity. Whitehead, on the other hand, claims that there is an infinite multiplicity of actual entities, each in a sense autonomous, each genuinely distinct. In his opinon, value is a basic factor in the universe. Value distinctions are maintained in the experience of God. Thus, in Whitehead's philosophy, Bradley's doctrine of actuality is simply inverted:

The point to be emphasized is the insistent particularity of things experienced and of the act of experiencing. Bradley's doctrine—Wolf-eating-Lamb as a universal qualifying the absolute—is a travesty of the evidence. *That* wolf ate *that* lamb at *that* spot at *that* time; the wolf knew it; the lamb knew it; and the carrion birds knew it.[118]

Whitehead points out that Bradley attempts to discuss internal relations in terms applicable to external relations.

He overlooks the obvious fact that a relationship is not a universal. It is a concrete fact, as concrete as the relata. Whitehead contends, further, that just as the relations modify the nature of the relata, so the relata modify the nature of the relations.[119] In short, Whitehead refuses to agree with Bradley that relations are "indiscretions of the Absolute." [120]

It has been observed that there is a place for a "timeless unity" in Whitehead's cosmology. God's consequent nature, though it grows by taking in new content, is timeless in the sense that none of its components fade. It differs from Bradley's Absolute in that it holds within its life phases of other actual entities *only after* these actual entities have, as such, passed out of existence. This phase of God's activity is a further manifestation of divine patience. Thus God's consequent nature does not deny the reality of evolving actual entities. Indeed God's consequent nature could not exist without data provided by other actual entities.

Bradley's excessive use of a "logical" criterion of reality, on the basis of which he denies the possibility of a plurality of reals, leaves him open to Whitehead's penetrating comment: "The only logical conclusion to be drawn, when a contradiction issues from a chain of reasoning, is that at least one of the premises involved in the inference is false." [121] In other words, Whitehead contends that if facts in immediate experience involve contradiction (in the opinion of a rationalist), that does not justify their reduction to nonentity.

Alexander

It will be recalled that Whitehead acknowledges especial indebtedness to S. Alexander's *Space, Time and Deity.* In his last book (*Modes of Thought*), Whitehead states that *space, time,* and *"Deity"* are general terms which facilitate the understanding of nature. In other words, Whitehead is re-emphasizing three of his basic notions: (a) process (*time*); (b) arrangement of data (*space*); (c) the lure of ideals

(*Deity*). In these emphases he is in general agreement with Alexander.[122] In *Process and Reality* Whitehead notes that his concept of *feeling* bears close analogy to Alexander's *enjoyment;* [123] and that Alexander's *principle of unrest* is expressed in his notion that an actual entity is a becoming and contributes to the becoming of other actual entities.[124] *Science and the Modern World* states that Whitehead's procedure is to start with the analysis of space and time, or— more accurately—the status of space-time.[125] However, once Whitehead commences his analysis, his basic divergences from Alexander become very obvious.

In the first place, he is convinced that space-time cannot be considered a self-subsistent entity. Rather, such relationships are characteristics of events. Hence they (or it) cannot exist apart from events (actual entities).[126] On the other hand, Alexander claims that space-time "is the stuff of which all existents are composed; and it breaks up of itself into these complexes within the all-embracing stuff." [127] Thus, Alexander rejects the relational theory of space-time. He claims that it is not in accordance with our direct experience of space-time.[128] He contends that space and time are not relations between autonomous actual entities; but rather, relationships between entities are due to the fact that they are aspects of the one all-inclusive space-time stuff.[129] There is a further drastic difference. Alexander states, for example, that particular existents are "complexes of motion differentiated within the one all-containing and all-encompassing system of motion." [130] In order to emphasize the point, he uses metaphors. Particulars may be regarded as whirlpools within the ocean of space-time or as crystals in that matrix. However, though crystals may be separated from their matrix, existents never can. In view of statements such as the preceding, Alexander recognizes the necessity of facing the question: Are the existents within space-time lost in space-time, or do they conserve their own reality? [131] His answer is briefly

this: All finite existents are incomplete. However, they have
a relative reality. He attempts to clarify this concept by
pointing out that "a configuration of motion is not destroyed
by its relation to the circumambient medium, but is, on the
contrary, sustained thereby." [132] Similarly a person, as a constituent member of a society, is not destroyed by the society
but is sustained by it. To repeat: Everything is reducible
to motion. One complex group of motions may be shattered
into its component motions, but each component motion is
a part of space-time and hence is real to that extent. Alexander summarizes his position thus: "Everything that truly
is is really. The One is the system of the Many in which they
are conserved, not the vortex in which they are engulfed." [133]
Yet, despite this attempt to retain individuality, it would
seem that to reduce every existent to motion (or complexes
of motion) is to blot out the individual uniqueness which
Whitehead discovers in each actual entity. In place of the
complex inner life, with a distinct subjective aim, characterized by unique subjective form, achieving its own private
completion and then passing on data for other actual entities; in place of the complex patterns of social interaction
whereby Whitehead accounts for our everyday world—in
place of this Alexander gives us "motions in a sea of motions." Where, then, is genuine individuality? "Empirical
things come into existence, because Space-Time of its own
nature breaks up into finites." [134] Where is the *self-creativity*
which Whitehead assigns to actualities?

This reduction is in apparent opposition to Alexander's
well-known emphasis on emergent evolution. For example:
"The new quality life emerges . . . therefore life is at once
a physiochemical complex and is not merely physical and
chemical, for these terms do not sufficiently characterize the
new complex." [135] However, confusing as it seems, a few
pages later he returns to his advocacy of reductionism. "Each
new type of existence when it emerges is expressible com-

pletely or without residue in terms of the lower stage . . .
mind in terms of living process . . . matter itself in terms of
motion." [136]

It will be recalled that in Whitehead's system all actualities manifest objective value. Here is a point at which Alexander is in substantial disagreement. Values are not inherent qualities of reality, present wherever an actual entity
is present, whether appreciated by others or not.[137] In Alexander's opinion, value arises in a complex whole in which
there is a valued object and valuing subjects.[138] The object
must be characterized by coherence. Coherence or incoher-
ence, though involving reality, are the result of our reactions.[139] Standards of evaluation are available as the result
of the co-operation and conflict of many minds.[140] Thus, to
repeat, this is a relational theory of value. "The value re-
sides in the relation between the two [subject and object]
and does not exist apart from them." [141] These values are
real in the sense that they are "tertiary qualities," generated
as specified.[142]

Alexander and Whitehead agree that in the universe there
is a being called God. Alexander's God has several aspects.
(a) "God is the whole world as possessing the quality of
deity." [143] Deity in this sense is the next highest quality beyond what we know. It is the quality beyond mind. (The
term *Deity* in its wider usage means "the next highest quality." In this sense it is possible that mind might be Deity
with reference to matter.) This Deity phase of God is not
actual but ideal. This emphasis on an ideal aspect of God
is somewhat similar to Whitehead's concept of the primordial nature of God. (b) The infinite world, with its *nisus*
(tendency) toward Deity, is the actual phase of God. The
ideal phase of God is termed his mind. The actual aspect
is his body.[144] In a very general way the "actual phase" of
Alexander's God is similar to the consequent nature of
Whitehead's God. However, the "saving function" stressed

by Whitehead is not mentioned by Alexander. There seems to be nothing in Alexander corresponding to Whitehead's "superject nature" of God. In passing it may be noted that Whitehead rejects the creative initiative which the emergent evolutionists assign to the *nisus*.[145]

There are other points of difference between Whitehead and Alexander. In Alexander's opinion there are no relations between universals.[146] In other words, there is nothing in Alexander's system corresponding to the function whereby God's primordial nature arranges eternal objects and makes them readily available for the use of actual entities. Alexander also differs from Whitehead concerning the internality of relations. "If to be internal means that a relation is a quality of its terms, or belongs to them as a quality does, then a relation is not internal to its terms." [147] Alexander uses the concept *substance* which Whitehead rejects.[148] His analysis of causality rules out Whitehead's emphasis on experienced force.[149] In Alexander's system categories are pervasive characters of things, whereas for Whitehead categories are principles which are not necessarily pervasive— i.e., always present (at least some of them are not).

Whitehead in common with Alexander stresses *identity, diversity, existence, order, reciprocity, intensity, whole, part, number.* He prefers not to use the terms *universal* and *particular.* Further, in Alexander's analysis the notion of universal involves repetition, something which Whitehead does not stress in his theory of eternal objects. Whitehead, like Alexander, uses the concepts of *individuality* and *relation* but in a more thoroughgoing and genuine fashion. Alexander's concept of *motion* may be regarded as, in a very general fashion, somewhat similar to Whitehead's *process.*

This barrage of differences should not blind one to the fact that there are some further points, of at least apparent similarity, which should be recorded. Alexander, like Whitehead, is convinced that the world is a world of events; [150] that philosophy should use an empirical approach to its problems; [151] that sense experience is not the only valid avenue to knowledge; that no experience is ever isolated.[152] It must be admitted that some of Whitehead's comments in *Science and the Modern World* concerning "creativity" [153] remind one very strongly of Alexander's discussion of space-time. However, his later books indicate that this interpretation is incorrect.

In concluding this comparison of Whitehead and Alexander, one seems justified in contending that while there are some general characteristics in common, these systems diverge unmistakably in crucial details.

Nunn

In the Preface of *Process and Reality,* Whitehead states that he is greatly indebted to Professor T. P. Nunn, of the University of London.[154]

A perusal of the papers which Nunn read before the Aristotelian Society indicates the importance of his contributions to philosophy in general. However, apart from a common devotion to a realistic epistemology, and one or two other points of general agreement, there seems to be little similarity between Whitehead's *mature* philosophy and that briefly sketched by Nunn.

Whitehead agrees with Nunn that in sense experience there is a direct experience of objects outside and independent of the "sensing." [155] Further, he concurs in the claim that (a) both primary and secondary qualities are really in objects whether we perceive them or not; (b) they exist as accurately perceived; (c) there is thus no need to postulate a "representative function" of sense data.[156] Nunn's suggestions concerning the interrelation of reals and their extension through space are other samples of a common viewpoint:

Physical bodies are not isolated reals, each wearing its own qualities without any regard to the condition of any other body. In certain cases, capable of empirical determination, bodies reciprocally "take note" (in Lotze's phrase) of one another's condition, and express this notice in their own states. Again a thing must not be thought of as limited by a precise spatial boundary. It may be necessary to think of it as filling an indefinite part of the material universe.[157]

Nunn's recognition of the scientific value of the "realist doctrine which takes as ultimate data a psychic monad opposed to a universe of independent objects," [158] is quite in accord with Whitehead's stand. This is equally true of Nunn's general emphasis on the importance of an analysis of mind in conative terms and his stress on the fundamental nature of affective experience. " 'Mind' . . . is essentially a mass of objects . . . organized into conative systems which exhibit at one time various degrees of synthesis." [159] In the work of both men there appears a serious and genuine respect for "common sense" views. Nunn expresses this conviction rather effectively in the following words: "In philosophising, though I may rectify and add to the plain man's view, I must not contradict or explain away any essential positive features of it." [160] In his presidential address to the Aristotelian Society [161] he mentions, with approval, Whitehead's criticism of the "bifurcation of nature." He also notes that his theory of a physical object (a set of sense data) finds support in Whitehead's contention that a point is to be understood as a set of volumes.[162]

It must be remembered, however, that Whitehead in his later philosophizing does not agree that a thing is nothing but a set of sense data. The complicated inner subjective life of an actual entity is a far cry from a mere aggregation of sensa. This then is a crucial difference. The rich inner life of reality which Whitehead stresses, in his mature philosophy, is omitted (apart from a few undeveloped hints) in Nunn's analysis. Even when one compares Whitehead's

earlier writings with those of Nunn there is a basic disagreement—as Nunn sadly admits. He finds in *The Concept
of Nature* an apparent tendency to assign to common-sense
objects and scientific objects equal right to be considered
actual components of nature.[163] Nunn rejects this point of
view because he contends that "scientific objects are not a
new order of things, but are merely common-sense things . . .
with relevant simplifications." [164]

In the work of Nunn, Whitehead apparently found support for the "provisional" realistic position presented in his
earlier books, and in parts of *Science and the Modern World*.
Whitehead's epistemology is consistently realistic. However,
it is not as free from doubt in its later expressions as it is in
the earlier ones. In any case, Whitehead's "reformed subjectivism" involves the complete abandonment of the shal-
low and lifeless realism of associations of sense data. In this
connection one might well recall his denunciations of reliance on clear-cut sense data. Thus, Whitehead's expressions
of appreciation concerning the work of Nunn should not
mislead one into assuming that they express, in any detailed
fashion, identical, or even similar, points of view.

Santayana

Whitehead's great contemporary Santayana commands his
respect because of his admirable *Scepticism and Animal Faith*.
This obviously was one of the books Whitehead "had in
mind" as he was writing *Process and Reality*. However, despite his respect for Santayana's virtuosity he disagrees with
the "sturdy make believe of 'animal faith' " [165] which denies
that there is any element of givenness (of an external world)
in the process of perception. Like other exponents of representative perception, Santayana is forced to content himself
with a phenomenal veil which hangs, inescapably, between
the perceiver and reality.[166] This epistemological gap is, in
Whitehead's opinion, most disastrously evident when San-

tayana contends that intuitions cannot be the data of other intuitions. (That is to say, one moment of experience cannot be experienced by another moment of experience.)

There are other important differences between Whitehead and Santayana. For example, Santayana's essences, though eternal, are "neutral in value," [167] while some of Whitehead's eternal objects are value ideals. Further, Santayana's essences are "democratic" in that they are not arranged in levels of importance. The close linkage between eternal objects and actual entities which one finds in Whitehead's philosophy is definitely missing in Santayana's. The realm of essence has no essential connection with the concrete realm of matter. Whitehead finds a definite place in the universe for a God. Santayana's skepticism restrains him. In general Whitehead tries to come to grips with facts of all sorts. Santayana sighs sadly, smiles faintly, and advocates the honest admission that one is hugging delusions. This must be remembered as one discovers that in Santayana there are many statements which have a Whiteheadian ring. For example:

Each center is equally actual and equally central, yet each is dependent on its neighbors for its position and on its predecessors for its genesis. The existential interval from one center to another is bridged naturally by generation or motion—by a transition actually taking place from one moment, place or character to another, in such a manner that the former moment, place or character is abandoned or lost.[168]

A son is not connected with his father merely by similarity and contiguity, though Hume, who was an old bachelor, might let us think so. [It will be recalled that Santayana also was a bachelor!] There is always physical continuity and qualitative inheritance in a natural process, however vast or sudden the transformations.[169]

William James

Like Whitehead, James stresses unities in experience and regards feeling as a basic activity accounting for connectedness. Whitehead shares with James an emphasis on process, the plurality of reals, and the refusal to bow to the dictates of rationalism. There is also the common rejection of the theory of substance.[170] In dealing with the problem of the unity of consciousness, James develops a theory which is strikingly like Whitehead's theory of actual entities. He discusses "pulses" of feeling growing out of prior pulses but functioning as a creative agent.[171]

The importance of the individual is also stressed by James. His denunciations of absolute idealism are well known.[172] James' doctrine that there are "lines of influence" between things is, in general, Whitehead's position, though he does not assign as wide a scope to these phenomena as does Whitehead. The contention that "oneness and manyness are absolutely co-ordinate . . . neither is primordial or more essential or excellent than the other" [173] is also in accordance with Whitehead's point of view. The famous "buzzing confusion" of vague experience to which James refers seems to be the same sort of experience which Whitehead terms "causal efficacy."

James' anti-rationalism does lead him close to the extreme position which Bergson sometimes reaches. This is so despite some expressions of appreciation concerning conceptualization. He states, for example: "Both theoretically and practically this power of forming abstract concepts is one of the sublimest of our human prerogatives." [174] He notes that such concepts give increased power and vision in concrete human activity. However, James hastens to decry the almost habitual transition from useful instrument to metaphysical monstrosity. Concepts are treated as a superior type of entity, utterly opposed in nature to the transient lower world.[175] Worse still, concepts are used as the disreputable instruments by which the autocratic intellect dictates what properties a concrete object supposedly can or cannot possess. Concepts become the "procrustean beds" into which things must fit.[176] James' basic criticism of concepts (agreeing with Bergson) is that concepts are discontinuous and fixed. From this position many difficulties arise. The only way in which we can conceptually grasp "life" is to assume arbitrarily that it is broken up into static, distinct parts. Having done this, it is evident that the intellect cannot do justice to the "flow" of our immediate experience. Since moments of time are infinitely divisible by the intellect, no moment of time can ever pass. Similarly motion from one point to another is proved impossible, by the intellect, since any distance is infinitely divisible. James, more fairly, admitted that concepts may give *knowledge about things,* but we can only genuinely know reality by sympathetic acquaintance with it. "The only way in which to apprehend a reality's thickness is either to experience it directly by being a part of reality one's self, or to evoke it in imagination by sympathetically divining some one else's inner life." [177]

Whitehead quite agrees with James that apprehension of another reality involves direct experience. However, the fact that he sets out to provide a "coherent, logical necessary system of general ideas in terms of which every element of our experience can be interpreted" indicates that he has more respect for the intellect than James can muster. This does not mean that Whitehead is suffering from any delusions. His keen analysis of the deficiencies of words has been noted. He has nothing but scorn for those who think that by defining the meaning of words they become acquainted with the facts.[178] However, speaking technically, Whitehead holds that concepts do provide a genuine awareness of the nature of reality. That is to say, actual entities are objectified by eternal objects. A conceptual prehension may not be a complete prehension of a real thing, but it may be a genuine prehension of some phase of a real thing. Whitehead's discussion of the "relational essence" of eternal objects indicates his refusal to accept James' theory of the exclusiveness of concepts. In a very real sense, eternal objects imply each other in varying degrees of relevance. The relation of eternal objects to actual entities, through the mediation of God's primordial nature, further indicates Whitehead's divergence from James. In short, it is Whitehead's opinion that concepts (eternal objects) are not metaphysical monstrosities to be avoided. Rather, they are essential elements in the normal experience of real things (actual entities). In all this, Whitehead claims to be reporting the experience of ordinary men. On this basis he outlines the function of the intellect and its concepts. James points to the misuses of the intellect. Having done so he tends to condemn it. Whitehead provides a more balanced judgment—more true to the facts. When a person uses a concept he does not ordinarily intend to cut into parts the living flow of experience. Rather, he describes the living flow of concrete experience by means of concepts. There is no death-dealing potency in a concept. As relatively static (in meaning) it enables us to discuss, intelligently, entities which are not static. That is a fact of our normal, unmetaphysicalized experience.

Despite his evident kinship with James, there are other phases of the thought of the great pragmatist which Whitehead cannot accept. James' analysis of the physical world involves statements which, if taken literally, seem absurd in the extreme. For example: "We carve out constellations, to suit our human purposes. . . . We break the flux of sensible reality into things . . . at our will." [179] For pragmatism, reality is still in the making and awaits the future for its completion. This latter point, generally speaking, Whitehead would accept. However, he regards the physical world as a complex society of actual entities. These actual entities are autonomous centers of life, contributing their data to other actual entities. Thus the components of the external world are responsible for their own patterns. They are active in the life of the observer. They make contributions to the inner life of the observer. From Whitehead's point of view, it is very difficult to justify the claim that "we break the flux of sensible reality into things at our will." It is true that we contribute to the future. But some aspects of the future will exist, quite apart from anything we can do. In fairness to James, it must be admitted that he also, on occasion, takes a less extreme position than the one which has just been discussed—one more in accordance with the facts of ordinary experience.[180]

Positivism

Whitehead's main criticism of positivism is that it rests content with an apprehension of *some* of the facts and refuses to seek for *"reasons"* behind the facts. But, unless reasons are sought, facts cannot be observed adequately because the search for reasons provides hypotheses directive of observation.[181] Further, positivism (in Whitehead's very wide use of the term) involves an atomism which forbids any possible explanation of the relationships which we find, and assume, to exist in the world of experience. He suggests that the positivists try both "to have their cake and to eat it." They strive to achieve simplicity and accuracy of statement. In order to do this, they concentrate on private sense data, as supposedly the only reliable evidence. Yet, paradoxically, reference is also made to the public world. Whitehead deplores this vacillation.[182] In summarizing his criticism of positivism, he emphasizes the following points: (a) There is a restriction of thought within predetermined limits; it is concerned only with the trivialities of sense data and tautologies. (b) This restriction is based on metaphysical assumptions dogmatically assumed.[183] With characteristic irony he remarked in the course of a lecture on positivism: "It is rather stupid for a Professor to sit up and lecture to a complex pattern of color patches."

Misplaced Concreteness

In criticizing the work of previous thinkers, Whitehead points to a persistent tendency on the part of many to perpetrate the Fallacy of Misplaced Concreteness. This, as the title indicates, consists in mistaking the abstract for the concrete.[184] More specifically it involves setting up distinctions which disregard the genuine interconnections of things. For example, (a) the old-fashioned "faculty psychology" discussed mere awareness, mere private sensation, mere emotion, mere purpose—each a separate and distinct faculty.[185] (b) Another general illustration of this error is the subfallacy of *Simple Location*. This fallacy occurs when one assumes that in expressing the space and time relations of a bit of matter it is unnecessary to say more than that it is present in a specific position in space at a specific time. It is Whitehead's contention that it is absolutely essential to refer to *other* regions of space and *other* durations of time.[186] Whitehead expresses this idea more clearly and briefly by stating that simple location means a mutually exclusive "individual independence."[187] (c) A third general illustration of the fallacy of Misplaced Concreteness is the *Substance-Quality* concept. This is the notion that each real entity is absolutely separate and distinct from every other real entity, and that the qualities of each have no essential relation to the qualities of others.[188]

As has been seen, Whitehead objects to these three variations of the Fallacy of Misplaced Concreteness because they involve a "break up" of the real continuity of experience. He admits the *practical* usefulness of these fallacies. His objection is to the use of these patterns of thought without recognizing their serious deficiencies. Whitehead suggests that this approach is useful in metaphysical speculation only with reference to the "subjective form."[189] If the notion of simple location is taken seriously (in general) the reality of temporal duration is denied. Memory and induction become hopeless mysteries.[190] If the subject (substance) - predicate (quality) notion is accepted uncritically the subject is confined to a private world of experience. Solipsism is inescapable.[191] Whitehead also notes that frequently the substance-quality form of thought involves the notion of "vacuous actuality"; that is, there is a denial of subjective experience to the ultimate realities.[192]

8

Whitehead's Philosophic Position

The discovery of Whitehead's philosophic position is greatly facilitated by an examination of his comments concerning science. It will be recalled that he holds an honored place in this area of human activity. His opinions in the realms of mathematics and physics are those of an expert.

Whitehead's Attitude Toward Science

Whitehead's philosophy—as has been indicated—is based, in part, on recent physics. It can also be understood as a repudiation of some of the fundamental notions of traditional physics. The inadequacies of the theory of "simple location" have already been discussed; also the deficiencies of the substance-attribute pattern of thought. The traditional physics, which embodies both these mistaken notions, was very useful for a number of practical purposes.[1] Yet this system of thought does not provide within itself an explanation of some of its own basic assumptions. For example, there is no reason why bits of matter characterized by mass, motion, and shape should exemplify the law of gravitation.[2] Further, in themselves, these bits of matter were senseless, valueless, purposeless.[3] The disastrous implications of this doctrine of "vacuous actuality" are stressed frequently by Whitehead. For example, the modern industrialized world manifests the lack of reverence for artistic or natural beauty. This, however, is involved unmistakably in the serious acceptance of the theory that nature is valueless.[4] Seventeenth-century science, in the interests of clarity and simplicity, engaged in the worship of abstractions. Matter and mind were hopelessly sundered. This approach ruined modern philosophy. It was thereby doomed to the fruitless juggling of lifeless abstractions and the denial of the reality of genuine interrelations. Neither the resultant dualism nor one of the possible monisms can provide an adequate philosophy. All are infected with error to begin with. This then is the baleful influence of traditional science on modern philosophy.

Concerning the deficiencies of *scientific procedure,* few writers have expressed themselves more "acidly" than Whitehead. His denunciation of the unfortunate tendency of many scientists to rely on the data of "presentational immediacy" has already been discussed. He points out that this devotion to a narrow circle of scientific concepts issues in an obnoxious dogmatism and a blindness with reference to other data.[5] In the course of a very interesting discussion of the origins of modern science, Whitehead suggests that it is essentially irrational and based on a naïve faith. Science is irrational in the sense that it disregards relevant data and can give no reasons for its basic concepts. Since it can give no reasons, it relies on faith—faith in the adequacy of its methods and the assumptions on which they are based. Within the areas of its operations, traditional science—and to a very considerable extent contemporary science also—is rigorously rational. That is to say there is a strong emphasis on the exact techniques of mathematics.[6]

The vaunted impartiality of scientific method is exposed to the stinging jab of Whitehead's criticism. In some cases an impartial approach is inadequate. One must take into consideration individual as well as universal factors.[7] In general, then, the core of Whitehead's criticism is that "the experiences on which accurate science bases itself are completely superficial." [8] That is to say, clear-cut sense data are not the only or the best indicators of the nature of reality.[9]

Some critics of Whitehead's work are appalled and incensed by his apparently flippant and unjust references to scientific experiment. "Discussions on the method of science wander off on to the topic of experiment. But experiment is nothing else than a mode of cooking the facts for the sake of exemplifying the law." [10] This iconoclastic statement can be understood only if it is placed in its proper context. It is part of his general denunciation of the widespread tendency to concentrate only on one segment of relevant data and dogmatically disregard the rest. It must be admitted that the remark under consideration is an overstatement of the point being made. Whitehead expresses high approval of some experimental work—for example, that of Michelson and the German opticians, as well as of Rayleigh and Ramsay. It is true that he does not make extensive references to specific experiments in physics, chemistry, and biology in the course of his metaphysical speculations. However, if experiment means controlled and verified observation, then it is obvious that he advocates and uses it in his study of human experience. Beyond all shadow of doubt he relies on valid experimental procedures, since he accepts and uses some of the recent developments in natural science. Whitehead is well aware of the fact that some of the greatest scientific minds, ancient as well as contemporary, refuse to be confined to clear-cut sense data. Some scientists search for reasons so thoroughly that it is difficult to decide whether they should be called scientists or philosophers. They cannot be accused of "naïve faith." If the term *faith* is used, it should be qualified by "rational" or "empirically justified." In short, Whitehead's "polemic" interests, his desire to correct the deficiencies of some scientific procedures, lead him into dangerous generalities concerning "science."

Thus, despite the inadequacies of both traditional and recent science, Whitehead admits that there is much of value to be found in contemporary science—indeed in science down through the years. There has been a very commendable attempt to find the basic facts and to relate them to fundamental general principles.[11] Within the field of science there is real tolerance. Conflicting theories are not the basis of internecine warfare: they are stimuli to creative effort.[12] Further, Whitehead argues, with considerable efficacy, that value is involved in the scientific approach in a very genuine sense.

In the physical sciences, value judgments are not part of the subject matter. However, no study of the motivation of scientific work can be accurate without a reference to value distinctions. The scientist undertakes a project because he considers it valuable. More specifically he is concerned with the moral value *truth*. He may frequently—if he is an applied scientist—be interest in *beauty*. Certainly he will be concerned with *utility*. Indeed the "pure" scientist finds *beauty* in an abstract system. And it may have considerable utility in bringing him intellectual satisfaction. Thus Whitehead contends that there would be no natural science unless there were first judgments of value.[13]

It has already been emphasized that Whitehead heartily approves the modern emphasis on "process," "interaction," "structure," and in general the implications of the relativity and quantum theories. It is very important to realize that he makes a comprehensive and serious attempt to show that his theory of actual entities is perfectly consistent with the latest developments in physics. He states that the general principles of physics are implied by the philosophy of organism.[14] For example, consider the experience of an actual entity "M" deriving data from other actual entities: A, B, C.

There is in fact a directed influx from A, B, C of quantitative feeling, arising from specific forms of feeling. The experience has a vector character, a common measure of intensity, and specific forms of feeling conveying that intensity. If we substitute the term 'energy' for the concept of a quantitative emotional intensity, and the term 'form of energy' for the concept of 'specific form of feeling,' and remember that in physics 'vector' means definite transmission from elsewhere, we see that this metaphysical description of the simplest elements in the constitution of actual entities agrees absolutely with the general principles according to which the notions of modern physics are framed. The 'datum' in metaphysics is the basis of the vector-theory in physics; the quantitative satisfaction in metaphysics is the basis of scalar localization of energy in physics; the 'sensa' in metaphysics are the basis of the diversity of specific forms under which energy clothes itself.[15]

The flow of feeling from one actual entity to another, with the actual entity requiring a duration for its self-creation, constitutes a situation which would be expected in view of modern quantum theory.[16] The term *potential difference,* as used in physics, is relevant to the situation in the experience of actual entities when two actual entities are contrasted with reference to their objective lures—i.e., the relevant patterns of eternal objects which are used in their process of self-creativity.[17] Whitehead's theory of contemporary actual entities is in accordance with the implications of the relativity theory. According to the traditional theory of time two contemporaries should belong to the same actual world. In the relativity theory this is not so. It will be recalled that Whitehead designates contemporary actual entities as those which do not belong to the actual world selected by the other.[18] He states that the causal independence of contemporaries is a principle which is implied clearly by the Einsteinian formula for the physical continuum.[19] Whitehead's theory of society enables him to show further relationships between the philosophy of organism and recent developments in physics. The notion that there are many space-time systems is what one would expect in view of the theory that there are numerous linear series (personal societies) of actual entities. Each of these linear series constitutes a space-time system.[20] Molecules and crystals are to be regarded as societies. Electrons and protons may be similarly considered.[21] "Wave transmission" is an important characteristic of physical nature because of the behavior of some personal societies. In a personal society with little novelty, the slight amount of spontaneity manifest by its component actual entities is the basis of wave-transmission phenomena.[22] Whitehead contends that his theory conciliates the corpuscular theory of light with the wave theory. Societies of actual entities may take the form of either a wave front or a corpuscle. The light phenomena may start as a corpuscular society—i.e., it may be characterized by strands of personal societies. Gradually these distinct societies may fade out and be replaced by a society which assumes the wave characteristic more obviously.[23] Vibration and rhythm appear in physical nature because in a society which constitutes an ordinary object there is an achievement of contrast within the unified experience of the component actual entities which form the enduring object's society. This contrast is achieved—as Whitehead has indicated—by conceptual reversion, transmutation, subjective harmony, and subjective intensity.[24]

As has been shown, Whitehead emphasizes the scientific basis of his metaphysics. It should be obvious from the preceding that many scientific data fully support the details of his philosophic system. Whitehead's discussion of the relations between his theory of reality and the findings of science are focused chiefly in the area of physical science. He also claims to make use of biological data.[25]

It is interesting to discover that at least two outstanding biologists are convinced that the data of biological science provide further verification for Whitehead's "descriptive generalization." W. E. Agar (Fellow of the Royal Society, Professor of Zoology at the University of Melbourne) has summarized a series of studies in a recent book entitled

A Contribution to the Theory of the Living Organism. He emphasizes his fundamental agreement with Whitehead's position. For instance he states: "The main thesis of this book is that all living organisms are subjects." [26] He regards Whitehead's philosophical system as a "self-consistent account of (a) the body-mind relation; (b) of the relation of efficient to final causation and (c) of the relation of the continuity we find in nature to the atomic character of natural processes." [27] It is his opinion that Whitehead's philosophy of organism is especially adapted to deal with the philosophical problems involved in the hypothesis which he (Agar) regards as inescapable—the hypothesis that organisms can only be understood as subjects, or as organizations (nexūs) of subjects. It must be admitted that sometimes Agar seems to abandon the Whiteheadian concept of nexus and replace it by the notion that an extensive subject (e.g., an organism) may include less extensive subjects (e.g., cells).[28]

This subjectivistic emphasis is developed in some detail. It is argued, for instance, that simple cells must be explained in terms of perception (prehension) and final causation. Thus he states: "It is not only legitimate but, as we shall maintain, necessary, for him [a biologist] to include in his explanatory schemes factors which are unnecessary for the explanatory schemes of the [classical] physicist—namely, such concepts as memory, anticipation, purpose, final causation— in a word, perception." [29] Like Whitehead, Agar suggests that purpose is not necessarily conscious [30] and that an event has a·duration.[31] Agar seems to misinterpret Whitehead's theory of the mental pole of an actual entity. He suggests that it has to do with the achievement of meaning. His discussion of satisfaction seems also to be erroneous, since it is said to involve a grasp of the meaning of the whole situation.[32] However, Agar offers an interesting defense of the use of subjectivistic concepts in biology. He claims that they are just as valid as those concepts involved in the "atomic" approach to matter. "They are justified by their success as explanatory systems, meaning by explanation the formulation of general principles of which apparently diverse phenomena can be shown to be special instances." [33]

An even more impressive indication of the applicability of Whitehead's philosophic concepts to the data of biology is provided by R. S. Lillie in his *General Biology and Philosophy of Organism*. Whitehead's theory of concrescence is echoed in Lillie's statement that every organism is a temporary organization of materials from the environment in accordance with a constant pattern.[34] Indeed he suggests that an organism is constituted by a synthetic process—a process of concretion.[35] He remarks further that some measure of uniqueness or autonomy belongs to each natural individual.[36] Thus each organism is internally determined and so escapes from complete control by the external environment. Like Whitehead, Lillie is willing to admit that the expression of this internal initiative depends on available external data. He refers to similar general conclusions reached by C. E. Coghill.[37]

The necessity of using subjectivistic (psychological) terms in describing the behavior of an organism is repeatedly emphasized by Lillie. "The act of integration [by which an organism is constituted] appears in itself as psychical rather than physical, no matter how dependent it may be upon physical factors for its execution." [38] It is to be noted that he incorporates Whitehead's concept "subjective aim" in his position.[39] Favorable reference is also made to Whitehead's theory of eternal objects. He feels that they help explain stability. They underlie and condition the repeated occurrence of similar events.[40]

Lillie when he advocates a double-aspect theory parts company with Whitehead. While admitting the importance of psychological data (to account for the facts of direction and novelty), he also stresses the inescapable presence of physical data to account for permanency in the organism.[41] However, it should be realized that he refers to psychical stability and admits that physical stability may be due to mental stability.[42] Further, he remarks that the permanent element in an organism is its pattern and not its material component.[43] In any case, while Lillie uses the term *physical* with the meaning it has in physical science, Whitehead (in discussing the physical pole of an actual entity) is employing the term in a sense which is best statable in a psychological context.

The Intelligibility of Whitehead's Language

There is an opinion, widely held, that much of Whitehead's philosophical language is unintelligible. Others go further and state that his philosophy is unintelligible. A few "hardy souls" contend that the language and the philosophy are intelligible, but that he would have been well advised to use simpler language and hence express his valuable insights more clearly.

Whitehead is not unaware of these comments—charitable and otherwise. Speaking to members of the Eastern Division of the American Philosophical Association, at a session held in his honor, he met this problem "head on." "Philosophy in its advance must involve obscurity of expression, and novel phrases." [44] Newly cut trails of course seem strange. With characteristic humor, he once remarked to his Harvard class on cosmology: "There is danger in clarity. I always comfort myself with that thought." He also referred, with a twinkle in his eye, to a reviewer who, in commenting on Whitehead's use of language, accused him of writing in the style of a second-rate female novelist. Speaking seriously on the point at issue, Whitehead contends that he is not telling the same old story in barbaric terminology. *He claims that you cannot express new ideas using old terms.* After all, novelty of expression is not, in all cases, an undesirable characteristic to be deplored by critics. As Whitehead aptly remarks,

modern mathematics now uses symbols which would have
been unintelligible less than a hundred years ago; similarly
in physics. Even in instances where the same symbols are
employed, in many cases there has been a drastic shift in
meaning.[45] The contention that philosophy already has an
adequate and clear-cut set of concepts is also effectively exposed to destructive Whiteheadian ridicule. He points out
that the term *proposition,* as used by the distinguished logi-
cian W. E. Johnson, is found to have twenty-two different
meanings by the equally distinguished critic H. W. B. Joseph.
Where then is the much-vaunted clarity of this basic, traditional concept? There is not a sentence which adequately
states its own meaning. "There is always a background of
presupposition which defies analysis by reason of its infinitude." [46] Ordinary language is concerned with obvious facts
which have a practical bearing on everyday experiences.[47]
Metaphysics, which is a search for underlying generalities,
cannot use "everyday" language with any degree of confidence. Ordinary language must be redesigned. "Words and
phrases must be stretched towards a generality foreign to their
ordinary usage." [48] This involves taking available words, at
present ill defined and ambiguous, and indicating as clearly
as possible exactly what meaning is being assigned to them.[49]
Whitehead notes that "however such elements of language be
stabilized as technicalities, they remain metaphors mutely
appealing for an imaginative leap." [50] This reference to an
"imaginative leap" does not involve an incoherent, blind,
frantic process. It seems to be merely another name for the
insight (intuition) which reveals the basic facts (some of
which have not yet been verbalized). Thus he states: "No
language can be anything but elliptical, requiring a leap of
the imagination to understand its meaning in its relevance to
immediate experience." [51] Whitehead contends that in formulating his technical terms he has applied the principle that
technical phraseology should be based on the usage of the

great men who have gone before.[52] However, the ultimate appeal is not to the great masters but rather to the facts. As he expressed it once to a group of students: "For God's sake look at things for yourself."

The discussion in Chapter 7 of Whitehead's relationship to the members of the philosophic family, from Plato to Bergson and Alexander, indicates that he expresses some ideas and uses some words which have a prominent place in the philosophic tradition. It is true, as he remarks, that other philosophers have not always applied the same emphasis. Some of Whitehead's technical terms are his own invention. However, if one examines their definitions and usage with sufficient care, it is quite possible to understand their meaning. Whether or not Whitehead's new philosophy is supported by the facts is a matter to be settled by individual examination of these facts. This process of verification is facilitated if one has abandoned preconceived notions concerning his system. In any case, as Whitehead aptly points out, there are many strands in the philosophic tradition. It is absurd dogmatism for the adherents of one strand to demand that devotees of other strands adhere to their particular version of what constitutes correct philosophic procedure.[53]

What Is Whitehead's Philosophic Position?

Whitehead refers to his philosophy as the "Philosophy of Organism." It is important to grasp the meaning which he assigns to this phrase. He uses the term *organism* in two chief senses: (a) An actual entity is an organism; that is to say, an actual entity is a process of synthesis whereby various data are woven into an organic whole. (b) A nexus (of actual entities) is also an organism; in other words, there is a process of constituative relationship between the members of the nexus.[54]

This is what Whitehead has in mind when he suggests

that there are organisms of organisms, or societies of societies.[55] The question, however, remains: Is he a realist, idealist, pragmatist, or logical positivist?

There are those who are prepared to argue that he is "neither fish nor fowl nor good red herring." Indeed Whitehead does not facilitate the application of technical labels. In *Science and the Modern World* he seems to suggest that his organic point of view might be accepted by either a realist or an idealist. However, he adopts a provisional realism.[56] This is done because he rejects the idealistic contention that cognitive mentality is inescapably involved in every detail of the real world.[57] He contends that even when some idealists *seem* to take the results of science seriously it is only a pose. In the last analysis they reduce everything to ideas in a Mind.[58]

In *Science and the Modern World* he also terms his position "Organic Mechanism." This involves a contrast with "Materialistic Mechanism." Whitehead's position is mechanistic in that physical ultimates, such as electrons, blindly run (i.e., there is for practical purposes no novelty in the conceptual prehensions of the component actual entities). However, when electrons are within a body, they are influenced by the fact. Hence there is an organic mechanism.[59] Whitehead also sketches, in more general terms, the contrast between an organic and a materialistic philosophy. The so-called materialistic philosophy starts with independently existing substances, matter and mind. "The organic starting point is from the analysis of process as the realization of events disposed in an interlocked community." [60] In *Process and Reality* Whitehead calls his position "Organic Realism." [61] In the preface of the same book, it is suggested that his system is a "transformation of some main doctrines of Absolute Idealism onto a realistic basis." [62]

Whitehead's emphasis on value as an essential component of reality, seems to place him in the camp of idealism. Yet in this he is in agreement with some of the new realists. As has been shown, Whitehead is a realist in epistemology. Things exist independently of being perceived. He is, therefore, a firm opponent of the idealism of Berkeley. His fundamental divergences from the essential features of the absolute idealism of Bradley have been discussed. Thus, despite the common emphasis on feeling, one must seriously question his statement that some of the main doctrines of absolute idealism have been given a realistic basis. It has been shown that his position is different from the idealism of Plato and of Leibnitz. However, in the last analysis, Whitehead is an *idealist in metaphysics.* He is unmistakably a pan-psychist. The final real things are actual entities. Actual entities are subjects. Apart from subjects there is nothing.[63] It must, of course, be remembered that only a few such subjects are conscious or have clear sensory experience. Thus Whitehead does not contend that all components of the universe have characteristics found in human beings at their best. Yet what we find in human experience gives the clue to the remaining entities in the universe.

In justifying this subjectivistic approach, Whitehead argues that it follows from the commonly accepted position that human experience is part of nature. If this be so, then factors which are involved in descriptions of human experience will also be involved in dealing with other parts of nature. The alternative is to contend that human experience is "beyond nature." [64] There is another argument, more in accord with Whitehead's claim to be offering a generalized description of the facts of nature; it states that "feeling" is a directly observed factor present in all actual entities which are available for careful inspection.[65]

In the preceding discussion of the relation of Whitehead to modern science, reference was made to his claim that the general principles of physics are implied by the philosophy of organism.[66] He contends that his theory of actual entities avoids the dualism of matter and mind which has plagued modern philosophy. Also it provides a simple explanation of how one level of existence can emerge from another. For example, the emergence of life from non-living material is to be explained by an enriched experience of actual entities involving memory and anticipation.[67] There is no mystery about the process. One does not need to posit a "nisus" or assign "dividing tendencies" to space-time.

This reference to the emergence of new qualities focuses attention on the fact that in a certain sense the philosophy of organism is an evolutionary philosophy. Indeed, White-head refers to the evolutionary theory of the philosophy of organism.[68] More specifically he discusses the emergent unity of the superject stage of an actual entity.[69] He agrees with the general principle of emergent evolution that what emerges is more than a mere "collection" of different component elements.[70] It is suggested that different modes of functioning result from methods of organization.[71] In general, he feels that his metaphysics provides a basis for a thoroughgoing evolutionary philosophy.[72] Yet, as the preceding discussion has indicated, Whitehead is in fundamental disagreement with one of the chief representatives of emergent evolution —S. Alexander.

He is also severely critical of many phases of the traditional evolutionary philosophy linked with the name of Darwin. He accords scant respect to a philosophy based on the "evolutionary" notions of "struggle for existence" and "adaptation to environment." Whitehead points out that this struggle does not explain the emergence of a general type of organism which has faint survival power.[73] For instance, in the universe are rocks which survive eight hundred million years, and insects which have a life expectancy of less than a year. How then can you account for the insect which obviously is poorly equipped for the struggle for survival? Then, too, there is man, who is concerned with trivialities and irrelevancies, as far as mere existence is concerned. More accurately, there are some men who forget the "necessities" of food, clothing, and shelter. They fix their attention on the gleam of the sunlight, the song of birds. They dream dreams—voyaging far beyond the actual. These activities are enjoyed for their own sake. There is no ulterior purpose.[74] Thus, in its obvious meaning, this principle is, in numerous instances, inoperative. Where it seems to have relevance, Whitehead aptly remarks that if "maladjustment to the environment" is the explanation of the disappearance of a species, you are saddled with a useless tautology. "The phrase is like the liturgical refrain of a litany, chanted over the fossils of vanished species." [75] It is further suggested that the usual evolutionary philosophy does not account for the fact that there has been evolution upward and that animals have adapted the environment to themselves.[76]

These criticisms of various phases of the evolutionary philosophy follow obviously from Whitehead's metaphysics. It will be recalled that, in his opinion, actual entities are not primarily engaged in ceaseless, ruthless struggle with one another. Rather, they provide "mutual aid" in the sense that data from all past actual entities are made available for the use of all present actual entities. And all present actual entities furnish data for the use of all future actual entities. It is true that "conflicting ideals" (eternal objects) may be selected by newly arising actual entities. It is equally possible that the ideals may be similar and hence involve the actual entities in co-operation in a common cause. After all, the concept *society* is basic in his philosophy.

Whitehead's emphasis on the organic interrelatedness of actual entities, and their mutual aid, does not lead him in the direction of Herbert Spencer's claim that an individual is made by his society. Whitehead's doctrine is that each actual entity is ultimately autonomous in the sense that it selects the data it uses in the process of its self-creation.

But not. conscious selection ! ?

On occasion he uses the term *cell* as a synonym for *actual entity*.[77] Some students of Whitehead have been misled by his statement that the ultimate metaphysical truth is atomism.[78] Preceding discussion has indicated that he repudiates traditional atomism with its implication of mutual exclusiveness. The term *atomism* means for Whitehead "distinguishable individuals." He emphasizes the point that there must be a proper balance between atomism and continuity. The continuous interaction of actual entities must be stressed equally with self-creative individuality.[79] He underlines the fact that his concept of feeling is diametrically opposed to the "neutral stuff" theory of some of the realists.[80]

It should be obvious that Whitehead's emphasis on process does not involve a denial of permanence: (a) There are the unchanging eternal objects. (b) There is another type of permanence discoverable in the creative flux of actual entities.[81] The reproduction here mentioned is the so-called process of "objectification" whereby data from a perishing actual entity are transferred to a newly arising actual entity. This may be a member of a society. (c) There is an additional type of permanence provided by the inclusion of some data from all actual entities in the experience of God.[82]

Despite his emphasis on self-directed creative process, Whitehead rejects *vitalism*. He objects to it because it involves an unresolved dualism. Mechanism remains only partly subjugated within living bodies. The gap between living and dead matter remains.[83] Notwithstanding his denunciation of *dualism,* there are those who claim to find obvious dualisms in Whitehead's philosophy. There are contrasts between the physical pole and mental pole; between God's primordial nature and God's consequent nature; between God and the World. In his presidential address to the American Philosophical Association, "Objects and Subjects," [84] Whitehead dealt with this point. He states that, superficially, it might appear that the position which he has outlined is an instance of the revolt against dualism. But in another, and more accurate, sense he has attempted to provide a defense of one type of dualism.[85] It is a type of dualism which does not hopelessly sunder entities. Rather it is a type of dualism

. . . found *within* each occasion of actuality. . . . The universe is dual because, in the fullest sense, it is both transient and eternal. The universe is dual because each final actuality is both physical and mental. The universe is dual because each actuality requires abstract character. The universe is dual because each occasion unites its formal immediacy with objective otherness. The universe is *many* because it is wholly and completely to be analyzed into many final actualities. . . . The universe is *one,* because of the universal immanence. There is thus a dualism in this contrast between the unity and multiplicity. Throughout the universe there reigns the union of opposites which is the ground of dualism.[86]

Thus, Whitehead's so-called dualism really avoids the chief characteristics of traditional dualism, namely exclusiveness of substances based on mutual independence. It must be admitted that his position with reference to epistemological dualism is not too clear. (See the preceding discussion, pp. 81–82.) In any case, it might have been better, in the interests of clarity, if he had invented a new term rather than used the familiar one. To repeat: the dualism Whitehead defends is not the traditional dualism. His position is dualism "differently interpreted." The difference is complete and ultimate.

Whitehead's rejection of traditional dualism seems to admit him into the charmed circle of modern *naturalism.* "The rather solitary figure of Whitehead deserves at least some mention among the pioneers of contemporary naturalism, for he has argued brilliantly and powerfully against dualisms." [87] It is noted, further, that Whitehead stresses the point that mankind is a factor in nature.[88] However, Randall refers to his "dubious naturalism" and mentions Dewey's suspicion of the principle of concretion.[89] Actually Whitehead is justified in replying that the principle of concretion is a factor within nature. Yet, despite the fact that Whitehead opposes dualism, supernaturalism, and reductionism, there can be no doubt that he does not meet one of the basic criteria of modern naturalism. That is its insistence on the universal and unrestricted applicability of scientific method. Whitehead has great respect for science. As previous discussion has indicated, he is equally aware of its serious deficiencies.

Whitehead's confusing manipulation of the term *dualism* has been noted. His use of the terms *one* and *many* also causes some difficulty. In a sense Whitehead is a pluralist. The universe is many. "It is wholly and completely to be analyzed into many final actualities." [90] In a sense the universe is one, since all actual entities contribute data to (any) one newly arising actual entity. However, in the traditional meaning of the terms, Whitehead is a pluralist (numerically) rather than a monist.

More specifically he states that each actual entity has *both* *internal* and *external* relations with all other available actual entities.[91] All actualities are positively prehended, directly or indirectly. All eternal objects are either positively or negatively prehended. In either case there is a genuine contribution to the new actual entity. Even a negative prehension makes a contribution to the subjective form of the new entity. It would, therefore, seem that all entities have internal relations with all other entities. However, as has been reiterated, an actual entity is not entirely determined or constituted by these internal relations. Further each entity is genuinely distinguishable from the others. The essential selfhood of any actual entity lies in the fact that it is an autonomous center of life. It feels all the other actual entities as it sees fit, in a uniquely individual fashion (within certain very wide possibilities of experience). Thus any actual entity is "other" with reference to the remaining actual entities. Further, the extreme tenuousness of an actual entity's relationship with its contemporaries and with future and distant past actual entities, constitutes another type of externality of relationship. This problem of relationship, as it arises with reference to eternal objects, is discussed in very technical fashion in the chapter on "Abstraction" in *Science and the Modern World*. It will be recalled that Whitehead contends that each eternal object has a relational essence. Its relations to all other eternal objects is an essential factor; hence the relationship is internal. However, the relational essence of an eternal object is not unique to that object.[92] Therefore, it is possible to exemplify one (or a limited set of) eternal object in any actual entity without thereby exemplifying all eternal objects. That is to say, it is possible to have finite truths.

As is obvious, Whitehead's theory of relations avoids two extreme alternatives. He rejects the claim of Bradley or Hegel that, if things are genuinely related to each other, this can only be explained in terms of their inclusion in a unified whole (absolute) in such a way that their essential individuality is lost. Many of those who deny this explanation of relationship have in the past been left with the uncomfortable alternative that finite persons and things must be regarded as hopelessly sundered from each other without any real bonds of interconnection. As long as the category of substance was accepted, explicit or implicitly, the problem of relations generated the difficulties noted above. Whitehead's denial of substance, and his description of an actual entity as a finite reality constituting itself by its relations with other actualities, involves an *internally* related plurality of reals. Yet they are mutually *external* in the sense that there is in each a core of genuine autonomy and hence individual distinctness.

In conclusion, then, Whitehead is a pluralist in the sense that he claims that, at any period in the history of the universe, there are many actual entities, not just one all-inclusive entity. However, it should be clear from preceding discussion that, in a sense, Whitehead is a monist, because all actual entities are the same type of "being." All actual entities are subjects, having the same *general* characteristics. This at least is Whitehead's opinion. It has been argued above that as a matter of fact the actual entity God is drastically different from other actual entities. To this extent Whitehead's purported "qualitative" monism is subject to serious question.

Whitehead deals with the problem of "purpose" or "design" in the universe. He contends that it is the supreme task of the creative process (as it is manifested in actual entities) to change an unorganized group of conflicting elements into a unity in which opposition has been transformed into fruitful contrast.[93] This occurs in God and also in ordinary actual entities.[94] Preceding discussion has shown that God has no absolute power to bring this purpose to final realization, except in his own experience.

It becomes clear that Whitehead's philosophy does not support the traditional postulate that there is an *ultimate* structure or order manifest in all experience. The so-called "laws of nature" are descriptions of the dominant characteristics of dominant societies of actual entities. The laws only come into being because of the characters of members of a society. It is to be further noted that a system of "laws" gradually rises into prominence, has a period of application, and then fades from view as its "supporting" society is replaced by another.[95] "The present type of order in the world has arisen from an unimaginable past, and it will find its grave in an unimaginable future." [96]

If this point of view is accepted, the terms *order* and *disorder* take on a relative meaning. Disorder means that the order found in one society of actual entities is not found in another. In other words, disorder is a type of order not found in the society which is the point of reference.[97] Whitehead uses the term *chaotic disorder* to refer to a state of affairs in which there are no prominent societies providing relatively obvious unities of activity.[98]

Whitehead's position with reference to the problem of primary and secondary qualities is that the so-called secondary qualities (and, for that matter, tertiary also) are just as much a part of the object as the so-called primary qualities. Colors and sounds are *found* in spatio-temporal relationships in nature.[99] Having considered the alternative position Whitehead brands it as "quite unbelievable." [100]

Whitehead makes several attempts to state the main concepts involved in his complex system. In *Science and the Modern World* he mentions *change, value, eternal objects, endurance, organism, interfusion.*[101] *Process and Reality* provides several lists of which the following is perhaps representative: *system, process, creative advance into novelty, individual unity of experience, feeling, time as perpetual perishing, endurance as re-creation, purpose, universals* as forms of definiteness, *particulars* as ultimate agents of stubborn fact.[102] In more general fashion, he states that the Category of the Ultimate involves *creativity, one, many,* as basic, constituent categories.[103] The most complete list of Whitehead's basic concepts is found in his impressive gallery of *categories* —the three notions involved in the Category of the Ultimate; the eight Categories of Existence; the twenty-seven Categories of Explanation; and the nine Categoreal Obligations. These various categories have been referred to at relevant points in the preceding discussion. Critical comment will be offered later. However, it should be observed, in passing, that the Categories of Explanation provide a series of comments concerning the entities listed in the Categories of Existence. This entails the introduction of a number of technical terms such as *subject, feeling, satisfaction, ingression, potentiality, subjective form, data.* The nine Categoreal Obligations involve further explanations of the Categories of Existence.

For example, the unity of an actual entity is stressed; the origin of conceptual feelings is discussed; the function of the subjective aim is noted; freedom and determinism are considered. It will have been realized that in the preceding chapters no attempt has been made to use the technical names and numerical designations of the four sets of categories. These technicalities seemed likely to add to the difficulties of a reader unfamiliar with them. However, they do provide an effective summary of Whitehead's point of view. He might have been wiser if he had placed them at the end of *Process and Reality*. There would then be less risk of frightening or puzzling a prospective reader. After all, Whitehead admits that "the whole of the . . . discussion in the subsequent parts either leads up to these categories . . . or is explanatory of them." [104]

9

Evaluation

Various objections to the details of Whitehead's metaphysics have been offered from time to time in the course of the preceding exposition. In this final chapter these objections are summarized and a few more mentioned. Also an attempt is made to recapitulate the favorable comments which have been made. It is the opinion of the author that the excellences far outweigh the deficiencies.

Incidentally, it is interesting to observe that some of the most penetrating criticisms of his philosophy have been formulated by Alfred North Whitehead himself. Speaking to the members of the American Philosophical Association, he remarked: "I am in general agreement as to the need of clarification or revision in my written works." [1] Part IV of *Process and Reality* is designed to correct previous mathematical discussions.[2] He refers to some of his work as provisional outlines.[3] As has been noted, in conversation Whitehead is very willing to admit weaknesses and unsolved problems. On one occasion, with customary candor and humility he said: "Half the time you can't do your best work but you have to do it anyway—hence error and inadequacy."

Alfred North Whitehead contends that it is possible to "frame a coherent, logical, necessary system of general ideas in terms of which every element of our experience can be interpreted." [4] His theory of actual entities is an attempt to construct an intellectual system of this sort. The question naturally arises: Has he succeeded? A careful and unbiased reader of his later works cannot help but be impressed by the extent to which he *has* achieved his goal. Whitehead and others have shown, in considerable detail, that it is possible to interpret the data of physics, biology, psychology, sociology, mathematics, morality, aesthetics, logic, and religion, in terms of the theory of actual entities. (There seems to be no reason why chemistry could not be similarly dealt with.) Whitehead not only argues that his conceptual scheme is applicable but also attempts to prove that it is an adequate and accurate interpretation. Here again his position seems very strong indeed. Its strength lies in the fact that to a great extent he has avoided the mistakes that have vitiated the work of other philosophers. He has attempted to provide a *generalized description* of the facts dealt with in various fields of human experience. There is no suggestion of the arbitrary imposition of a metaphysical straight jacket. His fusion of a wide-ranging empiricism and a chastened rationalism has provided a more comprehensive and balanced description of the facts than many of the traditional systems. The apparently naïve method of *intuition* (which is the heart of his empiricism) on closer examination takes on considerable plausibility when one discovers exactly what he is talking about. In general, the absence of dogmatism is a very refreshing factor in Whitehead's metaphysics.

[handwritten marginalia: ? HAS HIS OWN FORM OF DOGMATISM.]

These highly generalized favorable comments must be supplemented by more specific evaluations, some laudatory, others the reverse.[5] The discussions are arranged roughly in accordance with the preceding chapter sequence. (The following topic is an exception.)

A. Whitehead's Terminology

(1) In the first place it must be admitted that Whitehead's use of language is open to serious criticism. He frequently employs the same term with at least two different meanings. This is so even in the case of such "key concepts" as *feeling,*

ingression, realization, subjective form, satisfaction, objectification, living, mental, actual world, event, dualism, valuation, truth, beauty, goodness. This procedure is particularly unfortunate because it involves in some cases, first, the delineation of an apparently important distinction; and, then, the elimination of the distinction by extending the meaning of one of the terms used in making the distinction. For example: (a) *objectification* and (b) *ingression* are contrasted with (c) *feeling;* then the contrast is blotted out by using objectification and ingression as synonyms for feeling. In view of Whitehead's ability to coin terms, one might ask why he did not produce a few more, in the interests of clarity—rather than generate confusion by overworking some of his key terms. However, a careful reading of context will indicate the varying usages which Whitehead employs. Also he indicates very clearly a list of synonyms for such terms as *actual entity, eternal object,* and other basic concepts.[6] In any case it must be emphasized that one of the most frequent criticisms of Whitehead—that his language is unintelligible —is grossly unfair. True, he has developed a vast armory of technical terms. Unfortunately, there are shifts in meaning. Many of these terms have an honored place in the philosophic tradition. In short, Whitehead's language is difficult, but these terms are not unintelligible, *if* a person will devote sufficient time and effort to their mastery.

(2) There are several objections to Whitehead's discussion of categories. Categories of Explanation VI and VII are almost duplicated in Category of Explanation XXIV. Having introduced the Category of Conceptual Reversion, and made considerable use of it in the earlier part of *Process and Reality,* Whitehead states that once the primordial nature of God is introduced (as an explanatory factor), the Category of Reversion is unnecessary.[7] To put it mildly, that is a strange way to deal with a category! Whitehead's Principle of Intensive Relevance (anything in the universe "has its

own gradation of relevance . . . in the constitution of any one actual entity" [8]) is really the same thing as the Principle of Relativity (Category of Explanation IV). One wonders why, in view of its important status, subjective aim is not one of the Categories of Existence. (It is true that subjective aim is involved in the Category of Subjective Intensity, Categoreal Obligation VIII.) In the course of discussion Whitehead was willing to acknowledge several omissions from his list of categories, namely: Continuity, Emergence, God's Primordial Nature.

(3) One relatively minor criticism has to do with the organization of material in *Process and Reality*. It seems that it might have been wiser to place the present Part III at the end of Part I. Part III seems to fit in at this place because it proceeds to consider many of the categories stated in Part I. Part II (as it now stands) frequently involves reference to the forthcoming discussion of categories in Part III. Without this "looking ahead" to Part III, sections in Part II are not really intelligible.

(4) It must be pointed out that sometimes Whitehead is very *careless* in expressing his philosophical ideas. On occasion he makes statements which are not in accord with his actual position, as defined accurately. As has been noted, he sometimes refers to eternal objects as sensa, though he really means to say that sensa are *exemplifications* of eternal objects. In discussing God, he terms God's primordial nature an actual entity and assigns consciousness to God's consequent nature. As a matter of fact, he means that God in his entirety (as a union of primordial, and consequent and superject natures) is an actual entity. Under certain conditions, God experiences consciousness. Whitehead's statement that at any stage an actual entity is both subject and superject is, of course, incorrect. During its process of self-creation the actual entity is subject. When it has finished its life the superject stage has been reached. Whitehead sometimes applies the

term *objective datum* to what ordinarily, when he is striving for accuracy, he calls *initial datum*. He refers to an actual entity A feeling other actual entities, B. C. D. He suggests that B may also feel C and D. However, strictly speaking this is impossible since if A feels B. C. D. then they are all out of existence and B cannot feel C and D. The possibility of B. C. and D being "past" in different degrees with reference to A is apparently ruled out. A further apparent disregard of the usual analysis of the prehensive process is found in the statement that actual entity A may feel actual entity B, and actual entity B may feel A. This is quite impossible. If A feels B then B must have gone out of existence and hence cannot feel A.[9]

(5) In some instances Whitehead's statements are *misleading because of ambiguity*, though a careful reading of context makes possible the grasping of his real meaning. For example, there are his references to *creativity* which seem to imply that it is the fundamental reality possessing ultimate causal power. This, however, is not what he really means. His discussion of the *relational function* of eternal objects seems to imply that eternal objects, as such, constitute the linkage between actual entities. What actually happens in most cases is the transfer of concrete contents, which exemplify eternal objects. Whitehead's remark that "the universe is always one" is a rather misleading way of saying that one actual entity prehends the entire universe. This statement becomes even more clear when used in a wider context as in *Process and Reality*. Similarly the statement that the "many" become "one" and are increased by "one" is not entirely clear. However, it should be obvious, on careful thought, that the "many" which present data for the newly arising "one" are not the "many" (the "world") of which the newly created entity is a member. When Whitehead remarks that God solves all indeterminations, he is not to be taken literally. The reference is to indetermination among eternal objects, not actual

entities. There is a serious blurring of the distinction between eternal objects in their status of (a) available data
and (b) realized components of an actual world. His comments concerning the efficacy of subjective form are also
somewhat misleading unless the context is carefully examined. This is also true of his statement that there is a mutual
immanence of contemporaries. He really means that the subjective aim, not the subjective form, directs the process of
self-creation. Contemporaries, by their very nature, cannot
be immanent in any direct sense. This so-called immanence
is of a very tenuous sort. Whitehead's claim that the future
is in the present in a real sense turns out to be rather confusing. He actually means that the future as such is not present—only data which *may* be used by future actual entities
are present. His apparent localization of value in the realm
of eternal objects is seen, on closer examination, to be merely
a partial approach. His complete exposition indicates that
while, of course, value ideals are eternal objects, these ideals
are realized in the world of fact. Thus actual value is present as well as value ideals.

B. Actual Entities

(1) Whitehead's basic contention that the general characteristics found in human experience will also be present in
all actual entities seems open to serious objection. It is difficult to accept his claim that stones are composed of entities
which are constituted by feelings—particularly conceptual
feelings—and that these feelings are guided by subjective
aim and manifest subjective form. Is this not anthropo-
morphism and animism? True, Whitehead claims that our
experience of the physical world supports his position. Few
men have the competence in physics which he possesses.
There is also support from leading biologists for the claim
that this metaphysical theory applies in that field. It must
be remembered that physicists and biologists cannot agree

on the ultimate nature of reality. It *may be* that Whitehead is correct in his contention. After all it is a difficult problem for the layman (in science) to solve. Further, there is Whitehead's argument that only on the basis of his general point of view can it be contended that man is at home in the universe.

(2) Whitehead's claim that there can be feeling—both physical and conceptual, as well as subjective aim and subjective form—without consciousness being present, seems absurd. Granted that he uses the term *consciousness* in a special sense—the contrast of theory with fact. This perhaps removes most of the sting from the obvious criticism. But the fact remains that there seems little justification for this specialized use of the term *consciousness*. Whitehead might profitably have invented a new term to apply to the process which he calls *consciousness*.

(3) Vehement objection has been directed against Whitehead's doctrine that a "subject," or actual entity, is the emergent result of its feelings in the sense that it is constituted by them. Or to express this in another fashion: An actual entity *is not* something which exists prior to its feelings and originates them. As a matter of fact, an examination of human experience seems to indicate that there is more involved than Whitehead reports. It is true that a subject is built up by its feelings. But there appears to be something which possesses the feelings, something more than the sum of the feelings. There is a "center" which, in reacting to other centers, *has* feelings. The fact that these feelings are characterized by subjective form and are guided by subjective aim is due to the nature of the subject. While its feelings modify the nature of the subject, they cannot occur unless it is present to possess them. To repeat: The human subject seems to be more than the sum of integrated feelings. Even Whitehead's suggestion that the subject is an emergent unity does not seem to free him from this criticism when one exam-

ines exactly what he means by the statement. If there is, to begin with, no center of feeling to which the feelings add content, then the feelings appear to be substantives rather than relational processes. These feelings take on characteristics traditionally assigned to substantial subjects. These feelings have subjective forms, they have data. Somehow (since there is no underlying subject to provide it) a subjective aim appears in the midst of a flux of feelings. This flux, mysteriously unified by its subjective aim, constitutes the actual entity. This theory seems to bear witness to a fear of substance rather than a completely accurate report of observed fact. Why should one deny the existence of interacting, developing entities *more substantial* than those discussed by Whitehead?

The objection that Whitehead does not offer an adequate description of the human subject applies most obviously to his analysis of *adult* human experience. It is *possible* that his position is, in a general fashion, correct as a description of one phase of human experience. There does seem to be a stage in the early development of a child when selfhood emerges out of a welter of experiences—is constituted by them. However, it is very doubtful whether the *details* of Whitehead's analysis apply here—e.g., conceptual prehension and subjective aim. However, further, it should not be forgotten that the experience of "conversion" in any field of human experience, does seem to involve the emergence of a novel adult subject. Yet the fact remains that the appearance of new subjects out of old does not occur, in *adult* experience, with the *regularity and frequency* claimed by Whitehead.

(4) The preceding comment brings us to a further objection to Whitehead's theory of the nature of actual entities. He claims that an occasion of experience has a very brief duration. He argues that subjects rise and very quickly pass away. The so-called "self" is in reality a society—a tempo-

ral series of actual entities. In expounding this position, Whitehead does not take with sufficient seriousness the factor of endurance which characterizes the human self. The self which has its subjective aim and guides its process of feeling, does not endure for a brief instant and then "fade out." Its component feelings are of brief duration, but the self, with its subjective aim, may last for fifty years. True, it changes as its experiences change, as different feelings rise and pass away. The man of sixty-five is not the boy of fifteen. But *one* subjective aim may be the guiding principle of his fifty years of experience. In a real sense the self at the end of fifty years of experience is the same self. But, since the self has been enriched by this experience, it is in this sense different from what it was at the age of fifteen. It must, of course, be admitted that all subjects do not endure as long as fifty years. However, the fact remains that *the existence of a human subject does not seem to be as brief* as Whitehead contends. To this extent his analysis of human experience is incorrect. Even the theory that there is a "felt identity" of past occasions of experience within present occasions of experience does not do justice to all the facts.[10]

(5) An examination of human experience also casts some doubt on Whitehead's theory of "objectification." He contends that in some cases this involves a literal transfer of content from one actual entity to another. For example, the *same angry feeling* is transferred from a perishing actual entity to a newly arising actual entity. Is it not legitimate to suggest that since the actual entity which originally held the anger is different from the newly arising actual entity, therefore, the identically same anger cannot be present in both actual entities? This point is particularly relevant in view of Whitehead's insistence that no two actual entities can be exactly alike, and his emphasis on the importance of considering data in their context.

(6) Whitehead contends that actual entities are *causa sui.* Each actual entity determines which data shall be accepted and how these data shall be experienced. Is it not obvious that Whitehead is unduly optimistic concerning the powers of resistance possessed by human subjects (the prototype of all actual entities)? Is it not true that *most*—perhaps *all*— actual entities can conceivably be brought to the point where they can no longer resist the necessity of bowing to the pressure of externally imposed data? The general question may be raised as to whether Whitehead, in his examination of human experience, has taken into consideration the fact of individual differences.

(7) Whitehead's contention that mathematical forms cannot characterize subjective form (in its restricted meaning) is contrary to ordinary experience. It is correct, as he suggests, that there cannot be "squareness of emotion." But might not the emotion have an intensity denoted by the number three? (He mentions triplicity as an example of a mathematical form.)

(8) Upon careful examination it becomes apparent that, *in a sense,* Whitehead's metaphysical position implies that an actual entity is restricted to the experiencing of its own component elements. The data which an actual entity receives come from other actual entities. Yet they, as experienced, are part of the constituent content of the prehending actual entity. They do not now belong to the original source, since the actual entity which provides data must pass out of existence before these data are made available. The newly arising actual entity does not prehend any other actual entity, as such. This line of approach culminates in the theory that an actual entity never has direct experience of the contemporary world. Whitehead recognizes that a form of solipsism is involved in his position. He feels that there is a danger here, and that he has not been sufficiently careful in formulating his ideas at this point. However, the emphasis

on the *felt impact of data from without* frees him from most of the dangers involved in traditional solipsism.

(9) According to Whitehead, a society of actual entities possesses only those characteristics which are to be found in its (some or all) component actual entities. If this theory is to be taken in absolute literalness, rather strange consequences follow. It will be necessary, for example, to claim that a table is square because its component actual entities manifest the eternal object *squareness*. (This presents an initial difficulty. See preceding objection, number 7.) If a saw is used to make the table top round, then supposedly some (at least) of the component actual entities would be replaced by actual entities which had, with one accord, decided to exemplify the eternal object *roundness*. This does not seem very plausible. There is a further difficulty. It is really hard to conceive how, on the basis of Whitehead's position, one could account for a situation in which various entities composing a society came together in a *patterned unity*. The pattern may be the distinguishing feature of the society; yet it (the pattern) may be of the sort that it is *not,* as such, exemplified in the life of any of the component actual entities. Each might contribute its share to the realization of the pattern, but the pattern would not be exemplified in any one actual entity. How then can the principle hold that a society can only have the characteristics which are found in some or all of its component actual entities? In short, Whitehead, in attempting to trace all the characteristics of a society back to its constituent entities, apparently disregards the fact that frequently the whole is more than the sum of its parts. Thus, at this point he seems to be overlooking "creative emergence." In discussion, Whitehead was prepared to admit that he neglected to formulate a Category of Emergence to deal with this problem. In the theory of "transmutation" he attempted it but did not succeed.

In fairness to Whitehead it must be realized that his theory of "multiple contrast" seems to meet this difficulty, though apparently only at the cost of abandoning the principle that a society has only the characteristics found in some or all of its members. A multiple contrast involves pairs of contrasting elements (for example, pairs of complementary colors). However, Whitehead contends that it is not merely an aggregation of contrasting elements. In a sense it is "over and above" its component elements. Whitehead specifically points out that this is the basis of a theory of emergent evolution.[11]

(10) Whitehead's discussion of *living societies* involves him in serious difficulties. To begin with, technically speaking, "life" cannot be the defining characteristic of a society. This is so since life means novelty and a society involves repetition. Further, Whitehead contradicts himself by stating first that no single occasion can be called living—and then proceeding to do just that.

His attempt to differentiate *life* from *mentality* ensnares him in a dangerous contradiction. "Conceptual novelty" is supposed to be the distinguishing factor, yet conceptual novelty is found on the level of life as well as that of mind. Further, *all* entities have a mental pole. Also he leaves himself, open to the charge that he employs the same differentia to distinguish living from non-living as he does to distinguish mental from living. True, he contends that this distinction is a matter of degree. In this fashion he perhaps partially meets this criticism.

(11) His discussion of the extensive continuum also issues in apparent confusion. It is referred to as *both* (a) a distinct entity, real in its own right and (b) a relational characteristic of other realities.

(12) Whitehead involves himself in contradiction in his conflicting claims that (a) the relationship between actual entities may be that of *either* positive or negative prehension and (b) the contrasting suggestion that it (always) *must be*

positive prehension. Incidentally, a detailed analysis of positive prehension reveals that negative prehension is involved as a necessary ingredient.

(13) The Whiteheadian doctrine of eternal objects is at least a plausible one. A minority of thinkers have found, in their experience, justification for a theory of this type. Further, his discussion of the realm of eternal forms is certainly free of some of the usual difficulties—exclusiveness in location and reality.

In turning now to some "more favorable" comments concerning Whitehead's theory of actual entities in general, it should be realized that the preceding specific objections should not be interpreted as a complete denunciation—far from it. Whitehead's emphasis on the genuine plurality of real entities, their creative interaction, the equal inescapability of process and endurance, the constantly recurring appeal to both the simple facts of human experience and advanced technical investigations—all this cannot be too highly commended. The fact that Whitehead can be criticized with reference to details does not deny the impressive validity of his *main* position. This point is to be borne in mind as we proceed to evaluate other, more specific phases of his work. It may be objected that his analysis of the *subject* does not do complete justice to its substantialness and endurance. This, however, does not undermine the validity of his treatment of the creative interaction of subjects. The conviction that the content transferred from one actual entity to another cannot be *exactly* the same should not lead one to overlook the fact that Whitehead is emphasizing an important type of relationship. The difficulties outlined above are serious. However, here again it must be remarked that they are signs of an energetic wrestling with complex problems—problems primarily in the area of *application* of the theory of actual entities. A sympathetic critic will have little difficulty in concluding that *some* of Whitehead's suggestions in this phase of his work are fruitful.

C. *God*

(1) Whitehead's contention that eternal objects will be unorganized, and will have no relevance to the course of concrete events, without the functioning of God's primordial nature, is not self-evident. Why may not one claim, with Plato, that the realm of eternal objects subsists in a state of hierarchical arrangement? Whitehead experiences the fact of organization and postulates an organizer. Why not rest content with the discovered fact of organization? Further, why not accept, as a simple fact, the exemplification of eternal objects in actual entities and explain it only by reference to the activity of the actual entities in which the eternal objects are exemplified? This alternative approach to the problem seems more plausible than Whitehead's. He claims that the experience of God as primordial gives a feeling of refreshment which is a characteristic of religious experience. Is it not true that there are religions without God? Might not the mere fact that there is an orderly system of ideals arouse the religious experience?

(2) Despite Whitehead's claim that in his system God is not to be regarded as an "exception," there is a drastic difference between God and other (ordinary) actual entities. (a) An ordinary actual entity "perishes" when it is complete. Its life endures for only a brief period. On the other hand, God has the ability to combine creative advance with mutual immediacy. In other words, God endures. (b) This claim concerning God gives rise to another phase of the argument that God is different from other actual entities. Although God is supposed to provide data for objectification in other actual entities, he cannot do so in the fashion of ordinary actual entities. They function only when they have perished subjectively, while God supposedly never undergoes

this subjective perishing. Here again, in discussion, White-head was prepared to admit a serious weakness in his position. He has on his hands an unsolved problem as to how the data of God's consequent nature can be made available for other actual entities. (c) God's primordial nature involves an envisagement of all eternal objects, which are thus available for the use of other actual entities. They select some of these for exemplification in their experience. God does not have to seek eternal objects from some other source, as is the case with other actual entities. (d) The subjective aim of an ordinary actual entity may undergo change. God's subjective aim (his eternal envisagement, and his interest in the maximum richness of life for all actual entities) remains unchanged. (e) There is the further difficulty that White-head apparently regards God (primordial, consequent and superject natures) *and* ordinary actual entities as always present in the universe. Thus there is no first day of creation; therefore, God does not have temporal priority over ordinary actual entities. Yet (and here is where the difficulty arises) there *is* an element of temporal priority involved in the situation. God's consequent nature can arise only *after* ordinary actual entities have developed to the point that they are able to provide data. All ordinary actual entities have a birthday. God, in his completeness, depends on ordinary actual entities.

Is ·Whitehead consistent in claiming that the universe is eternal—that there have *always* been ordinary actual entities and God?

These obvious differences between Whitehead's description of ordinary actual entities and his description of God, lead one to question his statement that "God is not to be treated as an exception to all metaphysical principles, invoked to save their collapse. He is their chief exemplification." However, it must be admitted that some understanding of the unique experiences which Whitehead attributes to

God may be derived from an examination of the experience of an ordinary human being (the sort of experience which is the basis of Whitehead's theory of the nature of ordinary actual entities). For example, the knowledge of our "specious present" gives us some insight into what an eternal specious present would be like, an experience in which there would be the retention of immediacy and creative advance. Also it must not be forgotten that many of the general characteristics of ordinary actual entities are found in God. He, like them, has physical and conceptual prehensions and manifests creativity. Like other actual entities God "derives" and "contributes" data. Thus to a considerable degree ordinary categories are applicable to God. In any case there is no suggestion of supernaturalism.

(3) In his refusal to attribute overwhelming power to God, Whitehead claims to be giving expression to the insights of the "Carpenter of Nazareth." God is one among many realities. The distinction between good and evil is not swallowed up in an infinite being. God experiences both; as a fellow sufferer, he understands. God saves some things which otherwise would be lost. But he does not save everything. Here then is a philosophy which gives God a prominent place but not at the expense of denying the details of ordinary, or more technical, accurate observation. God is one fact among the many facts which Whitehead finds and includes in his comprehensive intellectual synthesis. This phase of his work constitutes a very valuable contribution to the search for truth in this area.

The practical religious implications of Whitehead's metaphysics are of considerable interest, but that topic does not fall within the scope of this study.

D. Philosophy of Mind

(1) Possible objections to Whitehead's philosophy of mind are in part those already listed in dealing with his general

theory of actual entities. In particular, it would seem that he does not succeed in doing justice to the fact of endurance in one's "self" experience. The objection that his language is sometimes confusing, since he applies different meanings to the same word, is also relevant here. This is particularly obvious with reference to *feeling, consciousness, life.*

(2) His contention that *representative perception* must be rejected does not find very adequate support in his discussion of the difficulty one has in determining "how much" of experienced data is really "out there."

(3) It would appear that Whitehead is open to serious objection when, in discussing the function of the body, he suggests that "the eye sees": " 'The eye as experiencing such and such sights' is passed on as a datum, from the cells of the retina, through the train of actual entities forming the relevant nerves, up to the brain." [12] The contention that vision occurs before the relevant nerve centers in the brain are aroused is contrary to the teaching of much of modern psychology and looks suspiciously like a return to the supposedly naïve mistake of Aristotle.

(4) Whitehead suggests that *presentational immediacy* is an outgrowth from the complex data provided by *causal efficacy*. It may be objected that here Whitehead is trying to link two types of perception which, as a matter of fact, are not always related in this fashion. There is at least a possibility that in some cases one is as primitive as the other. This seems to be supported by the statement that "the simplest grade of actual occasions must be conceived as experiencing a few sensa." [13] It will be recalled that sensa are the data experienced in presentational immediacy. It is, of course, open to Whitehead to reply that the fact of derivation may have occurred before the simplest type of actual entity has the experience of sensa.

(5) One might also object to his contention that a propo-

sition is composed of actual entities to which an eternal object is referred. Might it not be more in accordance with ordinary usage to state that a proposition is a relationalized group of eternal objects used to refer to actual entities?

(6) The suggestion concerning a non-statistical approach to probability (making use of the organization of eternal objects in the primordial nature of God) is ingenuous but does not seem particularly practical.

(7) On the other hand, some of Whitehead's "psychological" comments provide a sane and balanced correction for many of the extreme positions which have been taken in modern psychology. The emphasis on the complex nature of the human self (particularly its affective phase) is a valuable feature of his work. Equally important is his discussion of its relation to the environment. His criticisms of the unfortunate results of uncritical reliance on clear-cut sense data are well taken. Further they serve to illustrate one of his major themes—the genuine interrelations of the distinguishable elements of experience. His discussion of thinking involves a useful emphasis on both its practical and theoretical phases. The examination of the values and dangers involved in the use of language is an effective introduction.

(8) Whitehead's comments concerning the problem of sampling are worthy of attention. His distinction between judgments and propositions seems sound. His remarks on proof and on self-evidence are not likely to arouse widespread enthusiasm but they should be provocative of careful thought. The vehement warning against excessive and unjustified reliance on clear, consistent, logical systems is one of the great services which Whitehead performs in encouraging the acquisition and use of knowledge. He personally strives for clarity and systematization, but only when the nature of the situation permits it. He recognizes, as few men have, the sacrifice of fact which is frequently made in order to achieve

a clear system of thought. As he once remarked: "One should seek clarity but distrust it."

E. Value

(1) In saying that value denotes the intrinsic reality of an event—that value is inherent in reality—Whitehead is apparently prepared to find value everywhere. It may, obviously, be objected that this practical identification of fact and value denies the distinctive nature of value, rather than deals with it adequately. In reply, it should be remembered that this contention is merely the rigorous adherence to the principle of pluralism. Every actual entity is important, none can be disregarded. Speaking in traditional terms, this is a self-realization theory of value.

(2) When he turns to a specialized discussion of the exalted values *truth, beauty, goodness* (which are not present everywhere), Whitehead is open to considerable objection. He does not provide a clear answer to the question: Which is the supreme value? Further, as has been noted, some of his key terms—*valuation, truth, beauty, goodness*—have several meanings. This makes it difficult, on occasion, to follow his discussion. There are also statements which seem to suggest a rather severe dichotomy of fact and value. On careful examination it appears that this is not what he intends. However, his remarks have misled some critics.

(3) On the other hand, there are many excellent features in this study of value. It is part of a complex system, not an isolated and unsupported fragment. It is based on recent developments in science and a careful study of many phases of human behavior. It is a theory developed by one of the keenest and sanest minds of our time. Whitehead's theory of value is part of his general philosophy of organism. Ultimately it stands or falls with this system of thought. More specifically: Are there eternal objects—*truth, beauty, goodness, peace*—which may be exemplified in the experience of

actual entities? At least a minority of thoughtful men say: Yes. Are there actual entities? Here again the answer is the same.

(4) It may be objected that Whitehead's treatment is too general. True, he does not set out to tell you how to act in each and every imaginable particular situation, exactly what to say in order to achieve a particular truth, what to do in order to be beautiful in Boston in 1952. Whitehead has not written a *Shorter Catechism* or a *Handbook for Beginners in Art*. However, he has done something which in a real sense is more important. He provides a firm basis on which such detailed structures may be built. Further, there *are* numerous suggestions as to the *general conditions* which must be present if truth, beauty, and goodness are to be achieved. His contention that these conditional factors are numerous is very sound. He points out, for example, that beauty depends not merely on pattern. Other factors are just as essential. The importance of the economic environment is particularly emphasized. Actually he does not *confine* himself to generalities. A surprising number of practical, specific suggestions are made. Yet the basic fact remains: He does not undertake this project in any complete and systematic fashion. The *minute details* of practical guidance are left chiefly to others. After all, there are limits to what one man can attempt to do.

(5) The reminder that without adventure (creative change) the maximum of truth, beauty, and goodness cannot be obtained, is a worth-while one. The claim that while there are eternal, changeless value ideals, the actual value of a specific type of act or situation may change, seems to be a sensible synthesis of the conflicting contentions of absolutism and relativity. His characteristic sanity is shown in his approach to truth. We do well to remember that although the truth is very important, there are dangers in extreme devotion to it. We may become blindly dogmatic concerning

something which we think is truth (and we are mistaken).

(6) Whitehead does great service in his brief but effective plea for the use of *art* as a means for the achievement of the highest levels of living. His advocacy of *peace,* as one of the chief values, is a worth-while contribution to the general topic. His contention that the "lure of ideals" constitutes an ultimate source of dynamic is presented impressively. At the very least Whitehead provides a vigorous challenge to those who would "read value out of the universe."

F. Whitehead and Other Philosophers

(1) An examination of Whitehead's frequent references to other philosophers does indeed provide the desired conclusion: Whitehead's philosophy has numerous, close affinities with "the great tradition." However, on occasion, one gets the impression that some of the similarities are more apparent than real. Indeed Whitehead is prepared to admit that. This is particularly true in the cases of Plato and Locke. Further, some of Whitehead's grateful acknowledgments of insights derived from other thinkers are excessive and misleading. This is very obvious with reference to Plato, Spinoza, Bradley, Nunn, and Alexander.

(2) Whitehead's understanding of the great philosophers is, generally speaking, sound. His youthful study of philosophy laid a firm foundation on which he continued to build.

(3) He provides a number of penetrating criticisms of the "great names." They are, of course, criticized at points where they diverge from the philosophy of organism. In so far as the reader accepts Whitehead's position, he will regard these criticisms as correct. Particularly noteworthy is Whitehead's attempted refutation of Hume's discussion of "cause." The claim that Aristotle *avoided* many of the metaphysical mistakes usually attributed to him also merits careful examination.

G. *Whitehead and Science*

(1) Whitehead's evaluation of science is an excellent sample of his judicious and comprehensive approach to a problem. Speaking as a natural scientist of repute, he performs a great service in showing the serious limitations of science. By stressing the restricted area in which science works, the frequently defective methods and undesirable attitudes, the unfortunate results which often are involved in science (even contemporary science), he has saved many laymen from a misleading idolatry. Yet, at the same time, he stresses the great value of many phases of scientific attitude and procedure. His contention that there need be no ultimate dichotomy between scientific fact and human value is something which needs to be emphasized in the modern world.

H. *Summary*

There can be little doubt that Whitehead has provided a remarkably effective synthesis of data from the major fields of knowledge. The main concepts of his system do apply validly in the specialized areas of human experience. The modern emphasis on *process* (rather than "stuff"), which is obvious particularly in physics and psychology, has an essential place in his theory of actual entities. The concept of *organic interrelation* which is stressed in these sciences, as well as in biology and sociology, is also prominent in Whitehead's metaphysics. The biological notion of *evolution* has a place in his system, though purged of some of its extreme and unbalanced aspects. The facts of "endurance" stressed in all science—the observed uniformities—are not neglected by this great sage of the twentieth century. *Value distinctions* and *God* are also treated seriously.

Many venerable philosophical problems are handled by Whitehead in an impressive fashion. The familiar dualism of *matter* and *mind* is effectively dealt with by recognizing the validity of the distinction, but refusing to tolerate a thoroughgoing destruction of all relationship. The related problem of *internal* versus *external* relations is similarly put in proper focus by suggesting that there are *both* internal and external relations. The same approach is used with reference to the traditional distinctions of *subject* and *object; thought* and *feeling.* The subject is in contact with its object; yet the object does not depend for its existence on the subject; nor, of course, is the subject just a "pile" of objects. The old opposition of thought and feeling is resolved by Whitehead's notion that both are co-operating components of one entity. The distinctiveness of each individual entity is maintained, but the fact of fruitful, creative, inter-action between the plurality of reals is equally emphasized. Therefore, the technical difficulties and the "common-sense-denying" intricacies of traditional monism and pluralism are avoided. Whitehead believes that there is one world. It is a world which includes God as one of the interacting entities. True, God is different in some respects from ordinary actual entities, but the application of terms based on human experience is not ruled out. God does not exercise control by brute force or by some form of predestination. God influences by his example—if others will follow his lead. He gives something of himself, if others will accept the gift. He retains some things which do not seem of importance to others. In Whitehead's universe there is no iron-bound necessity of law, unchanging and inescapable. Laws change, "laws of nature" as well as "man-made" laws. All this indicates that the determination of individual action lies ultimately with the individual. This constitutes both a challenge and the basis of optimism. The gates of the future are open—though perhaps not wide open; there are limitations in available data. But, to repeat, individual initi-ative is a basic fact in the universe. Whitehead's approach to value and his theory of God provide justification for the conviction that the exercising of one's initiative is worth while.

Whitehead contends that an adequate philosophy should (a) be characterized by a serious facing of facts, possibilities, and ideals; (b) have practical value in every field of endeavor and, in particular, aid in the achievement of the highest levels of living. Most students of Whitehead will agree that his work is genuinely concerned with facts, possibilities, and ideals. It is also clear that the related suggestion that "philosophy should be a critic of abstractions" is applied with great vigor in his thinking. On the other hand, there are many who have grave doubts as to the practical usefulness of this thought system. Yet, as a matter of fact, many of Whitehead's ideas *have had extremely fruitful application in the realms of education, religion, morality, art, and politics as well as the more obvious fields of mathematics and the natural sciences.*[14]

One of the great excellences of Whitehead's work is that he opposes the modern "drift from reason." Despite his recognition of the blind alleys into which a pseudo-rationalism has led its befuddled devotees, he is prepared to make full use of a chastened reason, enlightened by an examination of matters of fact. Thus it is that Whitehead acquires his eminence as a great builder of intellectual bridges over man-made gulfs in the realm of thought—gulfs which are not really there in the world of fact. Whitehead calls attention to connections which others have overlooked because their philosophical systems have convinced them that there can be no connections. In the misty mazes of metaphysics where many grope almost blindly, Whitehead proceeds with relative clarity. His philosophy is an extremely important synthesis of scattered insights which have been developed in previously sundered systems, plus insights of his own. This is not a mere "marble bag" eclecticism. It is a genuine synthesis of data from the major fields of human experience.

The "epistemological objectivity" of the realist; the "value" and "organic" emphases of some realists and idealists; the "process" insight of modern science, Bergson, and James; the Platonic stress on "eternal forms"; the religious insight that God is an inescapable fact; the pragmatic emphasis on the "practical"—all these, and many more, constitute the diverse strands which have been woven skillfully into the complex tapestry which is the philosophy of Alfred North Whitehead. There is no mystery or magic here. By way of justification and proof Whitehead can only say: *Look for yourself.* This vast creation of Whitehead's genius is a careful generalization of the main features of the facts which men find about them. It is an attempt to describe these facts in a unified system of concepts. Its only justification lies in a reference to these facts as experienced by ordinary men and by those technically trained in the various special fields of knowledge.

Is it not true that most men are aware of *change* and *endurance,* the old giving way to the new? Is there not an ultimate distinctiveness about the *individual* persons and things we meet? Do not *value* distinctions seem inescapable, despite our glib talk of complete relativity? Is there not something in the universe which we call *God?* In so far as the answer is "Yes," Whitehead's philosophy receives general validation. It is, of course, possible to object to the detailed fashion in which he expresses these general insights. In some cases the objections are far-reaching. But in no case does Whitehead desert his fundamental observations.

Here then is a technical philosophy, the work of a great scientist and civilized gentleman. It stands on the foundation of ordinary experience and finds support and encouragement in the specialized labors of mathematicians, physicists, biologists, psychologists, sociologists, and workers in the fields of logics, ethics, aesthetics, as well as searchers after religious truth.

It is obvious, then, that this way of understanding the nature of things merits careful examination.

It may well be that the philosophy of Alfred North Whitehead will provide, for the twentieth century, the answers to those ultimate questions which confront reflective men in all ages.

Appendix A

WIHTEHEAD'S EARLY THOUGHT

In 1898 Whitehead published *A Treatise on Universal Algebra*. This mathematical study is an obvious indication of its author's interest in "modes of togetherness." Universal algebra is defined as "that calculus which symbolizes general operations . . . which are called addition and multiplication." [1] The practical nature of this undertaking is emphasized vigorously. In his opinion mathematics should be used in all areas of experience where data can be apprehended definitely and expressed precisely. However, even in the midst of his devotion to mathematics, Whitehead is well aware of the fact that there are other valid methods of thinking, valid in certain situations. In his classification of the genus "serious thought" he lists various species. In addition to mathematics developed by means of a calculus, he mentions philosophy, inductive reasoning, and imaginative thought. [2, 3]

A memoir "On Mathematical Concepts of the Material World" (1906) reveals Whitehead's dissatisfaction with the classical concept of the material world. It seems to him that this concept is unduly complicated. It involves the use of three mutually exclusive classes of entities: points of space, instants of time, and particles of matter. Further, Whitehead notes the inadequacy of the classic concept when it is applied to the changing world of everyday experience. He suggests the possibility of employing one class of ultimate physical entity (instants of time), and one type of relationship (intersection). It is interesting to realize that these ultimate physical entities are linear rather than punctual in nature—analagous to lines of force.[4] Thus, as early as 1905, Whitehead, writing as a mathematician, is suggesting to physicists that they use new entities and a new approach to relationship.

In a paper entitled "La Théorie Relationniste De L'Espace" (1914), Whitehead expounds a relational theory of space. Space is not to be regarded as a container for physical objects. Physical objects are in interaction. Space is merely a characteristic of this interaction.

During the years 1915–1917 Whitehead wrote three papers which are now most readily available as chapters 8 to 10 of *The Aims of Education*. These are "Space, Time and Relativity"; "The Organization of Thought"; "The Anatomy of Some Scientific Ideas." In these studies he stresses a number of important and influential ideas. There is, for example, the contention that both science and metaphysics are based on the foundation of immediate experience.[5] The basic importance of common-sense experience is also emphasized. "You may polish up common sense, you may contradict in detail, you may surprise it. But ultimately your whole task is to satisfy it." [6] Although in these essays he is not concerned with the development of a metaphysic, he recognizes the basic importance of such a study. He states, for example, that science does not lessen the need for a metaphysic.[7] Whitehead, despite his high place in the hierarchy of science, is well aware that the neat, simple, exact world which is the goal of classical scientific thought is not actually found in experience. Experience is essentially untidy and highly complex.[8] It is recognized clearly by Whitehead, at this stage in his intellectual development, that no element of our experience can really exist in isolation—traditional theories to the contrary.[9] He also emphasizes the rich variety of experience, pointing out that sense data do not constitute the only content of consciousness. In addition there are emotions, volitions, imaginations, conceptions, and judgments. One very important phase of Whitehead's thought at this period is expressed in the following significant statement: "We live in durations and not in instants . . . the present essentially occupies a stretch of time, the distinction between memory and immediate presentation cannot be quite fundamental; for always we have with us the fading present as it becomes the immediate past." [10] This emphasis on the extensive nature of a present moment of experience is in accord with his interest in those developments in physical science which contend that electrons are essentially fields of energy, neither distinctly localized nor mutually exclusive. Whitehead's discussion of methods for defining points, lines, and plane areas is a further demonstration of his concern to indicate that the notion of extensive relationship is a fundamental explanatory principle. For example, in his essay on "The Anatomy of Some Scientific Ideas," he shows in some detail how a point may be described as an ideal limit by indefinitely continuing the process of diminishing a volume. [11]

It is interesting to observe that at this time Whitehead regarded the so-called physical objects of ordinary experience as "inferential constructions." [12] "The creation of the world is the first unconscious act of speculative thought." [13] For example, the pyramids are a conceptualization based on the particular experiences of the various people who have "looked at them." [14]

Three important books (supplemented by several papers read before learned societies [15]) indicate Whitehead's continued interest in the topics discussed in the 1914–1917 papers. There is a further development and clarification of his thought. These books are *An Enquiry Concerning the Principles of Natural Knowledge; The Concept of Nature;* and *The Principle of Relativity.*

The Principles of Natural Knowledge attempts "to illustrate the principles of natural knowledge by an examination of the data and experimental laws fundamental for physi-

cal science." [16] In the preface of *The Concept of Nature*
Whitehead states: "The object of the present volume and of
its predecessor is to lay the basis of a natural philosophy
which is the necessary presupposition of a reorganized speculative physics." [17] *Principle of Relativity* continues this
work and adds a discussion of an alternative statement (to
that of Einstein) of the theory of relativity. [18] Whitehead contends that all his work in the field of science and the philosophy of science is concerned with what is evident in sense
experience. "Natural science is the science of nature. . . .
Nature is that which we observe in perception through the
senses. . . . In the philosophy of science we seek the general notions which apply to nature." [19]

A careful examination of nature reveals that it has two
sides. One "side" is characterized by creative advance. The
other aspect of nature is that of the permanence of things.
Because of these permanences, recognition of data can occur. [20] This observation is one basis of Whitehead's profound
dissatisfaction with the point of view of classical physics.
Classical physics explains the universe in terms of time, space,
and matter. There is a multiplicity of material entities,
diverse and disconnected. Time is conceived as a succession
of durationless instants. This theory, if taken seriously, denies the possibility of velocity, acceleration, momentum, and
kinetic energy. The unity found in a biological organism is
also "read out" of the universe. This is due to the fact that
the distinctive characteristics of life are not manifest at any
one instant. In language reminiscent of the English romantic
poets, Whitehead states that murder is necessary in order to
achieve the inclusion of biological data within the realm of
physical science. [21]

Whitehead's analysis of our experience of nature indicates
to him that our awareness of nature is an awareness of a
"whole," which can be discriminated into parts. The term
duration is used in a technical sense to apply to the present

totality of nature.[22, 23] The distinguishable parts of a duration are called finite *events*. Durations are also called *events*— infinite events. It is Whitehead's claim that events, infinite and finite, are the primary physical facts. The term *event* does not necessarily connote rapid or even obvious change. He gives the following examples of events: a block of marble, a house, the passage of a car, an accident.

In the summary chapter (8) of *The Concept of Nature*, Whitehead provides an excellent brief, non-technical exposition of this phase of his philosophy of nature. There is, for instance, a very useful analysis of his concept *event*. Taking a concrete illustration, he invites us to consider the event: "Yesterday a man was run over on the Chelsea Embankment." In discussing this event he notes that it occurred after tea and before dinner. Also we should be aware of the fact that it occurred in the proximity of two other events, a barge in the river and traffic in the Strand. Thus, according to Whitehead, nature is a complex of passing events. Within it we find definite mutual relations between component events. Some of these relations are spatial, others temporal. It is obvious that in referring to space and time you are not concerned with autonomous entities. Rather a description of certain characteristics of events is being provided.[24] After all, argues Whitehead, we have never experienced space or time in abstraction from events.[25] Further, when you attempt to disregard either the spatial or the temporal aspects of events, you are attempting a process of abstraction which disregards a basic fact of experience. We experience space and time factors as inescapably co-present. Space and time are co-present because they are phases of one fundamental relation between events. This relation is *extension*.[26]

Whitehead is convinced that the problem of accounting for the relation between events is a pseudo-problem. Events are experienced in a state of relationship. Those who insist on disregarding this fact are open to serious criticism. Whitehead employs the term *significance* to refer to the fact that our conscious experience of anything always reveals its relationships to other entities.[27] If we are aware of the specific characteristics of an entity, this is "cognizance by adjective." If, on the other hand, we are aware of entities merely in the sense that they must exist as part of a vaguely felt background, this is "cognizance by relatedness." [28]

Whitehead points out that recent developments of relativity theories in physics have great importance because of the emphasis which they place on the relatedness of entities and the relational nature of space and time.[29]

It is very essential to realize that, in his opinion, the fact of relationship is absolutely fundamental because it is constitutive.[30] Whitehead suggests that those who overlook the fundamental nature of the relationship between events are the victims of a faulty habit of thought. The habit is based on the assumption that "subjects" exist in absolute and utter disjunction, qualified only by their own predicates.[31]

His famous criticism of the "bifurcation of nature"—the protest against dividing nature into two species of reality— is part of his general protest against disregarding the fact of interaction among events. Those who bifurcate nature claim that the two types of reality are (a) the electrons of speculative physics; (b) minds and the objects of ordinary experience. According to this theory, mind is hopelessly shut off from the other reality. The results which follow from a serious acceptance of this point of view are disastrous. How can worth-while scientific work be accomplished when one assumes that there are two "natures," one conjecture, the other a private dream—between the two a bridgeless gap? Whitehead argues that as far as science and natural philosophy are concerned the only sensible attitude is to regard nature as one. Everything perceived is in this one nature.[32] Thus Locke's influential theory of "secondary qualities" is rejected with great vehemence. "We may not pick and choose.

For us the red glow of the sunset should be as much part of nature as are the molecules and electric waves by which men of science would explain the phenomenon." [33, 34]

Whitehead states that the relationship between events takes two distinguishable forms—extension and cogredience.

He claims that the continuity of nature is based on this fact of extension, temporal and physical. He contends that "every event extends over other events, and every event is extended over by other events." [35]

Whitehead's early discussion of the "extension" approach to basic physical concepts is given a very comprehensive development in the books and articles now under consideration. He shows, in great detail, that moments, points, straight lines, and planes can be thought of as complexes of relations between events or possible relations between events. Part III of *The Principles of Natural Knowledge* provides a very full technical discussion. An excellent, brief, non-technical statement is sketched in his contribution to the symposium on "Time, Space and Material."

A moment of a time-system is a route of approximation to the non-existent ideal of a duration without temporal extension. This route is composed of an infinite series of durations, extending over each other, the earlier in the series over the later, and so that there is no duration which they all cover. Such a series defines an instant of time, and will be here called a moment. . . . A point-series is an infinite series of events, each event extending over all the events subsequent to it in the series; the whole series converges towards an ideal of an event of no extension. . . . An instantaneous point is better named an "event-particle." [36]

Whitehead contends that this abstractive procedure is in accordance with ordinary methods of coming to grips with difficult problems. When we wish to understand something, we try to reduce the complexity of the situation to such an extent that it is within the range of understanding.[37] In any case, he argues that this method is very valuable in that it defines the meaning of concepts essential to physical science in terms of immediate sensory experience.[38] Further, it is in accordance with the notion of alternate temporal series which is required by the modern theory of electro-magnetic relativity.[39] Incidentally, Whitehead views with great approval the implication of the relativity theory that there is no sense in attempting to discuss the temporal beginning or end of nature.[40]

In a set of notes provided for the revised edition of *The Principles of Natural Knowledge* (1925), Whitehead states that extension, contrary to the apparent implications of some of his discussion, should not be regarded as uniquely important.[41] There is another type of relationship—*cogredience*. Cogredience is a relation between a finite event and duration, the relation of absolute spatial position in the duration. For example, when we experience nature we are experiencing it from a certain place (here) within the duration (which is the whole of nature now). This experience of "hereness" is a fundamental fact. The doctrine of cogredience is simply a statement of that fact.[42]

As has been observed, Whitehead is concerned to show that nature has two sides: (a) there is the becomingness of nature; (b) there is also a factor of permanence in nature. The theory of events is his exposition of becomingness. Whitehead's theory of "objects" is his attempt, at this stage in his development, to do justice to the fact of permanence.

Objects are the factors in nature which endure as self-identical amid changing circumstances. They are apprehended by either sense or intellect. They are the factors which make recognition possible. The concept of "possibility" is relevant to nature because objects can be present in many different events. Any particular object is not confirmed to one or a few present, past, or future events. For example, a specific shade of blue (Whitehead suggests "Cambridge blue") may be present in a coat or in the sky. This specific shade of blue, wherever it may be, is the same object, and is recognized as such when different events containing it are compared.[43]

Objects are of three main sorts: (a) sense objects; (b) perceptual objects; (c) scientific objects.

A particular color, a particular sound, a particular feeling —all these are sense objects. The relation of a sense object to the particular event (or events) in which it is found is called "ingression." Whitehead points out that the ingression of sense objects into events is a complicated process. Four main factors are involved: (a) percipient events; (b) situations; (c) active conditioning events; (d) passive conditioning events. The *percipient event* is "the relevant bodily state of the observer." The *situation* is the *event* where the sense object is located (i.e., where it seems to be). The *active conditioning events* are those events which are relevant for the determining of the situation event. The so-called perceptual object, the state of the immediate environment (light, etc.), mirrors in case of mirror vision—these are examples of active conditions. *Passive conditioning events* are the remaining events in nature and the general space-time relationships. In the case of a person looking directly at a blue flannel coat, under normal conditions, the coat would be a situation event in which the sense object *blue* had ingressed. The situation event, in the case of accurate perception, is the chief active conditioning event, although proper light and other factors would be necessary. The flip of a fish's tail in mid-Atlantic would be a passive conditioning event. Thus Whitehead makes his point that the situation in which a sense object is experienced depends on percipient events and active and passive conditioning events. In cases of delusive perception, an abnormal percipient event or abnormal conditions bring about a shift from valid experience. For example, when a person sees a blue coat which is apparently before him at arm's length, but which actually isn't, this may be due to uncritical use of alcohol or a mirror, which gives rise to a mistaken judgment.[44]

When a blue coat is perceived, what is perceived is an object other than a mere sense object. "The perceptual object is the outcome of the habit of experience. . . . It is the product of the association of sense-objects in the same situation."[45] For example, when you see a familiar coat, you "subconsciously" feel yourself wearing it, or you may be aware, by a process of association, of the aroma of tobacco. This complex of sense data, the blueness and the shape, plus the accretions provided by association, constitute a perceptual object. In Whitehead's opinion no act of judgment is involved at this stage. This arises only when an attempt is made at classification.[46]

A perceptual object is said to be a "physical object" when its situation event (i.e., *it*) is an active condition, and the same situation event is shared by an indefinite number of actual and possible percipient events (observers). (A delusive perceptual event is one which does not meet these two conditions.) Whitehead's discussion of physical objects is characterized by extreme "wavering" in his point of view.[47] First he states that a physical object is "nothing else than the habitual concurrence of a certain set of sense-objects in one situation."[48] Then, shifting his position drastically, he suggests that "a physical object is a condition for the occurrence of sense-objects other than those which are its components."[49] This latter point is made even more definitely when he states that perceptual objects should be regarded as "controls of ingression." "Thus in modern scientific phraseology, a perceptual object means a present focus and a field of force streaming out into the future."[50] Whitehead notes that this control function exercised by perceptual objects constitutes a refutation of Hume's claim that there is no evidence of causation in nature.

Scientific objects (e.g., electrons) are objects which are the bases of the most permanent characteristics of physical objects. Scientific objects provide a "simple expression" of the character of events." [51, 52] Whitehead argues that these are genuine objects, not merely formulae for calculations.[53] However, he admits in one discussion of this topic that they are conjectural.[54]

An important relation between the quantum theory and Whitehead's theory of scientific objects is worthy of careful note. It involves his previous emphasis on the fact that experience involves an expanse or extension.

An object which (in some sense) is located in an event extending throughout a duration is not necessarily located in any slice of that event contained in a duration which is a part of the original duration. For example, a molecule of iron and a tune both require a minimum time in which to express themselves. We may call such objects "non-uniform."

Having stated that in his opinion ultimate scientific objects are of this sort, Whitehead remarks: "The atomic property of objects and the non-uniformity of some types of objects are obviously the basis of the quantum properties of nature which are assuming such an important position in modern physics." [55]

Whitehead's statement that "Nature is closed to mind" [56] should be interpreted as an attempt to claim that nature is self-contained. Its apparent qualities are not due to sense awareness or thought. Whitehead hastens to point out that this does not imply any "metaphysical doctrine of the disjunction of nature and mind." This discussion is in the field of philosophy of science. It is not a metaphysics. The fact that value is not given a prominent place in *The Concept of Nature* but is emphasized in *Science and the Modern World* should not be considered surprising. In *The Concept of*

Nature it is suggested that "the values of nature are perhaps the key to the metaphysical synthesis of existence. But such a synthesis is exactly what I am not attempting." [57] Incidently, this remark should be borne in mind by those who attempt to interpret Whitehead's theory of actual entities almost entirely in terms of what he says in these earlier books.

Appendix B

MARGINAL NOTES BY WHITEHEAD

This appendix is composed of photostat reproductions of some marginal notes appended by Professor Whitehead, in 1937, to the rough draft of a manuscript. This material is included because it has a bearing on the problem of interpreting some of Whitehead's statements. In particular, these notes should help to clarify Whitehead's position with reference to (a) "creativity," (b) the relation of individual actual entities to God. It will be noted that Whitehead uses the symbol "XX" to indicate passages on which he comments in the margin or at the bottom of the page. The *absence of objection,* by Whitehead, to the details of the exposition of his position is significant.

(38)
(訂)

CHAPTER   III

GOD

      The fact that Whitehead postpones his discussion of God(apart from
a few scattered paragraphs) to the last short section of Process and
Reality,is no indication of the importance of this actual entity in
his cosmological scheme.God,one actual entity among others,(God is
an actual entity,and so is the most trivial puff of existence in far-off
empty space"P.28) serves as"the foundation of order","the goal toward
novelty" and makes possible a solution of the basic moral and aesthetic
problems.

      Like any other actual entity God has conceptual and physical poles.
These are
also referred to as the Primordial and Consequent natures of God.(ªGod is
not to be treated as an exception to all metaphysical principles.He is
their chief exemplification."P.521)---"The Primordial nature of God is
the concrescence of a unity of conceptual feelings,including among their
data-all eternal objects."(P.134)--"The Consequent nature of God is the
physical prehension by God of the actualities of the evolving universe"P134
God also has a"superject"nature in that he provides data to be used in
the self creative process of other actual entities.

THE PRIMORDIAL NATURE OF GOD

      Whitehead has seen fit to discuss the "natures" of God separately.
By a distinction of reason, God is first considered in the abstraction of
a primordial actuality. It is unfortunate,that on occasion Whitehead
almost suggests that these"factors in God","deficient in actuality",are
as a matter of fact actualities in their own right.- -Thus Whitehead

"yes. A great carelessness on my part
A.N.W.

(40)
(~~30~~)

In this exposition,Whitehead is,as usual,drawing on human experience
for his model.It is as tho a person,faced by a number of alternative
possibilities,reacted to them individually,with a certain feeling,ie subjective form of acceptance or rejection,so that,by this process they were
thence forth graded in order of relative importance.In this way patterns
of mutual interrelationship were set up.(this is what Whitehead terms
"valuation") This"chart"of the patterned relationships of eternal objects
is ~~thus~~ to be regarded as part of the available equipment for the self
creation of any person(actual entity).

A careful consideration of this general situation,reveals the fact
that all so called conceptual prehensions of eternal objects,are in
reality derived from,or based on hybrid physical prehensions of God.This
is evident from the fact that since the eternal objects are present as a
part of God's primordial nature,they can only be made available by a
hybrid physical prehension of God's P nature. (P.343;382)
                                         rimordial

Thus God's primordial nature fulfills two functions,-(1) It provides
for the relevance of eternal objects to each other(ie the patterned
relationships which they manifest) and also(2)God makes these eternal objects,
in their mutual relationships,available for the use of novel actual entities.
They are made available because God's primordial nature,in which they are
~~injustified~~ contained,is objectified in the newly arising actual entities.
"Apart from God,eternal objects unrealized in the actual world,would be
relatively non-existent for the concrescence in question"(P.46)

In addition to this,there is another phase of God's primordial nature
which requires consideration.--He has a desire that this work of his be used
by other actual entities.There is a "yearning after concrete fact-no particular facts,but after some actuality"(P.50)

(55)
(44)

The essential element in God's nature is the permanent unity of
vision(the conceptual prehension of eternal objects),-seeking physical
multiplicity.The essential element in the World (of actual entities)
is the vol*a*tile multiplicity of finite actual entities seeking a perfected
unity. These two elements in the universe grow,since they are"creatures"
manifesting "creativity".----In the process of growth,the primordial
                                              is God
unity of potentialities(eternal objects) acquires a multiplicity of
data from the external world.(In this sense only God is "many")--This
                           Thus God's Consequent nature arises
"multiplicity" God "absorbs into his own unity"(P.529) ------ ------
In the case of the "World"(That is to say, the many actual entities in
their physical finitude), the primordial multiplicity of vol*f*tile
entities"acquires(on the basis of a unifying subjective aim derived from
God) a consequent unity".That is to say,-a new actual entity emerges.
This new actual entity becomes"one" among the "Many" other actual entities.
This,apparently,is what Whitehead means when he says,-"It is absorbed into
the multiplicity of the primordial character"(P.529) On the strength of
this sort of exposition Whitehead claims;-"It is as true to say that
God is one and the World many,as that the World is one and God many."(P528)

    This tenuous analysis has been undertaken to show that Whitehead's
"literary" claim,that"the consequent nature of God is composed of a
multiplicity of elements with individual self-realization",is an overstatem-
                                                    (P   551
ent of the inter relations of God and the actual entities composing
the world.The fact of this interrelationship should have been expressed
in the more exact terms of previous sections of "Process and Reality".
Or,more accurately,-in the case of the "world"----composed of creatures".

(571
(45)

Guided by the subjective aim provided by his primordial nature,
God prehends every actuality for what it can be in a perfect system---
its sufferings,its sorrows,its failures,its triumphs,its immediacies of
joy-woven by rightness of feeling into the harmony of the universal feeling?
----"No element in fact is ineffectual:thus the struggle with evil is a (P.525)
process of building up a mode of utilization by the provision of ~~immediate~~
~~intermediate~~ intermediate elements introducing a complex structure of
harmony"(P.517) It is to be noted that this "aesthetic" harmonization in
God's nature is not to be equated with the superficially similar doctrine
of Absolute Idealism.In God's consequent nature all distinctions are
retained.Good and evil are not transmuted into colorless perfection.In
God good and evil elements are seen in their proper ~~perfect~~ status,given
                                  by reference to
their"position"~~against~~ the scale of values provided by God's evaluative
process.

    It is to be noted that all elements ,made available by actual elements,
are not retained(in God's consequent nature) unchanged.There is a process
of transforming(as to degree of importance);and elimination.---"The
revolts of destructive evil,purely self-regarding,are dismissed into their
triviality of merely individual facts".(P.525)(ie "transformed" or "transm-
                                  actuality
uted")--------"Each novel entity in the temporal world contributes such
                              (not all elements are present in God)
elements as it can to a realization in God"(P.134)-------Thus,in terms
of the familiar doctrine of objectification,---While there is no
elimination within God's nature as such,-there is of course elimination
of some of the data available for inclusion in God's nature.

    Against the background of the preceeding discussion it is possible
to grasp Whitehead's meaning when he ~~says~~ states;-God exercises a tender

1'Tragedy' is omitted in P.R. It is introduced in A.I, of neg. prehension

(62)
(~~16~~)

In this sense it is "_consequent_" (ie -dependent on the growth of other
actual entities which provide data for it) and "_incomplete_"(continually
grows by using this/available data in its reconstruction).God's consequent
nature is "_everlasting_" in the sense that mutual immediacy of content is
retained in his life.---The"past"within his nature never fades.The statement that God as consequent is "fully actual" is not exactly correct.What
Whitehead apparently means is that,because God,the actual entity,has a
physical pole(consequent nature) he is fully actual.(Not that the
physical pole,as such,is fully actual-since actualities, must have both poles.)
This same general criticism applies to the statement that"God as consequent
is conscious".In reality God is conscious when he has both physical and
mental poles,-so that fact,present by physical prehension,can be confronted
by alternatives(conceptual prehensions)In short,the mere fact of a
physical pole as such,does not render God conscious.

       On the basis of a careful examination of the writings under discussion,
one can find little jusitification for Miss Stebbing's righteous indignation,
voiced in these pathetic words,-"Prof.Whitehead's indefensible use of
language becomes nothing short of scandalous when he speaks of God.He
says that God is a term used for creativity,Aristotelian matter and modern
neutral stuff". (Mind /30) as a matter of fact,Whitehead says no such thing.Apparently
Miss Stebbing has been misled by the opening phrase of Process and
Reality,Part I Chap.3. Here it is stated that "_creativity_'is another
rendering of the Aristotelian 'matter' and the modern 'neutral stuff".
The use of the phrase"another rendering",following a paragraph in which
the consequent nature of God was being discussed might have led Miss

.`?2/`
(-57)

description is replaced by description of dynamic process."(p10)

It is true that an examination of the two passages which Mr Bidney
mentions,might be expected to lead one to suppose that Whitehead was
espousing a Spinozistic Monism.Howeverpreference to many other statements,
chiefly in"Process and Reality" and "Adventures of Ideas",as well as an
examination of the general tendency of his work-seems to indicate the
fallaciousness of this interpretation.

In "Process and Reality"(p31)Whitehead,discussing the "Category of
the "Ultimate",refers to "xxxxxx "Creativity" as "the Universal of
Universals characterizing ultimate matter of fact."Thus is broadly Platonic
language,"Creativity" is an "idea"(essence or form) which is exemplified
(present) in matters of fact(ie particular actual entities).Conversely,-
the creative process,whereby one actual entity appropriates data provided
by other actual entities,and so constitutes itself,--is an exemplification
of the "idea" -"Creativity".

That Creativity(Process,Passage or Activity)is not "one fundamental
substrate of which all things are modes"(Bidney p583) is indicated by
reference to "Adventures of Ideas"--"Each event,viewed in its separate
individuality,is an passage between two ideal termini,namely,its components
in their ideal disjunctive diversity passing into these components in their
concrete togetherness.----There is nothingin the universe other than
instances of this passage(ie actual entities)and components of these
instances."(A.303)----In short,there is no creativity apart from actual
entities.Creativity is a process of interaction(passage) between and
constitutive of actual entities.----"Creativity is not an external agency
with its own ulterior purposes.All actual entities share with God this
characteristic of self-causation"(P.339)

See apge 83

(85)

These paragraphs of mine are very carelessly phrased. But their meaning is, I think, sound & near to the point.

Indeed,it seems that if these are to be taken literally,and
as quoted,they imply that "Creativity" is to be regarded as an
"ultimate substrate".It would appear,then,that Prof.Whitehead
thinks of "Creativity" in two distinct and contrary senses.---
However,I believe that this conclusion can be denied on the
basis of a more careful examination of the passages in question.

In"Process and Reality" the problem of Creativity is
discussed in a more thorogoing fashion,than in"Science and
the Modern World".I shall refer to the passage quoted from the
former,first.--Whitehead is discussing the "I coherence" which
certain Philosophies manifest.That of Descartes,who posits
two(perhaps three) substances when by definition there can
be only one,is cited as an example.Prof.Whitehead notes,with
approval,Spinoza's reference to One Substance only.Like
Spinoza,Whitehead posits only one sort of Metaphysical entity.
But this is as far as the similarity goes. The one real Substance,
of Spinoza,is replaced,in the thought of Prof Whitehead, by
many,real,dynamic Actual Entities(each of which exemplifies the
Universal of Universals-"Creativity".)--"the modes now become
the sheer actualities--analysis of them do s not lead us to
the discovery of any higher grade of reality"(Process and Reality p10)

With this,and the preceeding discussion in mind,I think
it is possible to grasp the meaning of the debatable passage
in Science and the Modern World(p 87-Cambridge Edition)--For
Spinoza,the ultimately real is the one Substance,God.For Whitehead
the ultimately real things are Actual Entities.When Mr Whitehead

(

Whitehead.

speaks of " each event as an individual matter of fact arising from
an individualisation of the substrate activity creativity" and states
that "creativity is a character which underlies all occasions"---he apparently means that the Universal(essence,principle) "Creativity" is
exemplified(manifest,present)in particular actual entities(ie in the
process whereby actual entities are objectified in each other in the act
of self-creation.)

Another apparently troublesome phrase--referring to all actual
entities as "the ultimate creatures derivative from the creative process"
(P.124)----on examination,is seen to imply Whitehead's basic doctrine
that actual entities are "causa sui".That is to say,-The creative process
referred to is the process by which an actual entity creates itself.

This discussion serves to clarify problems presented to D.C.Moxley
by the relationship of "creativity" to God.Moxley asks,-How can Whitehead
consistently say that;-(A) "creativity" is a universal(eternal object);
(B) apart from God any eternal object is "indistinguishable from nonentity";yet(C) God is a creature of creativity.-----These apparent
paradoxes can be solved by bearing in mind the fact that the term
"creativity" is applied to"creativity" as essence(eternal object)(in this
sense "creativity" is the universal of universals) and to "creativity"
as exemplified in the self-creative process of an actual entity.The
phrase which refers to God as a "creature of creativity" is using the
term"creativity" in this second sense.That is to say,-God is the "creature"
or outcome of his own self directed processof self creation.

Mr Moxley calls attention to the problems created by Whitehead's
comparison of "creativity" and Aristotelian matter.("Creativity is another
rendering of Aristotelian matter")

(II.)

That creativity is not to be thought of as a passively receptive
substratum,is explicitly indicated by Whitehead;-"It(creativity) is
divested of the notion of passive receptivity,either of form or of
external relations"(P.46)-----The only point they have in common is the
general characteristic that each is without character of its own in the
concrete sense.In other words,--As an essence or eternal object,"creativity"
has a distinct meaning;but this essence has,of course,no particular
concrete character until it is actualized in some actual entity or other.
In this sense it is "without a character of its own".

    A further confusion is likely to arise unless one notes carefully,
another slightly different usage of the term"creativity".---Whitehead
sometimes refers to "God and the actual world jointly constituting the
character of creativity for the initial phase of the novel concrescence"
                                                        (P.374)
By"character of creativity",here,Whitehead apparently means God and the
actual world provide the data which are used in the concrete process of
self-creativity by which a new actual entity arises.In a short discussion
of creativity in"Adventures of Ideas"(p.239) he states "this factor of
activity(the actual world relative to that(new) occasion) is what I
have called Creativity." Here again,data used in the creative process
are called "creativity".

    The problems relating to the temporal origin of the universe and
the relative importance of the various beings and things which appear in
it,have provided the basis for much cosmological discussion.Whitehead's
approach is refreshingly sound.---Basing his position on an
appeal to the experience of men,and refusing to indulge in flights of

(40)
(55)

each other they are not themselves.Nor(as has been noted) does God confer
reality on any actual entity.Each actual entity is its own self creative
agent.God provides data for any actual entity and any actual entity
provides data for God.God's only claim to primacy lies in his function
of providing for the relevance of eternal objects.Thus God is brought to
the same level,asfar as actuality or reality is concerned,as any other
actual entity.Whitehead thus denies the claim of Augustine and Aquinas
(for example) that the more important is the more real or actual.

This discussion also throws light on another problem raised by a
recent criticism(D.Bidney).It is the question as to the relation between
"Potentiality" and "Actuality"..-----In Mr Bidney's opinion,Whitehead ,like
Bergson and Alexander,starts with an"ultimate substrate (which) is
indeterminate potentiality or feeling lacking any natural powers and
characteristics"(Bidney p587)------and is faced with the problem of
accounting for the origin of change andthe differentiation into finite
modes.The utter fallacy of this interpretation will be evident by reference
to the preceeding paragraph.It is based on Mr Bidney's mistaken notion
that "creativity" is a substrate from which temporally emerge,-God's
primordial nature,other actual entities and finally God's consequent nature.

In addition,~~—————————————~~-Whitehead's emphasis on the
Ontological Principle,shows most unmistakably that there is no potentiality
apart from actuality.----"Every condition to which the process of becoming
conforms in any particular instance,has its reason either in the character
of some actual entity in the actual world of concrescence,or in the
character of the subject which is in process of concrescence."(P.36)

Notes

The following abbreviations of titles are here used to refer to works by Alfred North Whitehead:

A.E.	*The Aims of Education* (New York: The Macmillan Company, 1929)
.A.I.	*Adventures of Ideas* (New York: The Macmillan Company, 1933)
C.N.	*The Concept of Nature* (Cambridge: Cambridge University Press, 1920)
E.S.P.	*Essays in Science and Philosophy* (New York: The Philosophical Library, 1947)
F.R.	*The Function of Reason* (Princeton: Princeton University Press, 1929)
"Imm."	"Immortality," in *The Philosophy of Alfred North Whitehead*, edited by P. A. Schilpp (Evanston, Illinois: Library of Living Philosophers, 1941)
"M.G."	"Mathematics and the Good," in *The Philosophy of Alfred North Whitehead*, edited by P. A. Schilpp (Evanston, Illinois: Library of Living Philosophers, 1941)
M.T.	*Modes of Thought* (New York: The Macmillan Company, 1938)
P.N.K.	*An Enquiry Concerning the Principles of Natural Knowledge* (Cambridge: Cambridge University Press, second edition, 1925)
P.R.	*Process and Reality* (New York: The Macmillan Company, 1929)
Rel.	*The Principle of Relativity* (Cambridge: Cambridge University Press, 1922)
"Remarks"	"Remarks," in *The Philosophical Review*, Vol. XLVI, 1937, pp. 175–86.
R.M.	*Religion in the Making* (New York: The Macmillan Company, 1926)
S.M.W.	*Science and the Modern World* (New York: The Macmillan Company, 1929 Edition)
Sym.	*Symbolism: Its Meaning and Effect* (New York: The Macmillan Company, 1927)
"Time"	"Time," in *Proceedings of the Sixth International Congress of Philosophy* (New York: Longmans, Green & Co., 1927)
"T.S.M."	Contribution to "Symposium: Time, Space and Material," in *Aristotelian Society, Supplementary Volume II* (London: Williams and Norgate, 1919)
T.U.A.	*A Treatise on Universal Algebra* (Cambridge: Cambridge University Press, 1898)

PREFACE

1. *A.I.*, p. vii.
2. See *P.R.*, p. vii.
3. See the following articles: "A Criticism of D. Bidney's 'Spinoza and Whitehead,' " in *The Philosophical Review*, Vol. XLV; "The Intelligibility of Whitehead's Philosophy," in *Philosophy of Science*, Vol. X; "Truth, Beauty and Goodness in the Philosophy of A. N. Whitehead," in *Philosophy of Science*, Vol. XI; "The Psychology of Alfred North Whitehead," in *The Journal of General Psychology*, Vol. XXXII; "Whitehead's Theory of Actual Entities: Defence and Criticism," in *Philosophy of Science*, Vol. XII; "Whitehead's Philosophy of History," in *Journal of the History of Ideas*, Vol. VII; "A. N. Whitehead's Theory of Intuition," in *The Journal of General Psychology*, Vol. XXXVII.

Chapter 1

INTRODUCTION TO THE THEORY OF ACTUAL ENTITIES

1. "Remarks," p. 178.
2. *A.I.*, p. 125.
3. In trying to account for facts and their interrelations, general principles or laws are sought. The difference between the philosophic search for general principles and the scientific search is one of degree of inclusiveness. See *P.R.*, pp. 14–15.
4. *S.M.W.*, p. 126. See also p. 203; and *A.I.*, pp. 179, 183, 187.
5. See *M.T.*, p. 234. See in general pp. 232–38.
6. See *M.T.*, pp. 30–31; *P.R.*, pp. 25–26.
7. See *S.M.W.*, p. x; *A.I.*, p. 204; *M.T.*, p. 237.
8. See *P.R.*, p. 23.
9. See *M.T.*, p. 87
10. *P.R.*, pp. vi, 4. It should be noted that Whitehead no longer agrees with the obvious implications of the idea, expressed in *The Concept of Nature*, that "the recourse to metaphysics is like throwing a match into the powder magazine" (p. 29).
11. See *P.R.*, p. 5.
12. See *P.R.*, pp. 4–5.
13. *P.R.*, p. 6; "Remarks," p. 179.
14. See *P.R.*, pp. x, 12–13.
15. See *M.T.*, p. 58; "Remarks," p. 181
16. See *P.R.*, pp. 25, 1–3, 20–21, 70–71.
17. See *P.R.*, p. 7. This involves the "play of free imagination" (*P.R.*, p. 7) and issues in the abandonment of "Occam's razor," in the traditional sense. (*A.I.*, p. 305.) See also *F.R.*, pp. 64–65.
18. See *P.R.*, pp. 7, 8, 19.
19. See *P.R.*, p. 19; *S.M.W.*, p. 227.
20. *P.R.*, p. 6. See also *M.T.*, p. 96.
21. See *A.I.*, pp. 379–80.
22. *S.M.W.*, p. 27. See also *P.R.*, pp. vii, 4.
23. See *S.M.W.*, pp. 288–89.
24. See *P.R.*, pp. 11–12, 15–16; *M.T.*, pp. 143–46.

25. *A.I.*, p. 228; *P.R.*, p. 32.
26. *S.M.W.*, pp. 97, 286. See also *A.I.*, pp. 177–78. It should be noted that when Whitehead uses the phrase *intuitive judgment* he is concerned with a different matter. See *P.R.*, pp. 413–18.
27. See *A.I.*, pp. 209–10.
28. See *P.R.*, p. 527; *R.M.*, pp. 79–80.
29. See *P.R.*, pp. 517–18.
30. See *F.R.*, p. 30.
31. See *P.R.*, p. 253.
32. See *M.T.*, p. 185.
33. See *F.R.*, p. 30.
34. See *M.T.*, p. 69.
35. See *R.M.*, pp. 64–67, 137–38.
36. See *S.M.W.*, pp. 165, 207, 219.
37. See Johnson, A. H., editor, *The Wit and Wisdom of Whitehead* (Boston: The Beacon Press, 1947), pp. 3–31.
38. An outline of this phase of Whitehead's work will be found in Appendix A of this book (pages 201–12).
39. See *M.T.*, p. 188; *S.M.W.*, p. 149; *M.T.*, p. 195; *P.R.*, pp. 121–22; *S.M.W.*, pp. 53–55.
40. See *M.T.*, p. 198.
41. See *A.I.*, pp. 238–39.
42. See *A.I.*, p. 202.
43. See *S.M.W.*, p. 54.
44. See *S.M.W.*, p. 146, and in general Chapter 6.
45. See *S.M.W.*, pp. 213–14.
46. *S.M.W.*, p. 97.
47. *S.M.W.*, p. 107.
48. *S.M.W.*, p. 27.
49. See *S.M.W.*, pp. 162, 278; *P.R.*, p. 74; *A.I.*, pp. 209–10.
50. *P.R.*, pp. 252–53.
51. See *P.R.*, p. 427; *R.M.*, pp. 104–05; "Remarks," p. 185.

Chapter 2

THE ANALYSIS OF ACTUAL ENTITIES

1. This is Category of Existence I. See *P.R.*, p. 32.
2. *P.R.*, p. 27.
3. See *M.T.*, p. 60.
4. *M.T.*, p. 228. See also *S.M.W.*, pp. 27–28.
5. Whitehead suggests that the terms *actual entity* and *actual occasion* may be used as synonyms (*P.R.*, pp. 33, 113). However, the term *actual occasion* is to be preferred when referring to the characteristic of extensiveness (*P.R.*, p. 119). Further, the term *actual occasion* is never applicable to God (*P.R.*, p. 135). In *Science and the Modern World* Whitehead uses the term *prehensive occasion* or *event* instead of the terms *actual entity* or *actual occasion* (*S.M.W.*, pp. 104–05). The term *event* when used in *Process and Reality* means a *nexus* or group of interrelated actual entities (*P.R.*, pp. 352, 113). *Science and the Modern World* also uses the term in this sense (*S.M.W.*, p. 175).

6. See *P.R.*, pp. 337–39.
7. See *P.R.*, p. 35; *S.M.W.*, p. 101.
8. See *P.R.*, p. 366.
9. See *P.R.*, p. 35; *A.I.*, p. 226.
10. See *P.R.*, pp. 68–73, 101–02.
11. See *P.R.*, pp. 35, 65, 184–246, 363–64; *A.I.*, p. 248.
12. See *P.R.*, p. 321.
13. See *P.R.*, p. 35. The term "feeling" is, on occasion, applied to *any* prehension. See *A.I.*, p. 297. See Category of Explanation XII (*P.R.*, p. 35).
14. See *P.R.*, pp. 38, 129, 336.
15. See *P.R.*, p. 35.
16. See *P.R.*, pp. 35, 246, 322.
17. See *A.I.*, pp. 227, 325; *P.R.*, p. 447.
18. See *P.R.*, p. 32.
19. See *P.R.*, p. 29.
20. *Contrast* is Category of Existence VIII. See *P.R.*, p. 33.
21. See *P.R.*, p. 45.
22. See *P.R.*, p. 82.
23. See *P.R.*, p. 36. This is Category of Explanation XVI. *Multiplicity* is Category of Existence VII. See *P.R.*, pp. 36, 33.
24. This is Category of Existence V. See *P.R.*, p. 32.
25. See *P.R.*, p. 32.
26. *P.R.*, p. 70. This is involved in Category of Explanation VII. See *P.R.*, p. 34
27. See "Time," p. 60; *P.R.*, pp. 70, 73, 446; *M.T.*, pp. 95, 117; and *F.R.*, p. 26. Whitehead prefers to abandon the old technical distinction between *universal* and *particular*. The distinction is now blurred because his actual entities are like the traditional universals in that they enter into the description of other actual entities. In a sense his eternal objects are particular. They are just what they are. See *P.R.*, p. 76.
28. See *P.R.*, p. 82.
29. See *S.M.W.*, pp. 239, 228–29; *P.R.*, p. 94.
30. See *S.M.W.*, p. 241.
31. See *P.R.*, p. 33.
32. See *S.M.W.*, p. 243.
33. See *S.M.W.*, pp. 229–30.
34. See *S.M.W.*, pp. 230–31.
35. See *S.M.W.*, pp. 230–31.
36. *P.R.*, p. 37. This is Category of Explanation XIX.
37. *P.R.*, p. 443.
38. *Prehension* is Category of Existence II. See also Category of Explanation VIII (*P.R.*, pp. 32, 34).
39. This is Category of Explanation X. See *P.R.*, p. 35.
40. *P.R.*, 35. This is Category of Explanation XI.
41. See *P.R.*, pp. 130–31.
42. See *P.R.*, p. 34; *M.T.*, pp. 29, 32.
43. See *P.R.*, p. 82. This is Category of Explanation XXIV (*P.R.*, p. 38). The term *ingression* apparently is used in *Science and the Modern World* with a different meaning. It is used to refer to the presence of a sense object in space-time. (*S.M.W.*, p. 103.) This, however, seems

to be the germ of a more fully developed theory found in *Process and Reality* (to which reference has just been made).

44. See *P.R.*, pp. 71, 322. It must be noted that Whitehead sometimes uses the term *objectification* as a synonym for *feeling*, meaning full inclusion of the data, See *P.R.*, pp. 34, 361. There is a further difficulty. "Feeling" also means the complete process of positive prehension, not merely the second phase. See *P.R.*, p. 35.
45. See *P.R.*, pp. 337–38.
46. See *P.R.*, pp. 483, 35; *A.I.*, pp. 334, 379.
47. See *M.T.*, p. 122.
48. See *P.R.*, p. 66.
49. See *S.M.W.*, p. 101.
50. See *M.T.*, p. 167.
51. See *P.R.*, pp. 47, 280. Whitehead suggests that among the numerous appetitions there is the appetition for "self-preservation."
52. See *P.R.*, pp. 34, 63, 280, 379, 444; *A.I.*, pp. 324, 254; *M.T.*, p. 96.
53. See *P.R.*, pp. 96–97, 174; *S.M.W.*, pp. 127, 151.
54. This interpretation was verified during the course of a series of discussions with Professor Whitehead (1936–37).
55. See *M.T.*, pp. 116, 121; *P.R.*, p. 444.
56. See *P.R.*, p. 82.
57. See *P.R.*, pp. 35, 66; and Category of Explanation VII (*P.R.*, p. 34).
58. See *P.R.*, pp. 445, 175–76. See also "M.G.," p. 679.
59. See *P.R.*, pp. 445, 366.
60. See *P.R.*, p. 378.
61. This type of feeling is an instance of what Whitehead calls the Category of Conceptual Valuation, Categoreal Obligation IV. See *P.R.*, pp. 39–40, 379.
62. See *A.I.*, p. 237; *M.T.*, p. 224.
63. Such feelings are instances of the Category of Conceptual Reversion, Categoreal Obligation V. See *P.R.*, p. 40.
64. See *P.R.*, p. 367.
65. See *P.R.*, p. 69.
66. See *S.M.W.*, p. 234.
67. See *S.M.W.*, pp. 237–38.
68. See *P.R.*, p. 280.
69. See *A.I.*, p. 326; *P.R.*, p. 446. My discussion of the distinctions between objective and subjective species of eternal objects in "Whitehead's Theory of Actual Entities: Defence and Criticism," in *Philosophy of Science*, Vol. XII, p. 248, is not completely accurate: the distinction is not entirely one of function.
70. See *P.R.*, p. 101; *A.I.*, p. 230.
71. This is Category of Explanation XX. See *P.R.*, p. 38.
72. This is Category of Explanation IV. See *P.R.*, p. 33.
73. *P.R.*, p. 246.
74. *P.R.*, p. 133. See also *P.R.*, pp. 174, 177, 323, 364, 375, 479–80, 347; *M.T.*, pp. 98, 219–20, 229.
75. See *P.R.*, p. 336. Whitehead suggests that this doctrine of *perishing* is the one foundation upon which the whole development of *Process and Reality* is built. See *E.S.P.*, p. 117.

76. See *P.R.*, pp. 44, 364.
77. See *A.I.*, p. 254.
78. See *P.R.*, pp. 363–64.
79. *A.I.*, pp. 255–56. That is to say, negative prehension occurs.
80. *P.R.*, p. 80. See also *P.R.*, pp. 321, 154, 517; *M.T.*, p. 115. This is the sort of context in which Whitehead remarks that the transfer of content occurs without loss of original subjectivity. (*P.R.*, 363–64.) What is being said is that there is no loss of *what* is transferred. Anger wells up from the past as anger felt in another moment of experience.
81. See *P.R.*, p. 323.
82. See *P.R.*, p. 323. Another difficulty arises which is involved in his use of the term *objectification*. It is supposedly used with reference to initial data, but he also uses it with reference to objective data. See *P.R.*, p. 361.
83. See *P.R.*, p. 230.
84. See *P.R.*, p. 361; *M.T.*, p. 91.
85. See *P.R.*, pp. 71, 133–34.
86. See *A.I.*, p. 248.
87. *P.R.*, pp. 249, 93.
88. *P.R.*, p. 295 (italics added). See also *P.R.*, p. 350.
89. See *P.R.*, p. 230.
90. See *P.R.*, p. 343.
91. See *P.R.*, p. 377. In the course of this discussion, Whitehead apparently uses the term *conceptual feeling* in its widest possible connotation referring to both pure conceptual feelings and impure feelings. It will be recalled that the datum of a pure conceptual feeling is an eternal object. In contrast, the datum of an impure prehension is a proposition or—to use a synonym—a theory. Speaking technically, a proposition has as its subject an actual entity or a group of actual entities. The predicate of a proposition is an eternal object or a group of eternal objects. (*P.R.*, p. 280.) It must be noted that occasionally Whitehead abandons the details of this analysis and calls propositions pure feelings. (*P.R.*, pp. 369–72.) *Proposition* is Category of Existence VI and it is discussed in Category of Explanation XV. See *P.R.*, pp. 32–33, 35–36.
92. See *P.R.*, p. 469.
93. See *S.M.W.*, p. 216; *P.R.*, p. 469; *A.I.*, p. 318.
94. See *P.R.*, p. 355.
95. See *P.R.*, p. 35. This is Category of Explanation XIV. *Nexus* is Category of Existence III. See *P.R.*, p. 32.
96. See *P.R.*, p. 40. This is the Category of Transmutation, Categoreal Obligation VI.
97. This is Category of Existence IV. See *P.R.*, p. 32. Whitehead seems also to use the term *energetic form of composition*. See *M.T.*, p. 129.
98. See *P.R.*, pp. 35, 37, 338, 479; *A.I.*, pp. 236, 309. This is Category of Explanation XIII. See *P.R.*, p. 35.
99. *A.I.*, p. 227. See also *A.I.*, p. 325; *P.R.*, p. 447.
100. *P.R.*, p. 444. See also *P.R.*, pp. 355–58; *A.I.*, pp. 303, 326–27.
101. See *P.R.*, pp. 357–58.
102. See Category of Explanation XVII (*P.R.*, pp. 33, 36).
103. *P.R.*, p. 286. He uses the term *aware* in a technical sense, as a synonym for *conscious*.

104. See *P.R.*, p. 368.
105. See Category of Subjective Harmony, Categoreal Obligation VII (*P.R.*, p. 41).
106. See *P.R.*, pp. 228, 37.
107. See Category of Subjective Intensity, Categoreal Obligation VIII (*P.R.*, p. 41).
108. See *P.R.*, pp. 343, 322, 470, and Category of Subjective Unity, Categoreal Obligation I (*P.R.*, p. 39).
109. See *P.R.*, p. 38. This is Category of Explanation XXII.
110. See *P.R.*, p. 41.
111. See *E.S.P.*, p. 206.
112. *P.R.*, p. 355.
113. See *P.R.*, p. 355.
114. See *P.R.*, p. 354.
115. See *P.R.*, p. 343.
116. See *M.T.*, p. 213.

Chapter 3

THE CHARACTERISTICS OF ACTUAL ENTITIES

1. See *P.R.*, p. 134.
2. See *P.R.*, p. 134.
3. See *P.R.*, pp. 361, 365.
4. *A.I.*, p. 237. The felt transition of data explains why this is called *efficient causation*. In the context of the Aristotelian universe of discourse, it might also be said to involve *material* causation since data (materials) are provided.
5. See *M.T.*, p. 225.
6. See subsequent discussion, pp. 39–41, 60–1.
7. See *P.R.*, pp. 420–21
8. See *P.R.*, pp. 423–26.
9. See *P.R.*, p. 470.
10. *P.R.*, p. 470.
11. See *P.R.*, pp. 165–366. It should be remembered that in an earlier discussion Whitehead suggested that only some occasions are bipolar. Some are mental occasions, others are physical occasions. See *R.M.*, pp. 102–03, 118.
12. See *P.R.*, pp. 48–49, 280. It is confusing to find that sometimes the term *pure mental feeling* applies to propositional feeling as well as conceptual feeling. See *P.R.*, pp. 369–70.
13. See *P.R.*, p. 423.
14. See *P.R.*, p. 380.
15. See *P.R.*, p. 436
16. *P.R.*, p. 135. See also *P.R.*, pp. 71, 130, 373; *A.I.*, pp. 327–28. This implies a drastic revision of the position taken in *Science and the Modern World*, where it is suggested that an occasion may be "completely determined by the past" (p. 253).
17. See *P.R.*, p. 168.
18. See *P.R.*, p. 202.
19. See *P.R.*, 135.

20. *P.R.*, p. 74. This involves the Category of Freedom and Determination, Categoreal Obligation IX. See *P.R.*, p. 41.
21. See Category of Explanation VI. See *P.R.*, p. 33.
22. See *P.R.*, p. 75.
23. See later discussion, pp. 46–7, 169–70.
24. See *P.R.*, p. 188. See exception in *S.M.W.*, p. 106.
25. See *A.I.*, p. 278.
26. See *A.I.*, p. 252.
27. See *S.M.W.*, p. 178.
28. See *S.M.W.*, p. 174.
29. Whitehead uses the term *atomic* here in the sense of (co-operating) *individual*—not in the sense of an individual with no relations to other individuals.
30. See *P.R.*, p. 71.
31. See *P.R.*, p. 374.
32. See *P.R.*, pp. 42, 52; *S.M.W.*, p. 106.
33. See *P.R.*, p. 43; *A.I.*, p. 354.
34. Category of Explanation I. See *P.R.*, p. 33.
35. See *P.R.*, pp. 113–14. See later discussion of the concept *society*.
36. See *P.R.*, pp. 92, 52.
37. *P.R.*, p. 126.
38. See *P.R.*, pp. 124–26, 321.
39. See *A.I.*, pp. 250–51.
40. See *P.R.*, pp. 72, 326–28, 336.
41. See *A.I.*, p. 246.
42. *P.R.*, p. 380. This statement should be borne in mind while reading Whitehead's reference to "temporal actual entities." See *P.R.*, p. 102.
43. "Time," p. 61.
44. See *P.R.*, p. 517.
45. See *P.R.*, pp. 433–44. Yet note *S.M.W.*, p. 181. Here the process of self-realization is called *temporal*.
46. See *P.R.*, p. 434.
47. See *P.R.*, p. 107. The term *duration* also means a cross section of the universe at one epoch. See *P.R.*, pp. 190, 485–90.
48. See *S.M.W.*, pp. 153, 183; *M.T.*, p. 122.
49. See *S.M.W.*, p. 185. Here Whitehead seems to be referring to what in his later books he calls a *society of actual entities*—perhaps, more specifically, a *personal society*. See later discussion of the concept *society*.
50. *P.R.*, p. 108. See also *P.R.*, p. 443.
51. See *P.R.*, pp. 434, 119–20.
52. See *P.R.*, p. 165.
53. See *P.R.*, p. 448.
54. See *S.M.W.*, pp. 220–21; *A.I.*, p. 271.
55. See *S.M.W.*, p. 180.
56. See *S.M.W.*, p. 96.
57. See *S.M.W.*, p. 181. Some of the general implications of spatio-temporal distinctions are outlined by Whitehead in somewhat rhetorical fashion in *Modes of Thought* (see pp. 139–40).
58. *P.R.*, p. 79.
59. See *P.R.*, p. 66.
60. See *P.R.*, p. 224.

61. See *P.R.*, pp. 39, 224.
62. See *P.R.*, p. 366.
63. See *P.R.*, pp. 337–38.
64. See *P.R.*, p. 322.
65. See *P.R.*, p. 435.
66. See *P.R.*, p. 321. See Category of Explanation V (*P.R.*, pp. 33–34).
67. *P.R.*, pp. 136, 252. See Category of Explanation IX (*P.R.*, p. 34).
68. See *P.R.*, p. 234.
69. See *P.R.*, pp. 135–36.
70. See *P.R.*, pp. 338, 35.
71. See *P.R.*, p. 339.
72. See *P.R.*, p. 35.
73. Category of Explanation XXIII. See *P.R.*, p. 38.
74. *P.R.*, p. 136.
75. See *P.R.*, p. 340.
76. See *P.R.*, p. 481.
77. *P.R.*, p. 253. See Category of Explanation XVIII (*P.R.*, pp. 36–37).
78. See *P.R.*, pp. 239, 252–53.
79. See *S.M.W.*, p. 174.
80. See *S.M.W.*, pp. 96, 107.
81. See *S.M.W.*, pp. 129–30.
82. See *P.R.*, p. 39. See also *P.R.*, p. 337. This is Category of Explanation XXVII. See *P.R.*, p. 39.
83. See Category of Explanation II (*P.R.*, p. 33).
84. See Category of Explanation III (*P.R.*, p. 33).
85. See Categories of Explanation IV, XXV (*P.R.*, pp. 33, 38).
86. See *P.R.*, pp. 72, 129, 336. The inner life of an actual entity is also called the *real essence* (*P.R.*, p. 82).
87. See Category of Explanation XXVI; also the Category of Objective Identity, Categoreal Obligation II (*P.R.*, pp. 38, 39).
88. The Category of Objective Diversity, Categoreal Obligation III. See *P.R.*, p. 39.
89. See *P.R.*, pp. 227–28, 233.
90. See *P.R.*, p. 227.
91. See *M.T.*, p. 121.
92. See *M.T.*, pp. 121, 127.
93. See *P.R.*, p. 35; *A.I.*, pp. 258–59. The term *event* is sometimes used to mean a nexus of actual entities, and sometimes in the sense of a nexus as objectified by universals (*P.R.*, p. 352).
94. See *A.I.*, p. 261.
95. See *A.I.*, p. 262. It is to be noted that in *Science and the Modern World* Whitehead deals with the problem of endurance in terms of a theory of events. "Endurance is the property of finding its pattern reproduced in the temporal parts of the total event" (p. 219). In other words he uses the term to apply to what in *Process and Reality* he calls both *actual entity* and *society*.
96. See *A.I.*, pp. 261–62.
97. See *P.R.*, pp. 92, 114, 123.
98. See *P.R.*, p. 301; *A.I.*, p. 263.
99. See *P.R.*, p. 50.
100. See *P.R.*, p. 52.

101. See *A.I.*, p. 264; and, in general, *P.R.*, Part II, Chapter 3.
102. See *P.R.*, pp. 151–52.
103. See *P.R.*, pp. 151–52.
104. See *S.M.W.*, pp. 160–61, 215.
105. See *A.I.*, pp. 260–61.
106. See *A.I.*, p. 266; *P.R.*, pp. 156, 166.
107. See *P.R.*, pp. 146–50.
108. See *A.I.*, p. 266.
109. See *M.T.*, pp. 205–06.
110. See *M.T.*, pp. 206–07.
111. See *M.T.*, p. 229.
112. See *P.R.*, p. 156.
113. See *P.R.*, pp. 165, 49.
114. See *P.R.*, p. 166.
115. See *P.R.*, p. 166.
116. See *M.T.*, pp. 37–38; *A.I.*, p. 179; *F.R.*, p. 21.
117. See *M.T.*, pp. 33–36; but for a different position see *A.I.*, p. 264.
118. See preceding discussion of the autonomy of actual entities, pp. 39–41.
119. See *M.T.*, pp. 38–39. For a somewhat different analysis see *P.R.*, p. 269.
120. See *P.R.*, p. 440.
121. See *P.R.*, p. 461.
122. See *P.R.*, p. 472.
123. *P.R.*, p. 500.
124. See *M.T.*, pp. 123–26.
125. *P.R.*, p. 103. See also *P.R.*, pp. 53, 147–48; *A.I.*, p. 258.
126. See *P.R.*, p. 112.
127. *A.I.*, p. 355.
128. *P.R.*, p. 496.

Chapter 4

GOD

1. See "Imm.," p. 698.
2. See *P.R.*, p. 521.
3. *P.R.*, p. 521.
4. See *P.R.*, p. 134. In the course of this discussion of Whitehead's concept of God, the term *he* will be used. To some the impersonal *it* might appear more suitable. However, in view of Whitehead's general "subjectivism" and the particular characteristics assigned to God, the personal pronoun seems at least possible. In any case, this is the usage employed by Whitehead.
5. See *P.R.*, pp. 522, 134, 73.
6. See *P.R.*, p. 48. This is the so-called Ontological Principle. See *P.R.*, pp. 36, 134; *R.M.*, pp. 104, 152–53.
7. See *P.R.*, p. 73. It should be noted that Whitehead also refers to eternal objects as *existents* (*M.T.*, p. 95).
8. See *P.R.*, p. 248. In discussing the availability of eternal objects in *Science and the Modern World* (p. 154), he seems to confuse with God's primordial nature what in *Process and Reality* he calls *creativity*.
9. See *P.R.*, pp. 374, 523; *S.M.W.*, pp. 256–57.

10. See *S.M.W.*, p. 257.
11. See *P.R.*, p. 161.
12. *P.R.*, p. 50.
13. See *P.R.*, pp. 104, 343, 373.
14. See *P.R.*, p. 38.
15. *P.R.*, p. 164.
16. See *P.R.*, p. 343. This must be borne in mind when one reads in *R.M.* (p. 159) that God solves all indeterminations. What he really means to say is that God removes indeterminations, or lack of patterned arrangement, in the realm of eternal objects. But the indetermination is removed only in this realm.
17. See *P.R.*, p. 70.
18. See *P.R.*, pp. 344, 521.
19. See *P.R.*, p. 382.
20. *P.R.*, p. 392 (italics added). See also *R.M.*, p. 157.
21. See *S.M.W.*, p. 256.
22. See *P.R.*, p. 47.
23. See *P.R.*, p. 382
24. See *P.R.*, p. 134.
25. See *P.R.*, p. 524; *M.T.*, p. 128. This phase of Whitehead's theory of God involves a very definite shift from the position outlined in *Religion in the Making*. In this earlier book he contends that God should not be regarded as a derivative from the world. However, it must be noted that there he is referring to the primordial nature of God only. (This point of view, concerning God's primordial nature, is retained in his later and more fully developed position.) In suggesting that the eternal objects envisaged in God's primordial nature are ideal *consequents* he is of course using the term *consequent* in a different sense from its meaning when employed in the phrase *consequent nature of God*. See *R.M.*, pp. 156–58.
26. See previous discussion, Chapter 2, pp. 28–9.
27. See *P.R.*, pp. 64, 527. It should be noted that in the former of these otherwise valuable passages, Whitehead carelessly refers to God's primordial nature as an actual entity.
28. *P.R.*, p. 134 (italics added).
29. See *P.R.*, p. 525.
30. *P.R.*, p. 531
31. See *P.R.*, pp. 524–25.
32. *P.R.*, p. 532.
33. See *P.R.*, p. 531.
34. See *R.M.*, p. 155.
35. See "Imm.," p. 698. God is referred to as "the fellow-sufferer who understands." *P.R.*, p. 532.
36. See *R.M.*, p. 154.
37. See *P.R.*, p. 525.
38. See *R.M.*, pp. 154–55.
39. See *A.I.*, pp. 380–81.
40. See *M.T.*, p. 164.
41. See "Imm.," p. 694.
42. See *M.T.*, p. 141.
43. See *P.R.*, p. 531.

44. See *P.R.*, p. 524.
45. See *P.R.*, p. 532.
46. *P.R.*, p. 377.
47. *P.R.*, p. 135. See also *M.T.*, p. 128.
48. *S.M.W.*, pp. 102–03. See also *S.M.W.*, pp. 157, 180, 225.
49. See *P.R.*, p. 31.
50. *P.R.*, p. 339. See *A.I.*, p. 303. Comments in similar vein are found in *Religion in the Making*. He states that creativity is one formative element along with eternal objects and God (p. 90). However, he very quickly points out that it should not be considered an actual entity. "There are not two actual entities, the creativity and the creature. There is only one entity which is the self-creating creature" (p. 102).
51. See *P.R.*, pp. 31, 135, 248.
52. See *P.R.*, pp. 10–11. This interpretation is based on discussion with Professor Whitehead during 1936 and 1937. See Appendix B, pp. 218–23.
53. See *P.R.*, p. 32.
54. *P.R.*, p. 374. See also *A.I.*, p. 230.
55. *P.R.*, p. 31.
56. *P.R.*, p. 32. See also *P.R.*, p. 321. Categories of Explanation, XXI and XXII seem to be involved here. See *P.R.*, p. 38.
57. See Chapter 2, pp. 28–9.
58. *P.R.*, p. 521.
59. For an apparently different approach, see *M.T.*, pp. 140–41.
60. See *P.R.*, pp. 521, 523, 528.
61. See *P.R.*, pp. 134, 531.

Chapter 5

WHITEHEAD'S PHILOSOPHY OF MIND

1. See *A.I.*, pp. 290–91; *P.R.*, p. 244.
2. See *A.I.*, p. 291. For a discussion of these methods see: introspection (p. 30); intuition (pp. 9–11); social institutions (pp. 8, 36); scientific methods (pp. 91–2, 152–5). It is very difficult to apply any general psychological label to Whitehead's work. He agrees with the Gestaltists in stressing organic interrelationships and denouncing atomism. He concurs with Freud in emphasizing that much of mental life is unconscious. He makes purpose fundamental and to this extent agrees with McDougall. On occasion he sounds like a Behaviorist. There are noticeable affinities with James and Dewey. However, Whitehead's position is unmistakably different from all these.
3. *A.I.*, p. 225.
4. *M.T.*, p. 228.
5. See *P.R.*, pp. 301, 163–67, 516; *M.T.*, p. 224. Whitehead suggests that each member of this series has "an emphatic experience of the self-identity of the past in the immediacy of the present" ("Imm.," p. 689). See also *A.I.*, p. 237; *P.R.*, p. 164; *M.T.*, p. 151.
6. See "Imm.," p. 689.
7. See *M.T.*, p. 156; *A.I.*, pp. 289–90; *P.R.*, pp. 161–67. Whitehead's reference to the final percipient route of occasions (mind) as "perhaps some thread of happenings wandering in 'empty' space amid the inter-

stices of the brain" (*P.R.*, p. 516) becomes meaningful when it is realized that a high degree of novelty of experience is possible when a personal society (mind) is set in a context which does not involve a strong tendency toward a repetition of past experience. This condition is found in the group of actual entities (subjects) which comprise the so-called empty space in question.

8. See *A.I.*, p. 243; *M.T.*, p. 218. It will be recalled that the dualism of mental and physical is overcome in each actual entity in that all actual entities have conceptual prehensions and physical prehensions as cooperating components. However, it must be remembered that both types of prehension are feelings.

9. See *M.T.*, p. 222.

10. See *A.I.*, p. 267. The same notion is apparently expressed, in very general terms, in Whitehead's discussion of immortality ("Imm.," pp. 693, 698).

11. See *P.R.*, pp. 524-25. In *Religion in the Making*, Whitehead states: "The doctrine here developed . . . is entirely neutral on the question of immortality" (pp. 110-11).

12. See *P.R.*, pp. 531, 97, 134.

13. See *P.R.*, pp. 184, 189, 266-67.

14. See *P.R.*, pp. 271, 185, 189.

15. See *P.R.*, p. 262.

16. See *P.R.*, p. 261.

17. See *P.R.*, p. 497-99.

18. See *P.R.*, p. 193.

19. See *P.R.*, p. 472.

20. See *A.I.*, p. 232; *P.R.*, p. 125. Kant is equally open to attack at this point. See *P.R.*, p. 263.

21. See *A.I.*, pp. 233-34.

22. It may be argued that Whitehead does not deal fairly with Hume. For example, when Hume discusses the independence of impressions, what he really means is that these impressions may be considered as such for purposes of examination but they are not actually in this sundered condition. Thus, Hume states that "objects bear to each other the relations of continuity and succession . . . like objects may be observed in several instances to have like relations; and . . . all this is independent of, and antecedent to the operation of the understanding" (*Treatise*, Book I, Part III, Section XIV, p. 168, Selby-Bigge edition).

23. See *A.I.*, p. 234; *P.R.*, pp. 202-03.

24. See *P.R.*, pp. 480-81.

25. See *S.M.W.*, p. 75; *A.I.*, pp. 235-37; *P.R.*, Part II, Chapter 5.

26. See *M.T.*, p. 153; *A.I.*, pp. 290, 293. However, on at least one occasion, Whitehead uses "introspection" as a synonym for "intuition." See *A.I.*, p. 273.

27. See *R.M.*, p. 124.

28. See *S.M.W.*, p. 216; *P.R.*, p. 163.

29. See *P.R.*, pp. 125, 216, 363, 370-71. In particular, Whitehead emphasizes his opposition to the representative realism of Descartes and Locke, and the critical realism of Santayana.

30. See *P.R.*, p. 100; *A.I.*, pp. 274-75, 322. This point is made in rather extreme fashion in the following statement. "The world for me is nothing else than how the functionings of my body present it for my experience.

The world is thus wholly to be discerned within those functionings. Knowledge of the world is nothing else than an analysis of the functions" (*M.T.*, p. 225).

31. See *A.I.*, pp. 317–18.

32. In writing his earlier books, Whitehead seems to have been more impressed by the difficulties involved in perception and to have been driven to a position which looks very much like epistemological dualism. See *P.N.K.*, pp. 83–85; *Rel.*, p. 33.

33. *P.R.*, p. 176 (italics added). In general, see *S.M.W.*, pp. 128–32.

34. See *P.R.*, p. 411. Whitehead's discussion of the problem of erroneous perception is not characterized by the amazing and ingenious complications of theoretical construction which are found in the work of some of the realists, for instance Nunn and Alexander. Nunn points out that there is no substantial difference between his theory of sense perception and the one developed by Alexander in *Space, Time and Deity*. (See *Proceedings of the Aristotelian Society*, 1923–24, p. 11.) For example, Nunn tries to account for the appearance of a bent stick in the water by saying that the visual sensa are "constituents of a complex thing composed of the stick plus the liquid" (*Ibid.*, p. 12). Thus, the sensa are not constituents of the stick taken by itself. Nunn suggests that the distinction between normal and abnormal sense can be made with the help of supplementary tactile sensa. Thus, the apparently bent stick, immersed in water, feels straight as one runs a finger along it. As has been noted, Whitehead does not try to deal with the difficulty of erroneous perception by setting up an artificial complex object composed of perceived object, medium, and (or) abnormal bodily conditions, and then claiming that the experienced sensa are real components of that complex object. Whitehead is prepared to admit that one may have real difficulty in deciding that the grass which appears green really is green. See *A.I.*, p. 322.

35. See *P.R.*, p. 40.

36. See *Sym.*, p. 58.

37. See *Sym.*, p. 24.

38. See *P.R.*, p. 261.

39. See *P.R.*, pp. 261, 272.

40. See *P.R.*, pp. 245–46. It must be admitted that he somewhat modifies this adverse judgment. In discussing consciousness of sense data, Whitehead notes a tendency which has been emphasized by the Gestaltists—the tendency to achieve large, inclusive units in perception. See *M.T.*, pp. 169–70.

41. In this connection Whitehead makes use of the term *instinct*. See *A.I.*, p. 58; *Sym.*, p. 78.

42. See *A.I.*, p. 347.

43. See *P.R.*, pp. 282–83, 394, 402–03. *P.R.*, pp. 397–98, provides a technical statement of how a propositional feeling originates.

44. See *P.R.*, pp. 283, 395–97.

45. See *P.R.*, pp. 291–93, 412–13. Whitehead's involved and highly technical discussion of judgments has been omitted from this study because of its specialized nature.

46. See *P.R.*, pp. 287, 396.

47. See *P.R.*, pp. 351–52, 310; also "Time."
48. *P.R.*, pp. 435–36. It will be recalled that Whitehead claims that in a certain very definite sense the future is in the present. See *A.I.*, pp. 250–51.
49. See *P.R.*, pp. 282–83.
50. See *P.R.*, p. 281.
51. See *P.R.*, p. 407.
52. See *P.R.*, p. 286.
53. See *P.R.*, p. 245.
54. See *P.R.*, pp. 283–84.
55. See *P.R.*, p. 35.
56. See *P.R.*, p. 177.
57. See *P.R.*, p. 256; *A.I.*, p. 237.
58. See *M.T.*, p. 49.
59. See *A.I.*, p. 59.
60. See *A.E.*, pp. 78–79.
61. *S.M.W.*, p. 268. See also *A.E.*, pp. 77–78, 127–28; *A.I.*, p. 114.
62. See *P.R.*, p. 519; "Imm.," p. 699; *M.T.*, p. 60.
63. See *F.R.*, pp. 6–7.
64. See *F.R.*, pp. 57–61.
65. *P.R.*, p. 122.
66. See *M.T.*, p. 50.
67. See *F.R.*, p. 27; *R.M.*, p. 39.
68. See *A.E.*, p. 69.
69. See *S.M.W.*, pp. 166–67; *M.T.*, p. 46.
70. See *P.R.*, pp. 310–11.
71. See *A.I.*, p. 143.
72. See *P.R.*, pp. 310–11.
73. See *A.I.*, pp. 250–51.
74. *A.I.*, p. 250. See Chapter 3, pp. 43–4.
75. See *A.E.*, p. 80.
76. See *P.R.*, pp. 308, 315.
77. See *A.I.*, pp. 59–60.
78. See *A.E.*, p. 46.
79. See *M.T.*, p. 63.
80. See *M.T.*, pp. 84–85.
81. "Imm.," p. 700. See also "Remarks," p. 186.
82. See *S.M.W.*, p. 268.
83. See *M.T.*, pp. 25–26, 101. His comments concerning scientific experiments are in similar vein. See Chapter 8, pp. 153–4.
84. See *A.I.*, p. 91.
85. See *A.I.*, p. 228; *M.T.*, p. 69. Whitehead's term *intuitive judgment* has a different, highly technical meaning. See *P.R.*, pp. 413–14.
86. See *S.M.W.*, p. 286. Introspection, the traditional technique for the internal observation of one's own mental activities, is criticized by Whitehead because it concentrates on the data of presentational immediacy. "It lifts the clear-cut data of sensation into primacy, and cloaks the vague compulsions and derivations which form the main stuff of experience" (*A.I.*, p. 290).
87. See *M.T.*, p. 66.
88. See *A.I.*, pp. 283–84.

89. See *F.R.*, p. 51.
90. See *S.M.W.*, pp. 262–63. See illustrations from the history of science, (*S.M.W.*, pp. 263–65).
91. See *Sym.*, pp. 2, 11, 66, 67.
92. See *Sym.*, p. 68.
93. See *P.R.*, pp. 278–79.
94. See *Sym.*, pp. 69, 87.
95. See *M.T.*, p. 57.
96. See *M.T.*, p. 49.
97. See *P.R.*, pp. 276–78.
98. See *R.M.*, p. 34; *M.T.*, p. 55.
99. See R.M., pp. 126–27.
100. Mill, J. S., *System of Logic* (London: Longmans, Green & Co., 1879), Book V, Chapter 3, p. 330.

Chapter 6

WHITEHEAD'S THEORY OF VALUE

1. *R.M.*, p. 100.
2. *S.M.W.*, p. 136. It is to be noted that Whitehead ordinarily uses the term *importance* as a synonym for the term *value*. (*A.E.*, p. 63; and *M.T.*, p. 16.) However, on occasion, he employs the term in a different sense. For example, it is suggested that values differ in importance (*S.M.W.*, p. 152); also that importance depends on *endurance*. Endurance is defined, in this technical context, as the retention through time of the achievement of value. See *S.M.W.*, pp. 278, 152, 174.
3. He is also keenly aware of the essential place which economic values hold in the life of man.
4. See *S.M.W.*, p. 136.
5. See *S.M.W.*, p. 136.
6. See *P.R.*, p. 97.
7. See *M.T.*, p. 28.
8. See "Imm.," p. 692.
9. See *M.T.*, p. 161
10. See *M.T.*, p. 44.
11. See *M.T.*, p. 11
12. "Imm.," pp. 695–96.
13. See "Imm.," pp. 695–96.
14. It will be recalled that *personal identity* is maintained when a number of actual entities form a linear succession such that an essential characteristic is successively derived by each entity from its predecessors. (*P.R.*, p. 301.) This essential quality remains as an enduring factor, though it is manifest in a succession of different and transitory actual entities.
15. See "Imm.," p. 689.
16. See *P.R.*, pp. 39–40.
17. See *P.R.*, p. 46.
18. See *P.R.*, p. 367.
19. See *P.R.*, p. 368.
20. See *P.R.*, p. 380.

21. See *R.M.*, p. 100.
22. See *P.R.*, p. 526.
23. See *P.R.*, p. 525. See also subsequent discussion of the problem of evil.
24. See *A.I.*, p. 309.
25. Whitehead notes that it is possible to generalize this definition and omit any explicit reference to appearance. Thus "a truth-relation will be said to connect the objective contents of two prehensions when one and the same identical partial pattern can be abstracted from both of them. They each exhibit the same partial pattern, though their omitted elements involve the differences which belong to their diverse individualities" (*A.I.*, p. 310).
26. See *A.I.*, pp. 269–70.
27. It will be recalled that a proposition, according to Whitehead, has as its logical subject an actual entity or a group (society) of actual entities (e.g., a stone is a society of actual entities). Its predicate is an eternal object or a group of eternal objects. (The term *pattern* is also used in place of the term *eternal object.*) A proposition is defined as "the possibility of *that* [a certain specified] predicate applying in that assigned way to *those* [specifically indicated] logical subjects" (*P.R.*, p. 394). See also *P.R.*, pp. 282–83; *A.I.*, p. 312.
28. See *A.I.*, pp. 313–15. In terms of the definition of truth noted above, it will be realized that the type of truth relation under consideration does not involve an identical pattern (eternal object) present *in the same fashion*, in both the thing and the proposition about the thing. For example, the proposition "This stone is grey" involves the eternal object *grey* as a *possibility*. The stone actually exemplifies the eternal object *grey.*
29. See *A.I.*, p. 316.
30. See *A.I.*, p. 317.
31. See *A.I.*, p. 318.
32. See *A.I.*, pp. 318–20.
33. See *P.R.*, p. 291; *A.I.*, p. 321.
34. See *P.R.*, p. 414.
35. See *P.R.*, p. 275. See *R.M.*, p. 28, for further criticism of the superficiality of the pragmatic approach.
36. See *F.R.*, p. 31.
37. See *A.I.*, pp. 309, 311.
38. See *S.M.W.*, pp. 262–63.
39. *S.M.W.*, p. 266.
40. See *S.M.W.*, pp. 266–67.
41. *P.R.*, p. 284. For a discussion of error in perception and in thinking, see Chapter 5, pp. 81–3, 91–4.
42. *A.I.*, p. 313.
43. See *P.R.*, p. 281.
44. See *M.T.*, p. 14.
45. See *A.I.*, p. 313.
46. See *A.I.*, p. 321.
47. See *A.I.*, p. 311.
48. See *S.M.W.*, p. 268.
49. See *Sym.*, p. 39; *P.R.*, p. 526.
50. See *A.I.*, p. 324.

51. "A distinction must now be made between two meanings of the term Beauty. There is the *primary* meaning [involved in the definition just quoted]. . . . But in the analysis of an occasion, some *parts* of its objective content may be termed Beautiful by reason of their conformal contribution to the perfection of the subjective form of the complete occasion" (*A.I.*, p. 328; italics added). This is the *secondary* meaning of Beauty. Whitehead, however, concentrates his attention on the primary meaning.
52. See *A.I.*, p. 324.
53. *A.I.*, p. 324.
54. See *A.I.*, p. 324.
55. See *A.I.*, p. 324.
56. See *A.I.*, p. 339.
57. See *A.I.*, p. 339.
58. See *A.I.*, pp. 330–31. Whitehead illustrates this point by very apt references to various cultures—Greek, Hellenistic, Byzantium, and Chinese. See *A.I.*, pp. 331–32.
59. See *A.I.*, p. 132.
60. "Remarks," p. 186. See also *M.T.*, p. 84.
61. See "M.G.," p. 678. See also *M.T.*, pp. 81–82.
62. See "Imm.," p. 692.
63. See *M.T.*, p. 164.
64. See *A.I.*, p. 348.
65. See *S.M.W.*, pp. 290–91.
66. See *A.I.*, p. 348.
67. See *S.M.W.*, p. 291.
68. See *A.I.*, pp. 348–51.
69. See "M.G.," pp. 672–73.
70. See "M.G.," p. 678. See preceding discussion of the importance of "disorder."
71. See *M.T.*, p. 19.
72. "M.G.," p. 679.
73. See "M.G.," p. 674; *M.T.*, pp. 104–07; and later reference to Whitehead's discussion of the difficulty involved in formulating minutely specific rules of conduct (p. 111).
74. *P.R.*, p. 171.
75. See *M.T.*, p. 109.
76. See *R.M.*, p. 98.
77. See *A.I.*, pp. 324, 331–32; *M.T.*, p. 108; *P.R.*, p. 171.
78. See "M.G.," p. 679. Whitehead also *distinguishes* triviality from evil. There is a triviality which "lies in the anaesthesia by which evil is avoided." From this point of view, "evil is the half-way house between perfection and triviality" (*A.I.*, p. 355).
79. See *S.M.W.*, p. 276.
80. See *P.R.*, p. 517; *A.I.*, p. 333.
81. See *R.M.*, p. 95.
82. See *A.I.*, p. 330.
83. See *R.M.*, p. 97.
84. See *M.T.*, pp. 69–70, 110; *P.R.*, p. 517; "Imm.," p. 692.
85. See *M.T.*, pp. 69–70.
86. See *R.M.*, p. 155.

87. *R.M.*, p. 155 (italics added).
88. *P.R.*, p. 531 (italics added).
89. See *A.I.*, pp. 374–75. In private conversation, Whitehead on occasion developed this theme at some length. The Ten Commandments, for example, should be construed with common sense. Can we really believe that no work whatever can be done on Sundays? In an apparently flippant mood (but only apparently) he characterized the Ten Commandments as "How to get along in Arabia."
90. *M.T.*, p. 165.
91. See *M.T.*, p. 20.
92. See *P.R.*, p. 526; *A.I.*, pp. 376–77. The spirit or attitude which underlies an adequate moral system is difficult to describe. In general it seems to be a tolerant, sympathetic respect for the value of the individual. Perhaps the best brief description of this attitude is found in Whitehead's comments concerning the state of mind which he terms *Peace*. (See later discussion of this concept pp. 116–117.)
93. See *P.R.*, Part I, Chapter 1.
94. *M.T.*, p. 18.
95. See *A.E.*, p. 23.
96. See *A.E.*, p. 49. There is a brief reference to "moral responsibility" which indicates the metaphysical basis of Whitehead's approach to this problem. "The point to be noticed is that the actual entity, in a state of process during which it is not fully definite, determines its own ultimate definiteness. This is the whole point of moral responsibility. Such responsibility is conditioned by the limits of the data, and by the categoreal conditions of concrescence" (*P.R.*, p. 390). See also *P.R.*, p. 339.
97. See *A.E.*, p. 49.
98. See *A.I.*, p. 48. (It is obvious that Whitehead is addicted to the use of capitals when referring to values.)
99. *A.I.*, pp. 341, 344, 345, 341, 342.
100. See Whitehead, "Autobiographical Notes," in *The Philosophy of Alfred North Whitehead,* edited by P. A. Schilpp (Evanston, Illinois: Library of Living Philosophers, 1941)
101. *A.I.*, p. 13 (italics added).
102. See *A.I.*, pp. 341–42
103. See *A.I.*, p. 342.
104. *A.I.*, p. 342.
105. *A.I.*, p. 344.
106. *A.I.*, p. 345.
107. See "Imm.," p. 697.
108. *A.I.*, p. 190.
109. "M.G.," p. 674 (italics added).
110. See "M.G.," p. 678.
111. See *A.I.*, p. 345.
112. See Whitehead, "An Appeal to Sanity," in *The Atlantic Monthly,* Vol. CLXIII, p. 315.
113. See Whitehead, "The Study of the Past: Its Uses and Its Dangers," in *Harvard Business Review,* Vol. XI (1932–33), p. 440.
114. See Whitehead, "The Study of the Past," p. 443.
115. See Whitehead, "Reconstruction," in *The Atlantic Monthly,* Vol. CLXIX, p. 173

116. See *S.M.W.*, pp. 280–81.
117. See *A.I.*, p. 332.
118. *A.I.*, p. 353.
119. See *A.I.*, p. 368.
120. See *A.I.*, p. 369.
121. See *P.R.*, pp. 523–33.
122. *A.E.*, pp. 62–63. See also *M.T.*, pp. 26–27.

Chapter 7

WHITEHEAD'S RELATION TO OTHER PHILOSOPHERS

1. *S.M.W.*, p. xi.
2. See *P.R.*, p. v.
3. See *P.R.*, p. vii.
4. Incidentally it will be observed that Whitehead is very energetic in undertaking the standard philosophic project of criticizing the concepts used by other thinkers.
5. Whitehead, "Harvard: The Future," in *The Atlantic Monthly*, Vol. CLVIII, p. 264.
6. See *A.I.*, p. 188.
7. See *P.R.*, pp. 63, 147. In order to make this similarity more obvious, the later Plato of the *Philebus* and the *Sophist* is here considered. He formulated a theory which ascribed reality to members of the "mixed class"; saw no problem in the relation of Idea to thing; and regarded all Ideas as mutually involving each other. This is the Plato of the period before the reduction of Ideas to numbers. Whitehead refers to this distinction. See *A.I.*, p. 197
8. See *A.I.*, pp. 171, 192, 197.
9. See *P.R.*, p. 70; and *M.T.*, pp. 92–93. Here, obviously, Whitehead is criticizing the Plato of the *Republic* and the *Phaedo*.
10. See *M.T.*, p. 95. In general, see *M.T.*, pp. 93–96, 111–12.
11. *Sophist*, 247e, 249a. See also *Philebus*, 25–26, where temporal actualities are described in terms of γ   s οὐσίαν.
12. See discussion of this point expressed in terms of his distinction between Law as *immanent* and as *imposed* (*A.I.*, pp. 154–55). It is also interesting to note, in passing, Whitehead's suggestion that his philosophy of organism agrees with the *Timaeus* in tracing back the origin of the present cosmic epoch to "an aboriginal disorder, chaotic according to our ideals" (*P.R.*, p 146).
13. See *A.I.*, pp. 189–90.
14. See *P.R.*, p. 63
15. *S.M.W.*, p. 249.
16. See *P.R.*, pp. 522–23.
17. *P.R.*, p. 64.
18. See *P.R.*, pp. 147, 319; also *E.S.P.*, p. 116.
19. See *A.I.*, p. 136.
20. See *A.I.*, pp. 181–82.
21. See *A.I.*, p. 193.
22. See *S.M.W.*, p. 43.
23. See *A.I.*, p. 196.

24. See *M.T.*, p. 21.
25. See *A.I.*, p. 150; *M.T.*, pp. 193–94.
26. See *A.I.*, pp. 170, 355–56.
27. See *A.I.*, pp. 354–56.
28. See *P.R.*, p. 45.
29. See *P.R.*, p. 81. It is to be noted that, in his discussion of Aristotle's theory of substance, Whitehead seems to be guilty of a serious misunderstanding. In *Metaphysics* (IV, 8) Aristotle states that the primary meaning of substance is "that which has predicates and is not predicted of anything else." In other words, a substance is anything that has qualities and relations but is itself neither a quality or a relation. Thus substance is not identical with matter or mind, it does not imply independence of status, it does not necessarily imply static endurance. It would seem that in claiming to criticize Aristotle's theory of physical substance Whitehead is really "attacking the notion of a permanent independent object as it has come to us from the Greek atomists" (J. D. Mabbott, "Substance," in *Philosophy*, Vol. X, p. 188).
30. See *S.M.W.*, pp. 60–61; *S.M.W.*, pp. 100–01.
31. See *S.M.W.*, pp. 62–66.
32. See *S.M.W.*, pp. 102–03.
33. See *S.M.W.*, p. 255.
34. *P.R.*, p. 10.
35. See *P.R.*, p. 27.
36. See *P.R.*, pp. 114, 125.
37. See *P.R.*, p. 135.
38. See *P.R.*, p. 37.
39. See *P.R.*, p. 320.
40. See *P.R.*, p. 82.
41. See *P.R.*, p. 223.
42. See *S.M.W.*, p. 213.
43. See *P.R.*, p. 129.
44. See *P.R.*, pp. 86, 210.
45. See Essay, II, XXIII.
46. See *P.R.*, pp. 222, 321.
47. *P.R.*, p. 93.
48. See *P.R.*, p. 91.
49. See *P.R.*, p. 37.
50. See *P.R.*, p. 92.
51. See *P.R.*, pp. 173, 214; *A.I.*, p. 225.
52. See *A.I.*, pp. 335–36.
53. See *S.M.W.*, pp. 101–02.
54. See *S.M.W.*, pp. 101–03.
55. *P.R.*, pp. 265–266.
56. *A.I.*, p. 237.
57. See *P.R.*, pp. 204, 266. In lighter vein, Whitehead remarks that "causation has emerged from its treatment by Hume like the parrot after its contest with the monkey" ("T.S.M.," p. 45).
58. See *P.R.*, p. 267.
59. See *P.R.*, pp. 209–11.
60. See *P.R.*, p. 208.
61. See *P.R.*, p. 208.

62. See *P.R.*, pp. 212–13.
63. See *P.R.*, p. 215.
64. *P.R.*, p. 253.
65. See *P.R.*, p. 64.
66. See *P.R.*, pp. 65–66.
67. See *P.R.*, p. 220.
68. See *P.R.*, p. 241.
69. *P.R.*, p. 228.
70. See *A.I.*, p. 244.
71. See *A.I.*, p. 145.
72. See *P.R.*, p. 124.
73. See *P.R.*, p. 47.
74. See *S.M.W.*, p. 95.
75. See *A.I.*, p. 168.
76. See *S.M.W.*, p. 224.
77. See *S.M.W.*, pp. 223–25.
78. See *P.R.*, p. 124.
79. See *A.I.*, p. 171.
80. See *P.R.*, p. 238.
81. See *A.I.*, p. 300.
82. See *P.R.*, pp. 172–73.
83. See *P.R.*, p. 112.
84. See *P.R.*, pp. 236, 135–36.
85. See *P.R.*, p. 289.
86. See *P.R.*, p. 254.
87. See G. Vlastos, "Organic Categories in Whitehead," in *The Journal of Philosophy*, Vol. XXXIV, pp. 256–58.
88. See *Symposium in Honor of the Seventieth Birthday of Alfred North Whitehead* (Cambridge, Mass.: Harvard University Press, 1932), p. 25.
89. See *C.N.*, pp. 53–55.
90. Bergson, Henri, *Creative Evolution* (London: Macmillan & Co., 1928), p. 261.
91. See Bergson, *Evolution*, pp. 1–7.
92. See *P.R.*, p. 108.
93. Bergson, *Evolution*, p. 262.
94. See *S.M.W.*, pp. 212, 74.
95. See *S.M.W.*, p. 74; *P.R.*, p. 319.
96. *P.R.*, p. 489.
97. Bergson, *Evolution*, p. 186.
98. See *P.R.*, p. 4; *E.S.P.*, p. 116. Here, Whitehead is assigning greater efficacy to intelligence than in the discussion on pp. 90–1.
99. Bergson, Henri, *An Introduction to Metaphysics* (London: Macmillan & Co., 1913), p. 59. See also Bergson, Henri, *The Creative Mind* (New York: The Philosophical Library, 1947), pp. 48, 71–72.
100. Bergson, *Evolution*, pp. 92, 263.
101. See Bergson, *Evolution*, p. 262; p. 12.
102. See Bergson, *Mind*, pp. 18–19.
103. See Bergson, *Mind*, p. 81.
104. See Bergson, *Mind*, p. 53.
105. See Bergson, *Mind*, p. 103.

106. See *P.R.*, pp. 65, 174.
107. See Bergson, *Introduction*, pp. 76–77.
108. See Bergson, *Mind*, p. 36.
109. See Bergson, *Introduction*, p. 3.
110. See *P.R.*, p. 45.
111. *P.R.*, p. vii.
112. *A.I.*, pp. 296–97.
113. See *S.M.W.*, p. 93.
114. Bradley, F. H., *Appearance and Reality* (Oxford: Oxford University Press, 1930), p. 460
115. Bradley, p. 128. See also Bradley, pp. 403, 432.
116. See *P.R.*, pp. 85, 237.
117. Bradley, p. 469.
118. *P.R.*, p. 69. See also *P.R.*, p. 305.
119. See *A.I.*, p. 201.
120. See *P.R.*, p. 350.
121. *P.R.*, p. 12.
122. See *M.T.*, p. 139.
123. See *P.R.*, p. 65.
124. See *P.R.*, pp. 42–43.
125. See *S.M.W.*, p. 93.
126. See *S.M.W.*, p. 96.
127. Alexander, Samuel, *Space, Time and Deity* (London: Macmillan and Co., 1920), II, p. 428.
128. See Alexander, I, p. 38
129. See Alexander, I, p. 238.
130. Alexander, I, p. 183.
131. See Alexander, I, p. 345.
132. Alexander, I, p. 346.
133. Alexander, I, p. 347.
134. Alexander, II, p. 47.
135. Alexander, II, p. 46.
136. Alexander, II, p. 67.
137. See Alexander, II, p. 237.
138. See Alexander, II, p. 246.
139. See Alexander, II, p. 243.
140. See Alexander, II, p. 241.
141. Alexander, II, p. 302.
142. See Alexander, II, p. 244.
143. Alexander, II, p. 353.
144. See Alexander, II, p. 420.
145. See, for example, Morgan, Lloyd, *Emergent Evolution* (London: Williams and Norgate, 1923), Chapter 1.
146. See Alexander, I, p. 224.
147. Alexander, I, p. 250.
148. See Alexander, I, pp. 269–80.
149. See Alexander, I, p. 290.
150. See Alexander, I, p. vi.
151. See Alexander, I, p. 4.
152. See Alexander, I, p. 23.

153. For example, pp. 102–03.
154. See *P.R.*, p. vii.
155. See *The Proceedings of the Aristotelian Society* (London: Williams and Norgate, 1923–24) , p. 7.
156. See *Proceedings*, 1909–10, p. 193.
157. *Proceedings*, 1909–10, p. 206.
158. *Proceedings*, 1907–08, p. 149. (However, he has some doubts concerning its metaphysical validity.)
159. *Proceedings*, 1907–08, p. 152. See also *Proceedings*, 1907–08, pp. 142–43.
160. *Proceedings*, 1909–10, p. 202.
161. See *Proceedings*, 1923–24.
162. See *Proceedings*, 1923–24, p. 14.
163. See *Proceedings*, 1923–24, p. 16.
164. *Proceedings*, 1923–24, p. 18.
165. See *P.R.*, p. 85.
166. See *P.R.*, p. 216.
167. See Santayana, George, *Scepticism and Animal Faith* (New York: Charles Scribner's Sons, 1923) , p. 78.
168. Santayana, George, *Realms of Being* (New York: Charles Scribner's Sons, 1942) , p. 203.
169. Santayana, *Realms of Being*, p. 633. See also pp. 206, 278, 739.
170. See *P.R.*, p. 79; *A.I.*, pp. 296–97; *S.M.W.*, pp. 205–06. However, while James uses the term *feeling* to refer to all states of consciousness, Whitehead uses the term to refer not merely to states of consciousness but to all activities. However, there is definite kinship in this common emphasis on feeling.
171. See James, William, *Principles of Psychology* (New York: Henry Holt & Co., 1890) , I, pp. 185–86, 336–42.
172. See James, William, "On Some Hegelisms," in *The Will to Believe;* Lectures II and III in *A Pluralistic Universe;* Lecture IV in *Pragmatism.*
173. James, William, *Pragmatism* (New York: Longmans, Green & Co., 1928) , p. 138.
174. James, William, *The Pluralistic Universe* (New York: Longmans Green & Co., 1928) , p. 217.
175. See James, *Universe*, p. 218.
176. See James, *Universe*, p. 254.
177. James, *Universe*, pp. 250–51.
178. See *P.R.*, p. 18. This is not to imply that Whitehead equates words and concepts.
179. James, *Pragmatism*, pp. 253–54.
180. See James, *Pragmatism*, pp. 206, 211–12, 225.
181. See *M.T.*, pp. 203–04; *A.I.*, pp. 159–64.
182. See *P.R.*, p. 502
183. See *A.I.*, p. 151
184. See *S.M.W.*, p. 75; *P.R.*, p. 11.
185. See *P.R.*, p. 27.
186. See *S.M.W.*, pp. 84, 71–75
187. See *P.R.*, p. 208; *S.M.W.*, p. 77.
188. See *P.R.*, p. 179.
189. See *P.R.*, p. 45.
190. See *S.M.W.*, pp. 75, 72–73.

191. See *S.M.W.*, p. 218.
192. See *P.R.*, pp. 43, 254. It must be realized that Whitehead does use the term *substance* but not in the sense in which he is criticizing it. See *S.M.W.*, pp. 180–81.

It has been claimed by Professor Lovejoy that Whitehead apparently uses the term *simple location* in "at least seven distinguishable senses" (*The Revolt Against Dualism*, p. 159) ; or, more accurately, in denying simple location he is opposing seven distinguishable theories. As a matter of fact these so-called seven distinguishable senses turn out to be variations of one central theme. In other words, the notion of simple location can be illustrated in various ways. Lovejoy seems to realize this when, having distinguished two meanings, he notes in connection with the third that simple location "seems often to have to do with a much more general issue: not merely (a) with the conceptual or existential isolability of a given region of space or time or space-time from ulterior regions, (b) nor merely with the isolability of the concept of position from that of matter or concrete objects, but (c) with the isolability of anything whatever from anything whatever" (*Revolt*, p. 163). Whitehead illustrates his denial of simple location—i.e., the denial of individual independence—by pointing out that in the opinion of modern science in a certain sense, everything is everywhere at all times (see *A.I.*, p. 202; *M.T.*, pp. 188–89). Lovejoy takes this *illustration* of the denial of simple location and tries to make of it not one but two distinguishable *meanings* of simple location involved in its denial, in terms of (a) multiplicity of spatial situations (Lovejoy's meaning number 4) and (b) universal diffusion (meaning number 6). Lovejoy suggests that in denying simple location Whitehead is, on occasion, asserting the notion that an object is not restricted to a single location. The same object may be embodied in many different locations at the same time (meaning number 5). Lovejoy's seventh meaning involves a denial of simple location in terms of aspects of something present somewhere else. But Lovejoy himself admits that this is one way of expressing the notion of "everything is everywhere" (*Revolt*, p. 173). Thus, to repeat, it would appear that in denying simple location Whitehead is affirming that in a sense everything is everywhere (Lovejoy's meaning number 3). All the other so-called distinguishable meanings are simply more specific ways of stating or illustrating the same general point. It should be noted, in passing, that some of Lovejoy's critical comments concerning Whitehead's position are inaccurate, particularly when he charges Whitehead with self-contradiction. For example, he states that in the *Principle of Relativity* Whitehead holds an atomic point of view; stresses (some) contingent relations (*Revolt*, p. 164). This, argues Lovejoy, is inconsistent with his emphasis on "everything everywhere." It should be realized that this is only an apparent contradiction. In *Principle of Relativity* Whitehead is dealing with the philosophy required by science. In *Science and the Modern World* he is going beyond the practical abstractions required by science and attempting a more comprehensive and accurate statement of the interrelation of events. Again Lovejoy is incorrect in stating that for Whitehead "mutual exclusion is an essential property of real things" (*Revolt*, p. 167)—meaning by this a denial of the interpenetration of things.

Whitehead tries to develop a kind of atomistic *continuity*. It must be admitted that Whitehead's full discussion of this point is not provided in *Science and the Modern World*. It appears in *Process and Reality*. Lovejoy apparently did not have the latter book before him when he was writing *The Revolt Against Dualism*. Finally Lovejoy, in stating that objects have no necessary relation "inter se" (*Revolt*, p. 175), is overlooking Whitehead's detailed discussion of the relational essence of eternal objects which occurred in *Science and the Modern World* (see p. 230).

Chapter 8

WHITEHEAD'S PHILOSOPHIC POSITION

1. See *M.T.*, pp. 176–77; *S.M.W.*, pp. 25–26.
2. See *M.T.*, p. 183.
3. See *S.M.W.*, p. 25.
4. See *S.M.W.*, p. 281.
5. See *P.R.*, p. 8. In his discussion of science, at this point, Whitehead seems to be thinking chiefly of natural science. However, at least by implication, he does not confine his remarks to this phase of science.
6. See S.M.W., pp. 23–24.
7. See *M.T.*, p. 40.
8. *M.T.*, p. 41.
9. See *A.I.*, p. 289.
10. *A.I.*, p. 111.
11. See *S.M.W.*, p. 3.
12. See *S.M.W.*, pp. 266–67.
13. See *A.E.*, pp. 228–29.
14. See *P.R.*, p. 178.
15. *P.R.*, p. 177. See also *P.R.*, pp. 375–76, 323–24; *A.I.*, p. 239; *M.T.*, p. 231.
16. See *S.M.W.*, pp. 193–98; *P.R.*, p. 389.
17. See *P.R.*, p. 133.
18. See *P.R.*, p. 102.
19. See *P.R.*, p. 95.
20. See *S.M.W.*, p. 181.
21. See *P.R.*, p. 152; *S.M.W.*, p. 155.
22. See *A.I.*, p. 332.
23. See *P.R.*, pp. 53–54.
24. See *P.R.*, pp. 425–26; *S.M.W.*, p. 193.
25. See *P.R.*, p. vi.
26. Agar, W. E., *A Contribution to the Theory of the Living Organism* (Melbourne: University of Melbourne Press, 1943), p. 7.
27. Agar, p. 77.
28. See Agar, pp. 11, 77.
29. Agar, p. 21. See also Agar, pp. 8, 9, 22, 23.
30. See Agar, p. 24.
31. See Agar, p. 69.
32. See Agar, pp. 71–72.
33. Agar, p. 9.
34. See Lillie, R. S., *General Biology and Philosophy of Organism* (Chicago: University of Chicago Press, 1945), p. 23.

35. See Lillie, pp. 30, 34.
36. See Lillie, p. 120.
37. See *Science*, Vol. LXXVIII, p. 135. See also Lillie, pp. 22, 106–7, 149.
38. Lillie, p. 41. See also Lillie, pp. 49, 89.
39. See Lillie, pp. 96, 196.
40. See Lillie, pp. 46, 145–6.
41. See Lillie, p. 43. Note, however, apparent indecision: Lillie, pp. 104, 158, 171, 50, 56, 60, 195, 201.
42. See Lillie, pp. 182, 187.
43. See Lillie, p. 28.
44. See "Remarks," p. 178.
45. See *A.I.*, p. 294.
46. "Imm.," p. 699. See also *A.I.*, p. 295.
47. See *R.M.*, p. 34; *A.I.*, p. 209.
48. *P.R.*, p. 6. In a sense philosophy is like poetry, trying to express in available words insights which defy completely adequate expression in words. See *M.T.*, pp. 68–69.
49. See *P.R.*, p. 19.
50. *P.R.*, p. 6.
51. *P.R.*, p. 20.
52. See *A.I.*, p. 301.
53. See *A.I.*, p. 301.
54. See *P.R.*, p. 327.
55. See *A.I.*, p. 264; *M.T.*, p. 31; *S.M.W.*, p. 161.
56. See *S.M.W.*, pp. 93, 105.
57. See *S.M.W.*, p. 132.
58. See *S.M.W.*, p. 93.
59. See *S.M.W.*, pp. 115–16, 156.
60. *S.M.W.*, p. 219. It will be obvious that Whitehead here uses the term "materialistic" in a special sense.
61. See *P.R.*, p. 471.
62. *P.R.*, p. viii. See discussion of Bradley, Chapter 7, pp. 135–7.
63. See *P.R.*, p. 254.
64. See *A.I.*, p. 237.
65. See *P.R.*, p. 268.
66. See *P.R.*, p. 178. See also *M.T.*, p. 205. The same claim can be made with reference to biology, as was noted previously.
67. See "Imm.," p. 695.
68. See *P.R.*, p. 146; *S.M.W.*, pp. 164, 192–93.
69. See *P.R.*, p. 71; *R.M.*, p. 93.
70. See *P.R.*, p. 349.
71. See *M.T.*, pp. 215–16.
72. See *S.M.W.*, p. 157.
73. See *F.R.*, p. 3.
74. See *M.T.*, pp. 42–43.
75. *F.R.*, p. 4.
76. Additional discussion of the general evolutionary point of view is involved in Whitehead's critical comments on the Malthusian law of population. (*A.I.*, pp. 91–99.) In his opinion, this law lacks universal application because in some cases there are intervening factors—for example, the expansion of commerce, the development of technology,

the discovery of empty continents. A final reflection is relevant: "There is something in the ready use of force which defeats its own object. Its main defect is that it bars coöperation" (*S.M.W.*, p. 297).

77. See *P.R.*, p. 334.
78. See *P.R.*, p. 53.
79. See *P.R.*, pp. 53, 365; *A.I.*, pp. 235–36.
80. See *P.R.*, p. 65.
81. See *P.R.*, p. 365.
82. See *P.R.*, p. 525.
83. See *S.M.W.*, p. 115.
84. This is Chapter 11 of *Adventures of Ideas*.
85. See *A.I.*, pp. 244, 268.
86. *The Philosophical Review*, Vol. XLI (1932), pp. 145–46 (italics in first sentence added).
87. Krikorian, Y. H., editor, *Naturalism and the Human Spirit* (New York: Columbia University Press, 1944), p. 367.
88. See *A.I.*, p. 99.
89. See Krikorian, p. 367.
90. *A.I.*, p. 245.
91. See *P.R.*, pp. 470–71.
92. See *S.M.W.*, p. 237.
93. See *P.R.*, p. 528.
94. See *P.R.*, p. 531.
95. See *P.R.*, p. 139; *M.T.*, p. 130.
96. *R.M.*, p. 160. See also *A.I.*, pp. 142–44; *M.T.*, p. 118.
97. See *P.R.*, p. 128.
98. See *P.R.*, p. 129.
99. See *S.M.W.*, p. 129.
100. See *S.M.W.*, p. 80.
101. See *S.M.W.*, p. 127.
102. See *P.R.*, pp. 91, 196–97; *A.I.*, p. 256; *M.T.*, pp. 159–61.
103. See *P.R.*, p. 31.
104. *P.R.*, p. 42. A much more useful introductory statement, though admittedly a very partial one, is the list of "nine habits of thought" which are *repudiated* by the philosophy of organism. See *P.R.*, p. viii.

Chapter 9

EVALUATION

1. "Remarks," p. 179.
2. See *P.R.*, p. 440.
3. See *S.M.W.*, p. 165.
4. See *P.R.*, p. 4.
5. References to Whitehead's writings, relevant to the topics under consideration in these evaluations, have been omitted, since they have been listed at the appropriate places in the foregoing sections of this book. See Index. (The few exceptions are provided with footnote references where necessary.)
6. See *P.R.*, pp. 32–33.
7. See *P.R.*, p. 382

8. *P.R.*, p. 224.
9. See *P.R.*, pp. 345, 436–37, 351.
10. See "Imm," p. 689.
11. See *P.R.*, p. 349.
12. *P.R.*, p. 180.
13. *P.R.*, p. 176.
14. Support for this statement can not legitimately be included in this study (already lengthy), which is an *introduction* to the theory of actual entities. It is, however, a topic which will be dealt with at a later date.

APPENDIX

WHITEHEAD'S EARLY THOUGHT

1. *T.U.A.*, p. 18.
2. See *T.U.A.*, p. viii.
3. Whitehead, *Principia Mathematica* (Cambridge: Cambridge University Press, 1910), Vol. I, further illustrates the stress on systematic inter-relation. For example, cardinal numbers, infinite numbers, the real number system, and geometry are all placed within a general science of classes and relations.
4. See Lowe, Victor, "Whitehead's Philosophical Development," in *The Philosophy of Alfred North Whitehead,* edited by P. A. Schilpp (Evanston, Illinois: Library of Living Philosophers, 1941), pp. 36–37.
5. See *A.E.*, p. 161.
6. *A.E.*, p. 160.
7. See *A.E.*, p. 229.
8. See *A.E.*, pp. 157–58.
9. See *A.E.*, p. 196.
10. *A.E.*, pp. 189–90.
11. See *A.E.*, p. 206.
12. See *A.E.*, p. 191.
13. *A.E.*, p. 246.
14. See *A.E.*, p. 243.
15. See the bibliography in *The Philosophy of Alfred North Whitehead,* edited by P. A. Schilpp (Evanston, Illinois: Library of Living Philosophers, 1941), pp. 713–17.
16. *P.N.K.*, p. 195.
17. *C.N.*, pp. vii–viii.
18. See *Rel.*, p. v.
19. *C.N.*, pp. 3, 28.
20. See *P.N.K.*, p. 98.
21. See "T.S.M.," p. 45. As has been noted (see *A.E.*, pp. 189–90), Whitehead contends that we do not actually ever experience discrete, knife-edge instants of time; rather, temporal experience is characterized by extensive duration. We are able to distinguish, within it, antecedents and subsequents.
22. See "T.S.M.," p. 46.
23. Whitehead admits that the term *duration* is perhaps an unfortunate one in that it suggests a mere abstract stretch of time. As has been noted, by *duration* he means all of nature now present for sense aware-ness. See *C.N.*, p. 53.

24. See *C.N.*, p. 165.
25. See *C.N.*, pp. 34, 66, 168.
26. See *C.N.*, pp. 185, 186; *Rel.*, pp. 67–68.
27. See *Rel.*, pp. 17–18.
28. When he makes this distinction in *The Concept of Nature,* Whitehead uses the terms *discerned* and *discernible* (pp. 49–52). In this discussion he suggests that signified events must include events in the remote past as well as events in the future. See *C.N.*, p. 52.
29. See *The Proceedings of the Aristotelian Society* (London: Williams and Norgate), 1921–22: A. N. Whitehead, "The Philosophical Aspects of the Principle of Relativity," pp. 222–23.
30. See *Rel.*, p. 26.
31. See *Rel.*, pp. 13–14.
32. See *C.N.*, pp. 26–31.
33. *C.N.*, p. 29.
34. It is obvious from the foregoing that Whitehead, at this stage of his intellectual development, was a realist rather than an idealist. His careful consideration of the apparent support for idealism provided by modern relativity theory issued in the conclusion: "I am denying . . . that some correlation with mentality can be proved to be essential for the very being of natural fact." (*Proceedings:* "Philosophical Aspects," p. 222.) See also *Proceedings,* 1922–23: A. N. Whitehead, "Uniformity and Contingency," p. 12.
35. *C.N.*, p. 59.
36. "T.S.M.," pp. 47–48. See also *C.N.*, pp. 62, 86.
37. See *P.N.K.*, p. 76.
38. See *C.N.*, pp. 61–62.
39. See *C.N.*, p. 85.
40. See "T.S.M.," pp. 49–50.
41. See *P.N.K.*, p. 202.
42. See "T.S.M.," p. 50; *C.N.*, p. 110.
43. See *P.N.K.*, pp. 62–67.
44. See *C.N.*, pp. 149–56; "T.S.M.," pp. 52–53.
45. *C.N.*, p. 155.
46. See *C.N.*, pp. 154–55; "T.S.M.," pp. 53–54.
47. Whitehead admits "a wavering between the 'class theory' of perceptual objects and the 'control theory' of physical objects, and . . . confusion between perceptual and physical objects." He then remarks: "I do not hold the class-theory now in any form, and was endeavoring . . . to get away from it" (*P.N.K.*, p. 204).
48. *C.N.*, pp. 157–58.
49. *C.N.*, p. 158.
50. *Proceedings:* "Uniformity and Contingency," p. 17.
51. See *C.N.*, p. 158.
52. It is to be noted that physical objects are called *scientific objects* in "T.S.M." See p. 55.
53. See *C.N.*, p. 158.
54. See "T.S.M.," p. 55.
55. "T.S.M.," pp. 56–57.
56. *C.N.*, p. 4.
57. *C.N.*, p. 5.

Bibliography

In addition to the books and articles written by Alfred North Whitehead listed on p. 225 the following items are relevant to the topic under consideration in this study. These books and articles are not a complete bibliography of all "treatments" of the philosophy of Whitehead. This is a "selected bibliography" dealing with the theory of "actual entities."

BOOKS PRIMARILY CONCERNED WITH "ACTUAL ENTITIES"

Blyth, J. W., *Whitehead's Theory of Knowledge*. Providence, Brown University Press, 1941.

Cesselin, F., *La Philosophie Organique de Whitehead*. Paris, Presses Universitaires de France, 1950.

Das, R., *The Philosophy of Whitehead*. London, J. Clarke & Co. Ltd., 1938.

Ely, S. L., *The Religious Availability of Whitehead's God*. Madison, The University of Wisconsin Press, 1942.

Emmet, D. M., *Whitehead's Philosophy of Organism*. London, Macmillan & Co. Ltd., 1932.

Foley, Rev. L. A., *A Critique of the Philosophy of Being of Alfred North Whitehead in the Light of Thomistic Philosophy*. Washington, D.C., The Catholic University of America Press, 1946.

Hammerschmidt, W. W., *Whitehead's Philosophy of Time*. New York, King's Crown Press, 1947.

Lintz, E. J., *The Unity of the Universe according to Alfred North Whitehead*. Fribourg, Switzerland, University of Fribourg Press, 1939.

Lowe, V.; Hartshorne, C.; Johnson, A. H., *Whitehead and the Modern World*. Boston, The Beacon Press, 1950.

Miller, D. L. and Gentry, G. V., *The Philosophy of A. N. Whitehead*. Minneapolis, Burgess Publishing Co., 1938.

Schilpp, P. A. (ed.), *The Philosophy of Alfred North Whitehead* (The Library of Living Philosophers, Vol. III). Evanston, The Library of Living Philosophers, Inc., 1941. (See subsequent references to specific chapters.)

Shahan, E. P., *Whitehead's Theory of Experience*. New York, King's Crown Press, 1950.

Wells, H. K., *Process and Unreality*. New York, King's Crown Press, 1950.

BOOKS DEALING, IN PART, WITH "ACTUAL ENTITIES"

Agar, W. E., *The Theory of the Living Organism*. Melbourne, Melbourne University Press, 1943.

Beer, S. H., *The City of Reason*. Cambridge, Mass., Harvard University Press, 1949.

Bowman, A. A., *The Sacramental Universe*. Princeton, N.J., Princeton University Press, 1939.

Emmet, D. M., *The Nature of Metaphysical Thinking*. London, The Macmillan Co., 1945.

Hallett, H. F., *Aeternitas*. Oxford, Oxford University Press, 1930.

Lillie, R. S., *General Biology and Philosophy of Organism*. Chicago, University of Chicago Press, 1945.

Mack, R. D., *The Appeal to Immediate Experience*. New York, King's Crown Press, 1945.

Metz, R., *A Hundred Years of British Philosophy*. London, George Allen & Unwin Ltd., 1938.

Morris, C. W., *Six Theories of Mind*. Chicago, The University of Chicago Press, 1932.

Ratner, J., "Introduction," *Intelligence in the Modern World, John Dewey's Philosophy*. New York, Random House, 1939.

Sheldon, W. H., *America's Progressive Philosophy*. New Haven, Yale University Press, 1942.

Smith, V. E., *Idea Men of Today*. Milwaukee, Bruce Publishing Co., 1950.

Stallknecht, N. P., *Studies in the Philosophy of Creation*. Princeton, Princeton University Press, 1934.

Taube, M., *Causation, Freedom, and Determinism*. London, George Allen & Unwin Ltd., 1936.

Ushenko, A. P., *Power and Events*. Princeton, Princeton University Press, 1946.

Weiss, P., *Reality*. Princeton, Princeton University Press, 1938.

ARTICLES

Alston, W. P., "Internal Relatedness and Pluralism in Whitehead," *The Review of Metaphysics*, V (1952), 535–58.

Alston, W. P., "Whitehead's Denial of Simple Location," *The Journal of Philosophy*, XLVIII (1951), 713–21.

Balz, A. G. A., "Whitehead, Descartes and the Bifurcation of Nature," *The Journal of Philosophy*, XXXI (1934), 281–97.

Bidney, D., "The Problem of Substance in Spinoza and Whitehead," *The Philosophical Review*, XLV (1936), 574–92.

Bixler, J. S., "Whitehead's Philosophy of Religion," in P. A. Schilpp (ed.), *The Philosophy of Alfred North Whitehead*, 487–511.

Blyth, J. W., "On Mr. Hartshorne's Understanding of Whitehead's Philosophy," *The Philosophical Review*, XLVI (1937), 523–28.

Bodkin, M., "Physical Agencies and the Divine Persuasion," *Philosophy*, XX (1945), 148–61.

Boodin, J. E., "Fiction in Science and Philosophy II," *The Journal of Philosophy*, XL (1943), 701–16.

Braham, E. G., "The Place of God in A. N. Whitehead's Philosophy," *London Quarterly Review*, CLXIV (1939), 63–69.

Brotherston, B., "The Wider Setting of 'Felt Transition,'" *The Journal of Philosophy*, XXXIX (1942), 97–104.

Christian, W. A., "The Mutual Exclusiveness of Whitehead's Actual Occasions," *The Review of Metaphysics*, II (1949), 45–75.

Coolidge, M. L., "Purposiveness without Purpose in a New Context," *Philosophy and Phenomenological Research*, IV (1943–1944), 85–93.

Cory, D., "Dr. Whitehead on Perception," *The Journal of Philosophy*, XXX (1933), 29–43.

Creegan, R. F., "The Actual Occasion and Actual History," *The Journal of Philosophy*, XXXIX (1942), 268–73.

De Burgh, W. G., "Professor Whitehead's *Modes of Thought*," *Philosophy*, XIV (1939), 205–11.

De Laguna, G., "Existence and Potentiality," *The Philosophical Review*, LX (1951), 155–76.

Dewey, J., "The Objectivism-Subjectivism of Modern Philosophy," *The Journal of Philosophy*, XXXVIII (1941), 533–42.

Dewey, J., "The Philosophy of Whitehead," in P. A. Schilpp (ed.), *The Philosophy of Alfred North Whitehead*, 641–61.

Dewey, J., "Whitehead's Philosophy," *The Philosophical Review*, XLVI (1937), 170–77.

Dunham, A. M., "Animism and Materialism in Whitehead's Organic Philosophy," *The Journal of Philosophy*, XXIX (1932), 41–47.

Forsyth, T. M., "Creative Evolution In Its Bearing On the Idea of God," *Philosophy*, XXV (1950), 195–208.

Forsyth, T. M., "The New Cosmology in Its Historical Aspect: Plato, Newton, Whitehead," *Philosophy*, VII (1932), 54–61.

Fries, H. S., "The Function of Whitehead's God," *The Monist*, XLVI (1936), 25–58.

Gentry, G. V., "Eternal Objects and the Philosophy of Organism," *Philosophy of Science*, 13 (1946), 252–60.

Gentry, G. V., "Prehension as an Explanatory Process," *The Journal of Philosophy*, XXXV (1938), 517–22.

Gentry, G. V., "The Subject in Whitehead's Philosophy," *Philosophy of Science*, XI (1944), 222–6.

Goheen, J., "Whitehead's Theory of Value," in P. A. Schilpp (ed.), *The Philosophy of Alfred North Whitehead*, 435–59.

Golightly, C., "Inquiry and Whitehead's Schematic Method," *Philosophy and Phenomenological Research*, XI (1951), 510–24.

Gregory, J. C., "Three Clues to Whitehead's Philosophy of Organism," *The Philosopher*, 3 (1951), 72–78.

Gross, M., "Whitehead's Answer to Hume," *The Journal of Philosophy*, XXXVIII (1941), 95–102.

Hall, E. W., "Of What Use Are Whitehead's Eternal Objects," *The Journal of Philosophy*, XXVII (1930), 29–44.

Harris, M. S., "Symbolic Logic and Esthetics," *The Journal of Philosophy*, XXXVII (1940), 533–46.

Hartshorne, C., "An Interpretation of Whitehead (Reply to John W. Blyth)," *The Philosophical Review*, XLVIII (1939), 415–23.

Hartshorne, C., "Is Whitehead's God the God of Religion?" *Ethics*, LIII (1942–1943), 219–27.

Hartshorne, C., "On Some Criticisms of Whitehead's Philosophy," *The Philosophical Review*, XLIV (1935), 323–44.

Hartshorne, C., "Organic and Inorganic Wholes," *Philosophy and Phenomenological Research*, III (1942), 127–36.

Herrmann, H., "The Unity of the Morphological and Functional Aspects of Living Matter," *Philosophy of Science*, 14 (1947), 254–60.

Hocking, W. E., "Whitehead on Mind and Nature," in P. A. Schilpp (ed.), *The Philosophy of Alfred North Whitehead*, 389–404.

Hooper, S. E., "A Reasonable Theory of Morality (Alexander and Whitehead)," *Philosophy*, XXV (1950), 54–67.

Hooper, S. E., "Whitehead's Philosophy: Actual Entities," *Philosophy*, XVI (1941), 285–305.

Hooper, S. E., "Whitehead's Philosophy: Eternal Objects and God," *Philosophy*, XVII (1942), 47–68.

Hooper, S. E., "Whitehead's Philosophy: Propositions and Consciousness," *Philosophy*, XX (1945), 59–75.

Hooper, S. E., "Whitehead's Philosophy: Space, Time and Things," *Philosophy*, XVIII (1943), 204–30.

Hooper, S. E., "Whitehead's Philosophy: The Higher Phases of Experience," *Philosophy* XXI (1946), 57–78.

Hooper, S. E., "Whitehead's Philosophy: The World as *Process*," *Philosophy*, XXIII (1948), 140–60.

Hooper, S. E., "Whitehead's Philosophy: Theory of Perception," *Philosophy*, XIX (1944), 136–58.

Hughes, P., "Comments and Criticism," *The Journal of Philosophy*, XXXVI (1939), 103–05.

Hughes, Percy, "Is Whitehead's Psychology Adequate," in P. A. Schilpp (ed.), *The Philosophy of Alfred North Whitehead*, 275–99.

Johnson, A. H., "A Criticism of D. Bidney's 'Spinoza and Whitehead,'" *The Philosophical Review*, XLVII (1938), 410–14.

Johnson, A. H., "A. N. Whitehead's Theory of Intuition," *The Journal of General Psychology*, 39 (1947), 61–66.

Johnson, A. H., "Recent Discussions of Alfred North Whitehead," *The Review of Metaphysics*, V (1951), 293–308.

Johnson, A. H., "The Intelligibility of Whitehead's Philosophy," *Philosophy of Science*, 10 (1943), 47–55.

Johnson, A. H., "The Psychology of Alfred North Whitehead," *The Journal of General Psychology*, 32 (1945), 175–212.

Johnson, A. H., "'Truth, Beauty and Goodness' in the Philosophy of A. N. Whitehead," *Philosophy of Science*, 11 (1944), 9–29.

Johnson, A. H., "Whitehead's Philosophy of History," *Journal of the History of Ideas*, VII (1946), 234–49.

Johnson, A. H., "Whitehead's Theory of Actual Entities: Defense and Criticism," *Philosophy of Science*, 12 (1945), 237–95.

Karlin, E., "The Nature of the Individual," *The Review of Metaphysics*, I (1947), 61–88.

King, H. R., "A. N. Whitehead and the Concept of Metaphysics," *Philosophy of Science*, 14 (1947), 132–51.

King, H. R., "Whitehead's Doctrine of Causal Efficacy," *The Journal of Philosophy*, XLVI (1949), 85–100.

Lawrence, N., "Locke and Whitehead on Individual Entities," *The Review of Metaphysics*, IV (1950), 215–38.

Lawrence, N., "Whitehead's Method of Extensive Abstraction," *Philosophy of Science*, 17 (1950), 142–63.

Lillie, R. S., "Biological Directiveness and the Psychical," *Philosophy of Science*, 14 (1947), 266–68.

Litman, A., "Prehension as Relation," *The Journal of Philosophy*, XLIV (1947), 234–40.

Loomer, B. M., "Ely on Whitehead's God," *The Journal of Religion*, XXIV (1944), 162–79.

Lowe, V., "Mr. Miller's Interpretation of Whitehead," *Philosophy of Science*, V (1938), 217–29.

Lowe, V., "The Development of Whitehead's Philosophy," in P. A. Schilpp (ed.), *The Philosophy of Alfred North Whitehead*, 17–124.

Lowe, V., "The Influence of Bergson, James and Alexander on Whitehead," *Journal of the History of Ideas*, X (1949), 267–96.

Lowe, V., "The Philosophy of Whitehead," *The Antioch Review*, 8 (1948), 223–39.

Lowe, V., "William James and Whitehead's Doctrine of Prehensions," *The Journal of Philosophy*, XXXVIII (1941), 113–26.

McCreary, J. K., "A. N. Whitehead's Theory of Feeling," *The Journal of General Psychology*, 41 (1949), 67–78.

McEwen, W. P., "Whitehead's View of Personal Growth," *The Personalist*, XXIV (1943), 46–56.

McGilvary, E. B., "Space-Time, Simple Location, and Prehension," in P. A. Schilpp (ed.), *The Philosophy of Alfred North Whitehead*, 209–39.

Menge, E. J., "Professor Whitehead's Philosophy," *The Catholic World*, 134 (1932), 420–28.

Miller, D. L., "Whitehead's Extensive Continuum," *Philosophy of Science*, 13 (1946), 144–49.

Moore, M. H., "Mr. Whitehead's Philosophy," *The Philosophical Review*, XL (1931), 265–75.

Morgan, C. L., "Subjective Aim in Professor Whitehead's Philosophy," *Journal of Philosophical Studies*, VI (1931), 281–94.

Morgan, G., Jr., "Whitehead's Theory of Value," *International Journal of Ethics*, XLVII (1936–1937), 308–16.

Morris, B., "The Art-Process and the Aesthetic Fact in Whitehead's Philosophy," in P. A. Schilpp (ed.), *The Philosophy of Alfred North Whitehead*, 461–86.

Moxley, D. C., "The Conception of God in the Philosophy of Whitehead," *Aristotelian Society Proceedings*, N.S. XXXIV (1933-4), 157–86.

Murphy, A. E., "Objective Relativism in Dewey and Whitehead," *The Philosophical Review*, XXXVI (1927), 121–44.

Murphy, A. E., "The Anticopernican Revolution," *The Journal of Philosophy*, XXVI (1929), 281–99.

Murphy, A. E., "What Is an Event?" *The Philosophical Review*, XXXVII (1928), 574–86.

Murphy, A. E., "Whitehead and the Method of Speculative Philosophy," in P. A. Schilpp (ed.), *The Philosophy of Alfred North Whitehead*, 351–80.

Needham, J., "A Biologist's View of Whitehead's Philosophy," in P. A. Schilpp (ed.), *The Philosophy of Alfred North Whitehead*, 241–71.

Northrop, F. S. C., "Whitehead's Philosophy of Science," in P. A. Schilpp (ed.), *The Philosophy of Alfred North Whitehead*, 175–207.

Page, F. H., "Whitehead's Philosophy," *The Dalhousie Review*, 28 (1948), 133–44.

Ritchie, A. D., "Whitehead's Defence of Speculative Reason," in P. A. Schilpp (ed.), *The Philosophy of Alfred North Whitehead*, 329–49.

Robson, J. W., "Whitehead's Answer to Hume," *The Journal of Philosophy*, XXXVIII (1941), 85–95.

Rotenstreich, N., "On Whitehead's Theory of Propositions," *The Review of Metaphysics*, V (1952), 389–404.

Schilpp, P. A., "Whitehead's Moral Philosophy," in P. A. Schilpp (ed.), *The Philosophy of Alfred North Whitehead*, 561–618.

Sellars, R. W., "Philosophy of Organism and Physical Realism," in P. A. Schilpp (ed.), *The Philosophy of Alfred North Whitehead*, 405–33.

Stace, W. T.; Blake, R. N.; Murphy, A. E., "Can Speculative Philosophy Be Defended?" *The Philosophical Review*, LII (1943), 116–43.

Stace, W. T., "The Problem of Unreasoned Beliefs," *Mind*, LIV (1945), 27–49; 122–47.

Stearns, I., "The Person," *The Review of Metaphysics*, III (1950), 427–36.

Taylor, A. E., "Dr. Whitehead's Philosophy of Religion," *Dublin Review*, CLXXX (1927), 17–41.

Taylor, H., "Hume's Answer to Whitehead," *The Journal of Philosophy*, XXXVIII (1941), 409–16.

Urban, W. M., "Elements of Unintelligibility in Whitehead's Philosophy," *The Journal of Philosophy*, XXXV (1938), 617–37.

Urban, W. M., "Whitehead's Philosophy of Language and its Relation to his Metaphysics," in P. A. Schilpp (ed.), *The Philosophy of Alfred North Whitehead*, 301–27.

Ushenko, A. P., "A Note on Whitehead and Relativity," *The Journal of Philosophy*, XLVII (1950), 100–02.

Ushenko, A. P., "Negative Prehension," *The Journal of Philosophy*, XXXIV (1937), 263–67.

Vlastos, G., "Organic Categories in Whitehead," *The Journal of Philosophy*, XXXIV (1937), 253–62.

Wahl, J., "La philosophie spéculative de Whitehead," *Revue Philosophique*, CXI (1931), 341–78; CXII (1931), 108–43.

Weber, P. L., "Significance of Whitehead's Philosophy for Psychology," *The Personalist*, XXI (1940), 178–87.

Weinberg, J., "The Idea of Causal Efficacy," *The Journal of Philosophy*, XLVII (1950), 397–407.

Winn, R. B., "Whitehead's Concept of Process, A Few Critical Remarks," *The Journal of Philosophy*, XXX (1933), 710–14.

N. B. *The Philosophy of Alfred North Whitehead* (P. A. Schilpp, ed.) contains a list of "selected reviews" of Whitehead's books. See pp. 701–25.

Supplementary Bibliography

BOOKS PRIMARILY CONCERNED WITH "ACTUAL ENTITIES"

Christian, W. A., *An Interpretation of Whitehead's Metaphysics.* New Haven, Yale University Press, 1959.

Leclerc, I., *Whitehead's Metaphysics: An Introductory Exposition.* London, George Allen & Unwin, and New York, Macmillan, 1958.

Mays, W., *The Philosophy of Whitehead.* London, George Allen & Unwin, and New York, Macmillan, 1959.

BOOKS DEALING, IN PART, WITH "ACTUAL ENTITIES"

Bochenski, I. M., *Contemporary European Philosophy.* Berkeley, University of California Press, 1956.

Harris, E. E., *Nature, Mind and Modern Science.* London, George Allen & Unwin, and New York, Macmillan, 1954.

Lawrence, N., *Whitehead's Philosophical Development.* Berkeley, University of California Press, 1956.

Leclerc, I. (ed.), *The Relevance of Whitehead.* London, George Allen & Unwin, 1961.

Levi, A. W., *Philosophy and the Modern World.* Bloomington, Indiana University Press, 1959.

Orsi, C., *La Filosofia Dell'Organismo di A. N. Whitehead.* Napoli, Libreria Scientifica Editrice, 1955.

Palter, R. M., *Whitehead's Philosophy of Science.* Chicago, University of Chicago Press, 1960.

Sherburne, D. W., *A Whiteheadian Aesthetic.* New Haven, Yale University Press, 1961.

Philosophical Essays for Alfred North Whitehead, New York, Longmans, Green & Co., 1936.

ARTICLES

Bakan, Mildred B., "On the Subject-Object Relationship," *The Journal of Philosophy,* LV (1958), 89-101.

Chappell, V. C., "Whitehead's Metaphysics," *The Review of Metaphysics,* XIII (1959), 278-304.

Chappell, Vere C., "Whitehead's Theory of Becoming," *The Journal of Philosophy,* LVIII (1961), 516-28.

Chiaraviglio, Lucio, "Strains," *The Journal of Philosophy*, LVIII (1961), 528-34.

Christian, William A., "Whitehead's Explanation of the Past," *The Journal of Philosophy*, LVIII (1961), 534-43.

Doan, Frank M., "On the Construction of Whitehead's Metaphysical Language," *The Review of Metaphysics*, XIII (1960), 605-622.

Eslick, Leonard J., "Substance, Change, and Causality in Whitehead," *Philosophy and Phenomenological Research*, XVIII (1958), 503-513.

Eslick, Leonard J., "Some Remarks in Reply to Professor Hartshorne," *Philosophy and Phenomenological Research*, XVIII (1958), 521-522.

Fitch, Frederic B., "Combinatory Logic and Whitehead's Theory of Prehensions," *Philosophy of Science*, XXIV (1957), 331-335.

Grunbaum, Adolf, "Whitehead's Method of Extensive Abstraction," *British Journal of the Philosophy of Science*, IV (1953), 215-226.

Harrah, David, "The Influence of Logic and Mathematics on Whitehead," *Journal of the History of Ideas*, XX (1959), 420-430.

Hartshorne, Charles, "Whitehead on Process: A Reply to Professor Eslick," *Philosophy and Phenomenological Research*, XVIII (1958), 514-520.

Hendel, Charles W., "The Subjective as a Problem," *The Philosophical Review*, LXII (1953), 327-354.

Hintz, Howard W., "A. N. Whitehead and the Philosophical Synthesis," *The Journal of Philosophy*, LII (1955), 225-243.

Johnson, A. H., "Hartshorne and the Interpretation of Whitehead," *The Review of Metaphysics*, VII (1954), 495-498.

Johnson, A. H., "Leibniz and Whitehead," *Philosophy and Phenomenological Research*, XIX (1959), 285-305.

Lawrence, Nathaniel, "The Vision of Beauty and the Temporality of Deity in Whitehead's Philosophy," *The Journal of Philosophy*, LVIII (1961), 543-553.

Leclerc, Ivor, "Whitehead and the Problem of Extension," *The Journal of Philosophy*, LVIII (1961), 559-565.

Levi, Albert William, "Substance, Process, Being," *The Journal of Philosophy*, LV (1958), 749-761.

Martin, R. M., "On Whitehead's Concept of Abstractive Hierarchies," *Philosophy and Phenomenological Research*, XX (1960), 374-382.

O'Keefe, Thomas A., "Emipiricism and Applied Mathematics in the Natural Philosophy of Whitehead," *The Modern Schoolman*, XXVIII (1950-51), 267-289.

Palter, Robert, "The Place of Mathematics in Whitehead's Philosophy," *The Journal of Philosophy*, LVIII (1961), 565-576.

Palter, Robert, "Philosophic Principles and Scientific Theory," *Philosophy of Science*, XXIII (1956), 111-135.

Reck, Andrew J., "Substance, Process, and Nature," *The Journal of Philosophy*, LV (1958), 762-772.

Rotenstreich, Nathan, "On Whitehead's Theory of Propositions," *The Review of Metaphysics*, V (1952), 389-404.

Seaman, Francis, "Whitehead and Relativity," *Philosophy of Science*, XXII (1955), 222-226.

Stebbing, L. Susan, "Concerning Substance," *Proceedings of the Aristotelian Society*, XXX (1930), 283-308.

Stebbing, L. S., Braithwaite, R. B., and Wrinch, D., "Symposium: Is the 'Fallacy of Simple Location' a Fallacy?," *Aristotelian Society, Mind, Objectivity and Fact*, Supplementary Volume VII (1927), 207-243.

Whittemore, Robert C., "Hegel's 'Science' and Whitehead's 'Modern World'," *Philosophy*, XXXI (1956), 36-54.

Whittemore, Robert C., "Time and Whitehead's God," *Tulane Studies in Philosophy*, IV (1955), 83-92.

Whittemore, Robert C., "Whitehead's Process and Bradley's Reality," *The Modern Schoolman*, XXXII (1954-55), 56-74.

Wyman, Mary A., "Whitehead's Philosophy of Science in the Light of Wordsworth's Poetry," *Philosophy of Science*, XXIII (1956), 283-296.

Index of Terms and Topics

N.B.: *Page numbers in parentheses refer to the "evaluation" chapter. Appendix A and Appendix B have not been included in this Index.*

CATALOGUE OF DOVER BOOKS

Books Explaining Science and Mathematics

WHAT IS SCIENCE?, N. Campbell. The role of experiment and measurement, the function of mathematics, the nature of scientific laws, the difference between laws and theories, the limitations of science, and many similarly provocative topics are treated clearly and without technicalities by an eminent scientist. "Still an excellent introduction to scientific philosophy," H. Margenau in PHYSICS TODAY. "A first-rate primer . . . deserves a wide audience," SCIENTIFIC AMERICAN. 192pp. 5⅜ x 8.　　　S43 Paperbound **$1.25**

THE NATURE OF PHYSICAL THEORY, P. W. Bridgman. A Nobel Laureate's clear, non-technical lectures on difficulties and paradoxes connected with frontier research on the physical sciences. Concerned with such central concepts as thought, logic, mathematics, relativity, probability, wave mechanics, etc. he analyzes the contributions of such men as Newton, Einstein, Bohr, Heisenberg, and many others. "Lucid and entertaining . . . recommended to anyone who wants to get some insight into current philosophies of science," THE NEW PHILOSOPHY. Index. xi + 138pp. 5⅜ x 8.　　　S33 Paperbound **$1.25**

EXPERIMENT AND THEORY IN PHYSICS, Max Born. A Nobel Laureate examines the nature of experiment and theory in theoretical physics and analyzes the advances made by the great physicists of our day: Heisenberg, Einstein, Bohr, Planck, Dirac, and others. The actual process of creation is detailed step-by-step by one who participated. A fine examination of the scientific method at work. 44pp. 5⅜ x 8.　　　S308 Paperbound **75¢**

THE PSYCHOLOGY OF INVENTION IN THE MATHEMATICAL FIELD, J. Hadamard. The reports of such men as Descartes, Pascal, Einstein, Poincaré, and others are considered in this investigation of the method of idea-creation in mathematics and other sciences and the thinking process in general. How do ideas originate? What is the role of the unconscious? What is Poincaré's forgetting hypothesis? are some of the fascinating questions treated. A penetrating analysis of Einstein's thought processes concludes the book. xiii + 145pp. 5⅜ x 8.　　　T107 Paperbound **$1.25**

THE NATURE OF LIGHT AND COLOUR IN THE OPEN AIR, M. Minnaert. Why are shadows sometimes blue, sometimes green, or other colors depending on the light and surroundings? What causes mirages? Why do multiple suns and moons appear in the sky? Professor Minnaert explains these unusual phenomena and hundreds of others in simple, easy-to-understand terms based on optical laws and the properties of light and color. No mathematics is required but artists, scientists, students, and everyone fascinated by these "tricks" of nature will find thousands of useful and amazing pieces of information. Hundreds of observational experiments are suggested which require no special equipment. 200 illustrations; 42 photos. xvi + 362pp. 5⅜ x 8.　　　T196 Paperbound **$2.00**

THE UNIVERSE OF LIGHT, W. Bragg. Sir William Bragg, Nobel Laureate and great modern physicist, is also well known for his powers of clear exposition. Here he analyzes all aspects of light for the layman: lenses, reflection, refraction, the optics of vision, x-rays, the photoelectric effect, etc. He tells you what causes the color of spectra, rainbows, and soap bubbles, how magic mirrors work, and much more. Dozens of simple experiments are described. Preface. Index. 199 line drawings and photographs, including 2 full-page color plates. x + 283pp. 5⅜ x 8.　　　T538 Paperbound **$1.85**

SOAP-BUBBLES: THEIR COLOURS AND THE FORCES THAT MOULD THEM, C. V. Boys. For continuing popularity and validity as scientific primer, few books can match this volume of easily-followed experiments, explanations. Lucid exposition of complexities of liquid films, surface tension and related phenomena, bubbles' reaction to heat, motion, music, magnetic fields. Experiments with capillary attraction, soap bubbles on frames, composite bubbles, liquid cylinders and jets, bubbles other than soap, etc. Wonderful introduction to scientific method, natural laws that have many ramifications in areas of modern physics. Only complete edition in print. New Introduction by S. Z. Lewin, New York University. 83 illustrations; 1 full-page color plate. xii + 190pp. 5⅜ x 8½.　　　T542 Paperbound **95¢**

CATALOGUE OF DOVER BOOKS

THE STORY OF X-RAYS FROM RONTGEN TO ISOTOPES, A. R. Bleich, M.D. This book, by a member of the American College of Radiology, gives the scientific explanation of x-rays, their applications in medicine, industry and art, and their danger (and that of atmospheric radiation) to the individual and the species. You learn how radiation therapy is applied against cancer, how x-rays diagnose heart disease and other ailments, how they are used to examine mummies for information on diseases of early societies, and industrial materials for hidden weaknesses. 54 illustrations show x-rays of flowers, bones, stomach, gears with flaws, etc. 1st publication. Index. xix + 186pp. 5⅜ x 8. T622 Paperbound **$1.35**

SPINNING TOPS AND GYROSCOPIC MOTION, John Perry. A classic elementary text of the dynamics of rotation — the behavior and use of rotating bodies such as gyroscopes and tops. In simple, everyday English you are shown how quasi-rigidity is induced in discs of paper, smoke rings, chains, etc., by rapid motions; why a gyrostat falls and why a top rises; precession; how the earth's motion affects climate; and many other phenomena. Appendix on practical use of gyroscopes. 62 figures. 128pp. 5⅜ x 8. T416 Paperbound **$1.00**

SNOW CRYSTALS, W. A. Bentley, M. J. Humphreys. For almost 50 years W. A. Bentley photographed snow flakes in his laboratory in Jericho, Vermont; in 1931 the American Meteorological Society gathered together the best of his work, some 2400 photographs of snow flakes, plus a few ice flowers, windowpane frosts, dew, frozen rain, and other ice formations. Pictures were selected for beauty and scientific value. A very valuable work to anyone in meteorology, cryology; most interesting to layman; extremely useful for artist who wants beautiful, crystalline designs. All copyright free. Unabridged reprint of 1931 edition. 2453 illustrations. 227pp. 8 x 10½. T287 Paperbound **$3.00**

A DOVER SCIENCE SAMPLER, edited by George Barkin. A collection of brief, non-technical passages from 44 Dover Books Explaining Science for the enjoyment of the science-minded browser. Includes work of Bertrand Russell, Poincaré, Laplace, Max Born, Galileo, Newton; material on physics, mathematics, metallurgy, anatomy, astronomy, chemistry, etc. You will be fascinated by Martin Gardner's analysis of the sincere pseudo-scientist, Moritz's account of Newton's absentmindedness, Bernard's examples of human vivisection, etc. Illustrations from the Diderot Pictorial Encyclopedia and De Re Metallica. 64 pages. **FREE**

THE STORY OF ATOMIC THEORY AND ATOMIC ENERGY, J. G. Feinberg. A broader approach to subject of nuclear energy and its cultural implications than any other similar source. Very readable, informal, completely non-technical text. Begins with first atomic theory, 600 B.C. and carries you through the work of Mendelejeff, Röntgen, Madame Curie, to Einstein's equation and the A-bomb. New chapter goes through thermonuclear fission, binding energy, other events up to 1959. Radioactive decay and radiation hazards, future benefits, work of Bohr, moderns, hundreds more topics. "Deserves special mention . . . not only authoritative but thoroughly popular in the best sense of the word," Saturday Review. Formerly, "The Atom Story." Expanded with new chapter. Three appendixes. Index. 34 illustrations. vii + 243pp. 5⅜ x 8. T625 Paperbound **$1.60**

THE STRANGE STORY OF THE QUANTUM, AN ACCOUNT FOR THE GENERAL READER OF THE GROWTH OF IDEAS UNDERLYING OUR PRESENT ATOMIC KNOWLEDGE, B. Hoffmann. Presents lucidly and expertly, with barest amount of mathematics, the problems and theories which led to modern quantum physics. Dr. Hoffmann begins with the closing years of the 19th century, when certain trifling discrepancies were noticed, and with illuminating analogies and examples takes you through the brilliant concepts of Planck, Einstein, Pauli, Broglie, Bohr, Schroedinger, Heisenberg, Dirac, Sommerfeld, Feynman, etc. This edition includes a new, long postscript carrying the story through 1958. "Of the books attempting an account of the history and contents of our modern atomic physics which have come to my attention, this is the best," H. Margenau, Yale University, in "American Journal of Physics." 32 tables and line illustrations. Index. 275pp. 5⅜ x 8. T518 Paperbound **$1.50**

SPACE AND TIME, E. Borel. Written by a versatile mathematician of world renown with his customary lucidity and precision, this introduction to relativity for the layman presents scores of examples, analogies, and illustrations that open up new ways of thinking about space and time. It covers abstract geometry and geographical maps, continuity and topology, the propagation of light, the special theory of relativity, the general theory of relativity, theoretical researches, and much more. Mathematical notes. 2 Indexes. 4 Appendices. 15 figures. xvi + 243pp. 5⅜ x 8. T592 Paperbound **$1.45**

FROM EUCLID TO EDDINGTON: A STUDY OF THE CONCEPTIONS OF THE EXTERNAL WORLD, Sir Edmund Whittaker. A foremost British scientist traces the development of theories of natural philosophy from the western rediscovery of Euclid to Eddington, Einstein, Dirac, etc. The inadequacy of classical physics is contrasted with present day attempts to understand the physical world through relativity, non-Euclidean geometry, space curvature, wave mechanics, etc. 5 major divisions of examination: Space; Time and Movement; the Concepts of Classical Physics; the Concepts of Quantum Mechanics; the Eddington Universe. 212pp. 5⅜ x 8. T491 Paperbound **$1.35**

Nature, Biology

NATURE RECREATION: Group Guidance for the Out-of-doors, William Gould Vinal. Intended for both the uninitiated nature instructor and the education student on the college level, this complete "how-to" program surveys the entire area of nature education for the young. Philosophy of nature recreation; requirements, responsibilities, important information for group leaders; nature games; suggested group projects; conducting meetings and getting discussions started; etc. Scores of immediately applicable teaching aids, plus completely updated sources of information, pamphlets, field guides, recordings, etc. Bibliography. 74 photographs. + 310pp. 5⅜ x 8½.   T1015 Paperbound **$1.75**

HOW TO KNOW THE WILD FLOWERS, Mrs. William Starr Dana. Classic nature book that has introduced thousands to wonders of American wild flowers. Color-season principle of organization is easy to use, even by those with no botanical training, and the genial, refreshing discussions of history, folklore, uses of over 1,000 native and escape flowers, foliage plants are informative as well as fun to read. Over 170 full-page plates, collected from several editions, may be colored in to make permanent records of finds. Revised to conform with 1950 edition of Gray's Manual of Botany. xlii + 438pp. 5⅜ x 8½.   T332 Paperbound **$2.00**

HOW TO KNOW THE FERNS, F. T. Parsons. Ferns, among our most lovely native plants, are all too little known. This classic of nature lore will enable the layman to identify almost any American fern he may come across. After an introduction on the structure and life of ferns, the 57 most important ferns are fully pictured and described (arranged upon a simple identification key). Index of Latin and English names. 61 illustrations and 42 full-page plates. xiv + 215pp. 5⅜ x 8.   T740 Paperbound **$1.35**

MANUAL OF THE TREES OF NORTH AMERICA, Charles Sprague Sargent. Still unsurpassed as most comprehensive, reliable study of North American tree characteristics, precise locations and distribution. By dean of American dendrologists. Every tree native to U.S., Canada, Alaska, 185 genera, 717 species, described in detail—leaves, flowers, fruit, winterbuds, bark, wood, growth habits etc. plus discussion of varieties and local variants, immaturity variations. Over 100 keys, including unusual 11-page analytical key to genera, aid in identification. 783 clear illustrations of flowers, fruit, leaves. An unmatched permanent reference work for all nature lovers. Second enlarged (1926) edition. Synopsis of families. Analytical key to genera. Glossary of technical terms. Index. 783 illustrations, 1 map. Two volumes. Total of 982pp. 5⅜ x 8.   T277 Vol. I Paperbound **$2.25**
                    T278 Vol. II Paperbound **$2.25**
                    The set **$4.50**

TREES OF THE EASTERN AND CENTRAL UNITED STATES AND CANADA, W. M. Harlow. A revised edition of a standard middle-level guide to native trees and important escapes. More than 140 trees are described in detail, and illustrated with more than 600 drawings and photographs. Supplementary keys will enable the careful reader to identify almost any tree he might encounter. xiii + 288pp. 5⅜ x 8.   T395 Paperbound **$1.35**

GUIDE TO SOUTHERN TREES, Ellwood S. Harrar and J. George Harrar. All the essential information about trees indigenous to the South, in an extremely handy format. Introductory essay on methods of tree classification and study, nomenclature, chief divisions of Southern trees, etc. Approximately 100 keys and synopses allow for swift, accurate identification of trees. Numerous excellent illustrations, non-technical text make this a useful book for teachers of biology or natural science, nature lovers, amateur naturalists. Revised 1962 edition. Index. Bibliography. Glossary of technical terms. 920 illustrations; 201 full-page plates. ix + 709pp. 4⅝ x 6⅜.   T945 Paperbound **$2.35**

FRUIT KEY AND TWIG KEY TO TREES AND SHRUBS, W. M. Harlow. Bound together in one volume for the first time, these handy and accurate keys to fruit and twig identification are the only guides of their sort with photographs (up to 3 times natural size). "Fruit Key": Key to over 120 different deciduous and evergreen fruits. 139 photographs and 11 line drawings. Synoptic summary of fruit types. Bibliography. 2 Indexes (common and scientific names). "Twig Key": Key to over 160 different twigs and buds. 173 photographs. Glossary of technical terms. Bibliography. 2 Indexes (common and scientific names). Two volumes bound as one. Total of xvii + 126pp. 5⅝ x 8⅜.   T511 Paperbound **$1.25**

INSECT LIFE AND INSECT NATURAL HISTORY, S. W. Frost. A work emphasizing habits, social life, and ecological relations of insects, rather than more academic aspects of classification and morphology. Prof. Frost's enthusiasm and knowledge are everywhere evident as he discusses insect associations and specialized habits like leaf-rolling, leaf-mining, and casemaking, the gall insects, the boring insects, aquatic insects, etc. He examines all sorts of matters not usually covered in general works, such as: insects as human food, insect music and musicians, insect response to electric and radio waves, use of insects in art and literature. The admirably executed purpose of this book, which covers the middle ground between elementary treatment and scholarly monographs, is to excite the reader to observe for himself. Over 700 illustrations. Extensive bibliography. x + 524pp. 5⅜ x 8.   T517 Paperbound **$2.45**

CATALOGUE OF DOVER BOOKS

COMMON SPIDERS OF THE UNITED STATES, J. H. Emerton. Here is a nature hobby you can pursue right in your own cellar! Only non-technical, but thorough, reliable guide to spiders for the layman. Over 200 spiders from all parts of the country, arranged by scientific classification, are identified by shape and color, number of eyes, habitat and range, habits, etc. Full text, 501 line drawings and photographs, and valuable introduction explain webs, poisons, threads, capturing and preserving spiders, etc. Index. New synoptic key by S. W. Frost. xxiv + 225pp. 5⅜ x 8. T223 Paperbound **$1.45**

THE LIFE STORY OF THE FISH: HIS MANNERS AND MORALS, Brian Curtis. A comprehensive, non-technical survey of just about everything worth knowing about fish. Written for the aquarist, the angler, and the layman with an inquisitive mind, the text covers such topics as evolution, external covering and protective coloration, physics and physiology of vision, maintenance of equilibrium, function of the lateral line canal for auditory and temperature senses, nervous system, function of the air bladder, reproductive system and methods—courtship, mating, spawning, care of young—and many more. Also sections on game fish, the problems of conservation and a fascinating chapter on fish curiosities. "Clear, simple language . . . excellent judgment in choice of subjects . . . delightful sense of humor," New York Times. Revised (1949) edition. Index. Bibliography of 72 items. 6 full-page photographic plates. xii + 284pp. 5⅜ x 8. T929 Paperbound **$1.65**

BATS, Glover Morrill Allen. The most comprehensive study of bats as a life-form by the world's foremost authority. A thorough summary of just about everything known about this fascinating and mysterious flying mammal, including its unique location sense, hibernation and cycles, its habitats and distribution, its wing structure and flying habits, and its relationship to man in the long history of folklore and superstition. Written on a middle-level, the book can be profitably studied by a trained zoologist and thoroughly enjoyed by the layman. "An absorbing text with excellent illustrations. Bats should have more friends and fewer thoughtless detractors as a result of the publication of this volume," William Beebe, Books. Extensive bibliography. 57 photographs and illustrations. x + 368pp. 5⅜ x 8½. T984 Paperbound **$2.00**

BIRDS AND THEIR ATTRIBUTES, Glover Morrill Allen. A fine general introduction to birds as living organisms, especially valuable because of emphasis on structure, physiology, habits, behavior. Discusses relationship of bird to man, early attempts at scientific ornithology, feathers and coloration, skeletal structure including bills, legs and feet, wings. Also food habits, evolution and present distribution, feeding and nest-building, still unsolved questions of migrations and location sense, many more similar topics. Final chapter on classification, nomenclature. A good popular-level summary for the biologist; a first-rate introduction for the layman. Reprint of 1925 edition. References and index. 51 illustrations. viii + 338pp. 5⅜ x 8½. T957 Paperbound **$1.85**

LIFE HISTORIES OF NORTH AMERICAN BIRDS, Arthur Cleveland Bent. Bent's monumental series of books on North American birds, prepared and published under auspices of Smithsonian Institute, is the definitive coverage of the subject, the most-used single source of information. Now the entire set is to be made available by Dover in inexpensive editions. This encyclopedic collection of detailed, specific observations utilizes reports of hundreds of contemporary observers, writings of such naturalists as Audubon, Burroughs, William Brewster, as well as author's own extensive investigations. Contains literally everything known about life history of each bird considered: nesting, eggs, plumage, distribution and migration, voice, enemies, courtship, etc. These not over-technical works are musts for ornithologists, conservationists, amateur naturalists, anyone seriously interested in American birds.

BIRDS OF PREY. More than 100 subspecies of hawks, falcons, eagles, buzzards, condors and owls, from the common barn owl to the extinct caracara of Guadaloupe Island. 400 photographs. Two volume set. Index for each volume. Bibliographies of 403, 520 items. 197 full-page plates. Total of 907pp. 5⅜ x 8½. Vol. I T931 Paperbound **$2.50**
Vol. II T932 Paperbound **$2.50**

WILD FOWL. Ducks, geese, swans, and tree ducks—73 different subspecies. Two volume set. Index for each volume. Bibliographies of 124, 144 items. 106 full-page plates. Total of 685pp. 5⅜ x 8½. Vol. I T285 Paperbound **$2.50**
Vol. II T286 Paperbound **$2.50**

SHORE BIRDS. 81 varieties (sandpipers, woodcocks, plovers, snipes, phalaropes, curlews, oyster catchers, etc.). More than 200 photographs of eggs, nesting sites, adult and young of important species. Two volume set. Index for each volume. Bibliographies of 261, 188 items. 121 full-page plates. Total of 860pp. 5⅜ x 8½. Vol. I T933 Paperbound **$2.35**
Vol. II T934 Paperbound **$2.35**

THE LIFE OF PASTEUR, R. Vallery-Radot. 13th edition of this definitive biography, cited in Encyclopaedia Britannica. Authoritative, scholarly, well-documented with contemporary quotes, observations; gives complete picture of Pasteur's personal life; especially thorough presentation of scientific activities with silkworms, fermentation, hydrophobia, inoculation, etc. Introduction by Sir William Osler. Index. 505pp. 5⅜ x 8. T632 Paperbound **$2.00**

Puzzles, Mathematical Recreations

SYMBOLIC LOGIC and THE GAME OF LOGIC, Lewis Carroll. "Symbolic Logic" is not concerned with modern symbolic logic, but is instead a collection of over 380 problems posed with charm and imagination, using the syllogism, and a fascinating diagrammatic method of drawing conclusions. In "The Game of Logic" Carroll's whimsical imagination devises a logical game played with 2 diagrams and counters (included) to manipulate hundreds of tricky syllogisms. The final section, "Hit or Miss" is a lagniappe of 101 additional puzzles in the delightful Carroll manner. Until this reprint edition, both of these books were rarities costing up to $15 each. Symbolic Logic: Index. xxxi + 199pp. The Game of Logic: 96pp. 2 vols. bound as one. 5⅜ x 8. **T492 Paperbound $1.50**

PILLOW PROBLEMS and A TANGLED TALE, Lewis Carroll. One of the rarest of all Carroll's works, "Pillow Problems" contains 72 original math puzzles, all typically ingenious. Particularly fascinating are Carroll's answers which remain exactly as he thought them out, reflecting his actual mental process. The problems in "A Tangled Tale" are in story form, originally appearing as a monthly magazine serial. Carroll not only gives the solutions, but uses answers sent in by readers to discuss wrong approaches and misleading paths, and grades them for insight. Both of these books were rarities until this edition, "Pillow Problems" costing up to $25, and "A Tangled Tale" $15. Pillow Problems: Preface and Introduction by Lewis Carroll. xx + 109pp. A Tangled Tale: 6 illustrations. 152pp. Two vols. bound as one. 5⅜ x 8. **T493 Paperbound $1.50**

AMUSEMENTS IN MATHEMATICS, Henry Ernest Dudeney. The foremost British originator of mathematical puzzles is always intriguing, witty, and paradoxical in this classic, one of the largest collections of mathematical amusements. More than 430 puzzles, problems, and paradoxes. Mazes and games, problems on number manipulation, unicursal and other route problems, puzzles on measuring, weighing, packing, age, kinship, chessboards, joiners', crossing river, plane figure dissection, and many others. Solutions. More than 450 illustrations. vii + 258pp. 5⅜ x 8. **T473 Paperbound $1.25**

THE CANTERBURY PUZZLES, Henry Dudeney. Chaucer's pilgrims set one another problems in story form. Also Adventures of the Puzzle Club, the Strange Escape of the King's Jester, the Monks of Riddlewell, the Squire's Christmas Puzzle Party, and others. All puzzles are original, based on dissecting plane figures, arithmetic, algebra, elementary calculus and other branches of mathematics, and purely logical ingenuity. "The limit of ingenuity and intricacy," The Observer. Over 110 puzzles. Full Solutions. 150 illustrations. vii + 225pp. 5⅜ x 8. **T474 Paperbound $1.25**

MATHEMATICAL EXCURSIONS, H. A. Merrill. Even if you hardly remember your high school math, you'll enjoy the 90 stimulating problems contained in this book and you will come to understand a great many mathematical principles with surprisingly little effort. Many useful shortcuts and diversions not generally known are included: division by inspection, Russian peasant multiplication, memory systems for pi, building odd and even magic squares, square roots by geometry, dyadic systems, and many more. Solutions to difficult problems. 50 illustrations. 145pp. 5⅜ x 8. **T350 Paperbound $1.00**

MAGIC SQUARES AND CUBES, W. S. Andrews. Only book-length treatment in English, a thorough non-technical description and analysis. Here are nasik, overlapping, pandiagonal, serrated squares; magic circles, cubes, spheres, rhombuses. Try your hand at 4-dimensional magical figures! Much unusual folklore and tradition included. High school algebra is sufficient. 754 diagrams and illustrations. viii + 419pp. 5⅜ x 8. **T658 Paperbound $1.85**

CALIBAN'S PROBLEM BOOK: MATHEMATICAL, INFERENTIAL AND CRYPTOGRAPHIC PUZZLES, H. Phillips (Caliban), S. T. Shovelton, G. S. Marshall. 105 ingenious problems by the greatest living creator of puzzles based on logic and inference. Rigorous, modern, piquant; reflecting their author's unusual personality, these intermediate and advanced puzzles all involve the ability to reason clearly through complex situations; some call for mathematical knowledge, ranging from algebra to number theory. Solutions. xi + 180pp. 5⅜ x 8. **T736 Paperbound $1.25**

MATHEMATICAL PUZZLES FOR BEGINNERS AND ENTHUSIASTS, G. Mott-Smith. 188 mathematical puzzles based on algebra, dissection of plane figures, permutations, and probability, that will test and improve your powers of inference and interpretation. The Odic Force, The Spider's Cousin, Ellipse Drawing, theory and strategy of card and board games like tit-tat-toe, go moku, salvo, and many others. 100 pages of detailed mathematical explanations. Appendix of primes, square roots, etc. 135 illustrations. 2nd revised edition. 248pp. 5⅜ x 8. **T198 Paperbound $1.00**

MATHEMAGIC, MAGIC PUZZLES, AND GAMES WITH NUMBERS, R. V. Heath. More than 60 new puzzles and stunts based on the properties of numbers. Easy techniques for multiplying large numbers mentally, revealing hidden numbers magically, finding the date of any day in any year, and dozens more. Over 30 pages devoted to magic squares, triangles, cubes, circles, etc. Edited by J. S. Meyer. 76 illustrations. 128pp. 5⅜ x 8. **T110 Paperbound $1.00**

CATALOGUE OF DOVER BOOKS

THE BOOK OF MODERN PUZZLES, G. L. Kaufman. A completely new series of puzzles as fascinating as crossword and deduction puzzles but based upon different principles and techniques. Simple 2-minute teasers, word labyrinths, design and pattern puzzles, logic and observation puzzles — over 150 braincrackers. Answers to all problems. 116 illustrations. 192pp. 5⅜ x 8.
T143 Paperbound **$1.00**

NEW WORD PUZZLES, G. L. Kaufman. 100 ENTIRELY NEW puzzles based on words and their combinations that will delight crossword puzzle, Scrabble and Jotto fans. Chess words, based on the moves of the chess king; design-onyms, symmetrical designs made of synonyms; rhymed double-crostics; syllable sentences; addle letter anagrams; alphagrams; linkograms; and many others all brand new. Full solutions. Space to work problems. 196 figures. vi + 122pp. 5⅜ x 8.
T344 Paperbound **$1.00**

MAZES AND LABYRINTHS: A BOOK OF PUZZLES, W. Shepherd. Mazes, formerly associated with mystery and ritual, are still among the most intriguing of intellectual puzzles. This is a novel and different collection of 50 amusements that embody the principle of the maze: mazes in the classical tradition; 3-dimensional, ribbon, and Möbius-strip mazes; hidden messages; spatial arrangements; etc.—almost all built on amusing story situations. 84 illustrations. Essay on maze psychology. Solutions. xv + 122pp. 5⅜ x 8.
T731 Paperbound **$1.00**

MAGIC TRICKS & CARD TRICKS, W. Jonson. Two books bound as one. 52 tricks with cards, 37 tricks with coins, bills, eggs, smoke, ribbons, slates, etc. Details on presentation, misdirection, and routining will help you master such famous tricks as the Changing Card, Card in the Pocket, Four Aces, Coin Through the Hand, Bill in the Egg, Afghan Bands, and over 75 others. If you follow the lucid exposition and key diagrams carefully, you will finish these two books with an astonishing mastery of magic. 106 figures. 224pp. 5⅜ x 8. T909 Paperbound **$1.00**

PANORAMA OF MAGIC, Milbourne Christopher. A profusely illustrated history of stage magic, a unique selection of prints and engravings from the author's private collection of magic memorabilia, the largest of its kind. Apparatus, stage settings and costumes; ingenious ads distributed by the performers and satiric broadsides passed around in the streets ridiculing pompous showmen; programs; decorative souvenirs. The lively text, by one of America's foremost professional magicians, is full of anecdotes about almost legendary wizards: Dede, the Egyptian; Philadelphia, the wonder-worker; Robert-Houdin, "the father of modern magic;" Harry Houdini; scores more. Altogether a pleasure package for anyone interested in magic, stage setting and design, ethnology, psychology, or simply in unusual people. A Dover original. 295 illustrations; 8 in full color. Index. viii + 216pp. 8⅜ x 11¼.
T774 Paperbound **$2.25**

HOUDINI ON MAGIC, Harry Houdini. One of the greatest magicians of modern times explains his most prized secrets. How locks are picked, with illustrated picks and skeleton keys; how a girl is sawed into twins; how to walk through a brick wall — Houdini's explanations of 44 stage tricks with many diagrams. Also included is a fascinating discussion of great magicians of the past and the story of his fight against fraudulent mediums and spiritualists. Edited by W.B. Gibson and M.N. Young. Bibliography. 155 figures, photos. xv + 280pp. 5⅜ x 8.
T384 Paperbound **$1.35**

MATHEMATICS, MAGIC AND MYSTERY, Martin Gardner. Why do card tricks work? How do magicians perform astonishing mathematical feats? How is stage mind-reading possible? This is the first book length study explaining the application of probability, set theory, theory of numbers, topology, etc., to achieve many startling tricks. Non-technical, accurate, detailed! 115 sections discuss tricks with cards, dice, coins, knots, geometrical vanishing illusions, how a Curry square "demonstrates" that the sum of the parts may be greater than the whole, and dozens of others. No sleight of hand necessary! 135 illustrations. xii + 174pp. 5⅜ x 8.
T335 Paperbound **$1.00**

EASY-TO-DO ENTERTAINMENTS AND DIVERSIONS WITH COINS, CARDS, STRING, PAPER AND MATCHES, R. M. Abraham. Over 300 tricks, games and puzzles will provide young readers with absorbing fun. Sections on card games; paper-folding; tricks with coins, matches and pieces of string; games for the agile; toy-making from common household objects; mathematical recreations; and 50 miscellaneous pastimes. Anyone in charge of groups of youngsters, including hard-pressed parents, and in need of suggestions on how to keep children sensibly amused and quietly content will find this book indispensable. Clear, simple text, copious number of delightful line drawings and illustrative diagrams. Originally titled "Winter Nights Entertainments." Introduction by Lord Baden Powell. 329 illustrations. v + 186pp. 5⅜ x 8½.
T921 Paperbound **$1.00**

STRING FIGURES AND HOW TO MAKE THEM, Caroline Furness Jayne. 107 string figures plus variations selected from the best primitive and modern examples developed by Navajo, Apache, pygmies of Africa, Eskimo, in Europe, Australia, China, etc. The most readily understandable, easy-to-follow book in English on perennially popular recreation. Crystal-clear exposition; step-by-step diagrams. Everyone from kindergarten children to adults looking for unusual diversion will be endlessly amused. Index. Bibliography. Introduction by A. C. Haddon. 17 full-page plates. 960 illustrations. xxiii + 401pp. 5⅜ x 8½.
T152 Paperbound **$2.00**

Entertainments, Humor

ODDITIES AND CURIOSITIES OF WORDS AND LITERATURE, C. Bombaugh, edited by M. Gardner. The largest collection of idiosyncratic prose and poetry techniques in English, a legendary work in the curious and amusing bypaths of literary recreations and the play technique in literature—so important in modern works. Contains alphabetic poetry, acrostics, palindromes, scissors verse, centos, emblematic poetry, famous literary puns, hoaxes, notorious slips of the press, hilarious mistranslations, and much more. Revised and enlarged with modern material by Martin Gardner. 368pp. 5⅜ x 8.   T759 Paperbound **$1.50**

A NONSENSE ANTHOLOGY, collected by Carolyn Wells. 245 of the best nonsense verses ever written, including nonsense puns, absurd arguments, mock epics and sagas, nonsense ballads, odes, "sick" verses, dog-Latin verses, French nonsense verses, songs. By Edward Lear, Lewis Carroll, Gelett Burgess, W. S. Gilbert, Hilaire Belloc, Peter Newell, Oliver Herford, etc., 83 writers in all plus over four score anonymous nonsense verses. A special section of limericks, plus famous nonsense such as Carroll's "Jabberwocky" and Lear's "The Jumblies" and much excellent verse virtually impossible to locate elsewhere. For 50 years considered the best anthology available. Index of first lines specially prepared for this edition. Introduction by Carolyn Wells. 3 indexes: Title, Author, First lines. xxxiii + 279pp.
T499 Paperbound **$1.35**

THE BAD CHILD'S BOOK OF BEASTS, MORE BEASTS FOR WORSE CHILDREN, and A MORAL ALPHABET, H. Belloc. Hardly an anthology of humorous verse has appeared in the last 50 years without at least a couple of these famous nonsense verses. But one must see the entire volumes—with all the delightful original illustrations by Sir Basil Blackwood—to appreciate fully Belloc's charming and witty verses that play so subacidly on the platitudes of life and morals that beset his day—and ours. A great humor classic. Three books in one. Total of 157pp. 5⅜ x 8.   T749 Paperbound **$1.00**

THE DEVIL'S DICTIONARY, Ambrose Bierce. Sardonic and irreverent barbs puncturing the pomposities and absurdities of American politics, business, religion, literature, and arts, by the country's greatest satirist in the classic tradition. Epigrammatic as Shaw, piercing as Swift, American as Mark Twain, Will Rogers, and Fred Allen, Bierce will always remain the favorite of a small coterie of enthusiasts, and of writers and speakers whom he supplies with "some of the most gorgeous witticisms of the English language" (H. L. Mencken). Over 1000 entries in alphabetical order. 144pp. 5⅜ x 8.   T487 Paperbound **$1.00**

THE PURPLE COW AND OTHER NONSENSE, Gelett Burgess. The best of Burgess's early nonsense, selected from the first edition of the "Burgess Nonsense Book." Contains many of his most unusual and truly awe-inspiring pieces: 36 nonsense quatrains, the Poems of Patagonia, Alphabet of Famous Goops, and the other hilarious (and rare) adult nonsense that place him in the forefront of American humorists. All pieces are accompanied by the original Burgess illustrations. 123 illustrations. xiii + 113pp. 5⅜ x 8.   T772 Paperbound **$1.00**

MY PIOUS FRIENDS AND DRUNKEN COMPANIONS and MORE PIOUS FRIENDS AND DRUNKEN COMPANIONS, Frank Shay. Folksingers, amateur and professional, and everyone who loves singing: here, available for the first time in 30 years, is this valued collection of 132 ballads, blues, vaudeville numbers, drinking songs, sea chanties, comedy songs. Songs of pre-Beatnik Bohemia; songs from all over America, England, France, Australia; the great songs of the Naughty Nineties and early twentieth-century America. Over a third with music. Woodcuts by John Held, Jr. convey perfectly the brash insouciance of an era of rollicking unabashed song. 12 illustrations by John Held, Jr. Two indexes (Titles and First lines and Choruses). Introductions by the author. Two volumes bound as one. Total of xvi + 235pp. 5⅜ x 8½.
T946 Paperbound **$1.25**

HOW TO TELL THE BIRDS FROM THE FLOWERS, R. W. Wood. How not to confuse a carrot with a parrot, a grape with an ape, a puffin with nuffin. Delightful drawings, clever puns, absurd little poems point out far-fetched resemblances in nature. The author was a leading physicist. Introduction by Margaret Wood White. 106 illus. 60pp. 5⅜ x 8.
T523 Paperbound **75¢**

PECK'S BAD BOY AND HIS PA, George W. Peck. The complete edition, containing both volumes, of one of the most widely read American humor books. The endless ingenious pranks played by bad boy "Hennery" on his pa and the grocery man, the outraged pomposity of Pa, the perpetual ridiculing of middle class institutions, are as entertaining today as they were in 1883. No pale sophistications or subtleties, but rather humor vigorous, raw, earthy, imaginative, and, as folk humor often is, sadistic. This peculiarly fascinating book is also valuable to historians and students of American culture as a portrait of an age. 100 original illustrations by True Williams. Introduction by E. F. Bleiler. 347pp. 5⅜ x 8.
T497 Paperbound **$1.35**

THE HUMOROUS VERSE OF LEWIS CARROLL. Almost every poem Carroll ever wrote, the largest collection ever published, including much never published elsewhere: 150 parodies, burlesques, riddles, ballads, acrostics, etc., with 130 original illustrations by Tenniel, Carroll, and others. "Addicts will be grateful . . . there is nothing for the faithful to do but sit down and fall to the banquet," N. Y. Times. Index to first lines. xiv + 446pp. 5⅜ x 8.
T654 Paperbound **$2.00**

DIVERSIONS AND DIGRESSIONS OF LEWIS CARROLL. A major new treasure for Carroll fans! Rare privately published humor, fantasy, puzzles, and games by Carroll at his whimsical best, with a new vein of frank satire. Includes many new mathematical amusements and recreations, among them the fragmentary Part III of "Curiosa Mathematica." Contains "The Rectory Umbrella," "The New Belfry," "The Vision of the Three T's," and much more. New 32-page supplement of rare photographs taken by Carroll. x + 375pp. 5⅜ x 8.
T732 Paperbound **$1.65**

THE COMPLETE NONSENSE OF EDWARD LEAR. This is the only complete edition of this master of gentle madness available at a popular price. A BOOK OF NONSENSE, NONSENSE SONGS, MORE NONSENSE SONGS AND STORIES in their entirety with all the old favorites that have delighted children and adults for years. The Dong With A Luminous Nose, The Jumblies, The Owl and the Pussycat, and hundreds of other bits of wonderful nonsense. 214 limericks, 3 sets of Nonsense Botany, 5 Nonsense Alphabets, 546 drawings by Lear himself, and much more. 320pp. 5⅜ x 8.
T167 Paperbound **$1.00**

THE MELANCHOLY LUTE, The Humorous Verse of Franklin P. Adams ("FPA"). The author's own selection of light verse, drawn from thirty years of FPA's column, "The Conning Tower," syndicated all over the English-speaking world. Witty, perceptive, literate, these ninety-six poems range from parodies of other poets, Millay, Longfellow, Edgar Guest, Kipling, Masefield, etc., and free and hilarious translations of Horace and other Latin poets, to satiric comments on fabled American institutions—the New York Subways, preposterous ads, suburbanites, sensational journalism, etc. They reveal with vigor and clarity the humor, integrity and restraint of a wise and gentle American satirist. Introduction by Robert Hutchinson. vi + 122pp. 5⅜ x 8½.
T108 Paperbound **$1.00**

SINGULAR TRAVELS, CAMPAIGNS, AND ADVENTURES OF BARON MUNCHAUSEN, R. E. Raspe, with 90 illustrations by Gustave Doré. The first edition in over 150 years to reestablish the deeds of the Prince of Liars exactly as Raspe first recorded them in 1785—the genuine Baron Munchausen, one of the most popular personalities in English literature. Included also are the best of the many sequels, written by other hands. Introduction on Raspe by J. Carswell. Bibliography of early editions. xliv + 192pp. 5⅜ x 8.
T698 Paperbound **$1.00**

THE WIT AND HUMOR OF OSCAR WILDE, ed. by Alvin Redman. Wilde at his most brilliant, in 1000 epigrams exposing weaknesses and hypocrisies of "civilized" society. Divided into 49 categories—sin, wealth, women, America, etc.—to aid writers, speakers. Includes excerpts from his trials, books, plays, criticism. Formerly "The Epigrams of Oscar Wilde." Introduction by Vyvyan Holland, Wilde's only living son. Introductory essay by editor. 260pp. 5⅜ x 8.
T602 Paperbound **$1.00**

MAX AND MORITZ, Wilhelm Busch. Busch is one of the great humorists of all time, as well as the father of the modern comic strip. This volume, translated by H. A. Klein and other hands, contains the perennial favorite "Max and Moritz" (translated by C. T. Brooks), Plisch and Plum, Das Rabennest, Eispeter, and seven other whimsical, sardonic, jovial, diabolical cartoon and verse stories. Lively English translations parallel the original German. This work has delighted millions, since it first appeared in the 19th century, and is guaranteed to please almost anyone. Edited by H. A. Klein, with an afterword. x + 205pp. 5⅝ x 8½.
T181 Paperbound **$1.15**

HYPOCRITICAL HELENA, Wilhelm Busch. A companion volume to "Max and Moritz," with the title piece (Die Fromme Helena) and 10 other highly amusing cartoon and verse stories, all newly translated by H. A. Klein and M. C. Klein: Adventure on New Year's Eve (Abenteuer in der Neujahrsnacht), Hangover on the Morning after New Year's Eve (Der Katzenjammer am Neujahrsmorgen), etc. English and German in parallel columns. Hours of pleasure, also a fine language aid. x + 205pp. 5⅝ x 8½.
T184 Paperbound **$1.00**

THE BEAR THAT WASN'T, Frank Tashlin. What does it mean? Is it simply delightful wry humor, or a charming story of a bear who wakes up in the midst of a factory, or a satire on Big Business, or an existential cartoon-story of the human condition, or a symbolization of the struggle between conformity and the individual? New York Herald Tribune said of the first edition: ". . . a fable for grownups that will be fun for children. Sit down with the book and get your own bearings." Long an underground favorite with readers of all ages and opinions. v + 51pp. Illustrated. 5⅜ x 8½.
T939 Paperbound **75¢**

RUTHLESS RHYMES FOR HEARTLESS HOMES and MORE RUTHLESS RHYMES FOR HEARTLESS HOMES, Harry Graham ("Col. D. Streamer"). Two volumes of Little Willy and 48 other poetic disasters. A bright, new reprint of oft-quoted, never forgotten, devastating humor by a precursor of today's "sick" joke school. For connoisseurs of wicked, wacky humor and all who delight in the comedy of manners. Original drawings are a perfect complement. 61 illustrations. Index. vi + 69pp. Two vols. bound as one. 5⅜ x 8½.
T930 Paperbound **75¢**

Say It language phrase books

These handy phrase books (128 to 196 pages each) make grammatical drills unnecessary for an elementary knowledge of a spoken foreign language. Covering most matters of travel and everyday life each volume contains:

Over 1000 phrases and sentences in immediately useful forms — foreign language plus English.

Modern usage designed for Americans. Specific phrases like, "Give me small change," and "Please call a taxi."

Simplified phonetic transcription you will be able to read at sight.

The only completely indexed phrase books on the market.

Covers scores of important situations: — Greetings, restaurants, sightseeing, useful expressions, etc.

These books are prepared by native linguists who are professors at Columbia, N.Y.U., Fordham and other great universities. Use them independently or with any other book or record course. They provide a supplementary living element that most other courses lack. Individual volumes in:

Russian 75¢	Italian 75¢	Spanish 75¢	German 75¢
Hebrew 75¢	Danish 75¢	Japanese 75¢	Swedish 75¢
Dutch 75¢	Esperanto 75¢	Modern Greek 75¢	Portuguese 75¢
Norwegian 75¢	Polish 75¢	French 75¢	Yiddish 75¢
Turkish 75¢		English for German-speaking people 75¢	
English for Italian-speaking people 75¢		English for Spanish-speaking people 75¢	

Large clear type. 128-196 pages each. 3½ x 5¼. Sturdy paper binding.

Listen and Learn language records

LISTEN & LEARN is the only language record course designed especially to meet your travel and everyday needs. It is available in separate sets for FRENCH, SPANISH, GERMAN, JAPANESE, RUSSIAN, MODERN GREEK, PORTUGUESE, ITALIAN and HEBREW, and each set contains three 33⅓ rpm long-playing records—1½ hours of recorded speech by eminent native speakers who are professors at Columbia, New York University, Queens College.

Check the following special features found only in LISTEN & LEARN:

- **Dual-language recording. 812 selected phrases and sentences,** over 3200 words, spoken first in English, then in their foreign language equivalents. A suitable pause follows each foreign phrase, allowing you time to repeat the expression. You learn by unconscious assimilation.
- **128 to 206-page manual** contains everything on the records, plus a simple phonetic pronunciation guide.
- **Indexed for convenience. The only set on the market** that is completely indexed. No more puzzling over where to find the phrase you need. Just look in the rear of the manual.
- **Practical.** No time wasted on material you can find in any grammar. LISTEN & LEARN covers central core material with phrase approach. Ideal for the person with limited learning time.
- **Living, modern expressions,** not found in other courses. Hygienic products, modern equipment, shopping—expressions used every day, like "nylon" and "air-conditioned."
- **Limited objective.** Everything you learn, no matter where you stop, is immediately useful. You have to finish other courses, wade through grammar and vocabulary drill, before they help you.
- **High-fidelity recording.** LISTEN & LEARN records equal in clarity and surface-silence any record on the market costing up to $6.

"Excellent . . . the spoken records . . . impress me as being among the very best on the market," **Prof. Mario Pei,** Dept. of Romance Languages, Columbia University. "Inexpensive and well-done . . . it would make an ideal present," CHICAGO SUNDAY TRIBUNE. "More genuinely helpful than anything of its kind which I have previously encountered," **Sidney Clark,** well-known author of "ALL THE BEST" travel books.

UNCONDITIONAL GUARANTEE. Try LISTEN & LEARN, then return it within 10 days for full refund if you are not satisfied.

Each set contains three twelve-inch 33⅓ records, manual, and album.

SPANISH	the set $5.95	GERMAN	the set $5.95
FRENCH	the set $5.95	ITALIAN	the set $5.95
RUSSIAN	the set $5.95	JAPANESE	the set $5.95
PORTUGUESE	the set $5.95	MODERN GREEK	the set $5.95
MODERN HEBREW	the set $5.95		

Americana

THE EYES OF DISCOVERY, J. Bakeless. A vivid reconstruction of how unspoiled America appeared to the first white men. Authentic and enlightening accounts of Hudson's landing in New York, Coronado's trek through the Southwest; scores of explorers, settlers, trappers, soldiers. America's pristine flora, fauna, and Indians in every region and state in fresh and unusual new aspects. "A fascinating view of what the land was like before the first highway went through," Time. 68 contemporary illustrations, 39 newly added in this edition. Index. Bibliography. x + 500pp. 5⅜ x 8. T761 Paperbound **$2.00**

AUDUBON AND HIS JOURNALS, J. J. Audubon. A collection of fascinating accounts of Europe and America in the early 1800's through Audubon's own eyes. Includes the Missouri River Journals —an eventful trip through America's untouched heartland, the Labrador Journals, the European Journals, the famous "Episodes", and other rare Audubon material, including the descriptive chapters from the original letterpress edition of the "Ornithological Studies", omitted in all later editions. Indispensable for ornithologists, naturalists, and all lovers of Americana and adventure. 70-page biography by Audubon's granddaughter. 38 illustrations. Index. Total of 1106pp. 5⅜ x 8.
T675 Vol I Paperbound **$2.25**
T676 Vol II Paperbound **$2.25**
The set **$4.50**

TRAVELS OF WILLIAM BARTRAM, edited by Mark Van Doren. The first inexpensive illustrated edition of one of the 18th century's most delightful books is an excellent source of first-hand material on American geography, anthropology, and natural history. Many descriptions of early Indian tribes are our only source of information on them prior to the infiltration of the white man. "The mind of a scientist with the soul of a poet," John Livingston Lowes. 13 original illustrations and maps. Edited with an introduction by Mark Van Doren. 448pp. 5⅜ x 8.
T13 Paperbound **$2.00**

GARRETS AND PRETENDERS: A HISTORY OF BOHEMIANISM IN AMERICA, A. Parry. The colorful and fantastic history of American Bohemianism from Poe to Kerouac. This is the only complete record of hoboes, cranks, starving poets, and suicides. Here are Pfaff, Whitman, Crane, Bierce, Pound, and many others. New chapters by the author and by H. T. Moore bring this thorough and well-documented history down to the Beatniks. "An excellent account," N. Y. Times. Scores of cartoons, drawings, and caricatures. Bibliography. Index. xxviii + 421pp. 5⅝ x 8⅜. T708 Paperbound **$1.95**

THE EXPLORATION OF THE COLORADO RIVER AND ITS CANYONS, J. W. Powell. The thrilling first-hand account of the expedition that filled in the last white space on the map of the United States. Rapids, famine, hostile Indians, and mutiny are among the perils encountered as the unknown Colorado Valley reveals its secrets. This is the only uncut version of Major Powell's classic of exploration that has been printed in the last 60 years. Includes later reflections and subsequent expedition. 250 illustrations, new map. 400pp. 5⅝ x 8⅜.
T94 Paperbound **$2.25**

THE JOURNAL OF HENRY D. THOREAU, Edited by Bradford Torrey and Francis H. Allen. Henry Thoreau is not only one of the most important figures in American literature and social thought; his voluminous journals (from which his books emerged as selections and crystallizations) constitute both the longest, most sensitive record of personal internal development and a most penetrating description of a historical moment in American culture. This present set, which was first issued in fourteen volumes, contains Thoreau's entire journals from 1837 to 1862, with the exception of the lost years which were found only recently. We are reissuing it, complete and unabridged, with a new introduction by Walter Harding, Secretary of the Thoreau Society. Fourteen volumes reissued in two volumes. Foreword by Henry Seidel Canby. Total of 1888pp. 8⅜ x 12¼. T312-3 Two volume set, Clothbound **$20.00**

GAMES AND SONGS OF AMERICAN CHILDREN, collected by William Wells Newell. A remarkable collection of 190 games with songs that accompany many of them; cross references to show similarities, differences among them; variations; musical notation for 38 songs. Textual discussions show relations with folk-drama and other aspects of folk tradition. Grouped into categories for ready comparative study: Love-games, histories, playing at work, human life, bird and beast, mythology, guessing-games, etc. New introduction covers relations of songs and dances to timeless heritage of folklore, biographical sketch of Newell, other pertinent data. A good source of inspiration for those in charge of groups of children and a valuable reference for anthropologists, sociologists, psychiatrists. Introduction by Carl Withers. New indexes of first lines, games. 5⅜ x 8½. xii + 242pp. T354 Paperbound **$1.75**

Art, History of Art, Antiques, Graphic Arts, Handcrafts

ART STUDENTS' ANATOMY, E. J. Farris. Outstanding art anatomy that uses chiefly living objects for its illustrations. 71 photos of undraped men, women, children are accompanied by carefully labeled matching sketches to illustrate the skeletal system, articulations and movements, bony landmarks, the muscular system, skin, fasciae, fat, etc. 9 x-ray photos show movement of joints. Undraped models are shown in such actions as serving in tennis, drawing a bow in archery, playing football, dancing, preparing to spring and to dive. Also discussed and illustrated are proportions, age and sex differences, the anatomy of the smile, etc. 8 plates by the great early 18th century anatomic illustrator Siegfried Albinus are also included. Glossary. 158 figures, 7 in color. x + 159pp. 5⅝ x 8⅜.   T744 Paperbound **$1.50**

AN ATLAS OF ANATOMY FOR ARTISTS, F Schider. A new 3rd edition of this standard text enlarged by 52 new illustrations of hands, anatomical studies by Cloquet, and expressive life studies of the body by Barcsay. 189 clear, detailed plates offer you precise information of impeccable accuracy. 29 plates show all aspects of the skeleton, with closeups of special areas, while 54 full-page plates, mostly in two colors, give human musculature as seen from four different points of view, with cutaways for important portions of the body. 14 full-page plates provide photographs of hand forms, eyelids, female breasts, and indicate the location of muscles upon models. 59 additional plates show how great artists of the past utilized human anatomy. They reproduce sketches and finished work by such artists as Michelangelo, Leonardo da Vinci, Goya, and 15 others. This is a lifetime reference work which will be one of the most important books in any artist's library. "The standard reference tool," AMERICAN LIBRARY ASSOCIATION. "Excellent," AMERICAN ARTIST. Third enlarged edition. 189 plates, 647 illustrations. xxvi + 192pp. 7⅞ x 10⅝.   T241 Clothbound **$6.00**

AN ATLAS OF ANIMAL ANATOMY FOR ARTISTS, W. Ellenberger, H. Baum, H. Dittrich. The largest, richest animal anatomy for artists available in English. 99 detailed anatomical plates of such animals as the horse, dog, cat, lion, deer, seal, kangaroo, flying squirrel, cow, bull, goat, monkey, hare, and bat. Surface features are clearly indicated, while progressive beneath-the-skin pictures show musculature, tendons, and bone structure. Rest and action are exhibited in terms of musculature and skeletal structure and detailed cross-sections are given for heads and important features. The animals chosen are representative of specific families so that a study of these anatomies will provide knowledge of hundreds of related species. "Highly recommended as one of the very few books on the subject worthy of being used as an authoritative guide," DESIGN. "Gives a fundamental knowledge," AMERICAN ARTIST. Second revised, enlarged edition with new plates from Cuvier, Stubbs, etc. 288 illustrations. 153pp. 11⅜ x 9.   T82 Clothbound **$6.00**

THE HUMAN FIGURE IN MOTION, Eadweard Muybridge. The largest selection in print of Muybridge's famous high-speed action photos of the human figure in motion. 4789 photographs illustrate 162 different actions: men, women, children—mostly undraped—are shown walking, running, carrying various objects, sitting, lying down, climbing, throwing, arising, and performing over 150 other actions. Some actions are shown in as many as 150 photographs each. All in all there are more than 500 action strips in this enormous volume, series shots taken at shutter speeds of as high as 1/6000th of a second! These are not posed shots, but true stopped motion. They show bone and muscle in situations that the human eye is not fast enough to capture. Earlier, smaller editions of these prints have brought $40 and more on the out-of-print market. "A must for artists," ART IN FOCUS. "An unparalleled dictionary of action for all artists," AMERICAN ARTIST. 390 full-page plates, with 4789 photographs. Printed on heavy glossy stock. Reinforced binding with headbands. xxi + 390pp. 7⅞ x 10⅝.   T204 Clothbound **$10.00**

ANIMALS IN MOTION, Eadweard Muybridge. This is the largest collection of animal action photos in print. 34 different animals (horses, mules, oxen, goats, camels, pigs, cats, guanacos, lions, gnus, deer, monkeys, eagles—and 21 others) in 132 characteristic actions. The horse alone is shown in more than 40 different actions. All 3919 photographs are taken in series at speeds up to 1/6000th of a second. The secrets of leg motion, spinal patterns, head movements, strains and contortions shown nowhere else are captured. You will see exactly how a lion sets his foot down; how an elephant's knees are like a human's—and how they differ; the position of a kangaroo's legs in mid-leap; how an ostrich's head bobs; details of the flight of birds—and thousands of facets of motion only the fastest cameras can catch. Photographed from domestic animals and animals in the Philadelphia zoo, it contains neither semiposed artificial shots nor distorted telephoto shots taken under adverse conditions. Artists, biologists, decorators, cartoonists, will find this book indispensable for understanding animals in motion. "A really marvelous series of plates," NATURE (London). "The dry plate's most spectacular early use was by Eadweard Muybridge," LIFE. 3919 photographs; 380 full pages of plates. 440pp. Printed on heavy glossy paper. Deluxe binding with headbands. 7⅞ x 10⅝.   T203 Clothbound **$10.00**

THE AUTOBIOGRAPHY OF AN IDEA, Louis Sullivan. The pioneer architect whom Frank Lloyd Wright called "the master" reveals an acute sensitivity to social forces and values in this passionately honest account. He records the crystallization of his opinions and theories, the growth of his organic theory of architecture that still influences American designers and architects, contemporary ideas, etc. This volume contains the first appearance of 34 full-page plates of his finest architecture. Unabridged reissue of 1924 edition. New introduction by R. M. Line. Index. xiv + 335pp. 5⅜ x 8. T281 Paperbound **$2.00**

THE DRAWINGS OF HEINRICH KLEY. The first uncut republication of both of Kley's devastating sketchbooks, which first appeared in pre-World War I Germany. One of the greatest cartoonists and social satirists of modern times, his exuberant and iconoclastic fantasy and his extraordinary technique place him in the great tradition of Bosch, Breughel, and Goya, while his subject matter has all the immediacy and tension of our century. 200 drawings. viii + 128pp. 7¾ x 10¾. T24 Paperbound **$1.85**

MORE DRAWINGS BY HEINRICH KLEY. All the sketches from Leut' Und Viecher (1912) and Sammel-Album (1923) not included in the previous Dover edition of Drawings. More of the bizarre, mercilessly iconoclastic sketches that shocked and amused on their original publication. Nothing was too sacred, no one too eminent for satirization by this imaginative, individual and accomplished master cartoonist. A total of 158 illustrations. lv + 104pp. 7¾ x 10¾. T41 Paperbound **$1.85**

PINE FURNITURE OF EARLY NEW ENGLAND, R. H. Kettell. A rich understanding of one of America's most original folk arts that collectors of antiques, interior decorators, craftsmen, woodworkers, and everyone interested in American history and art will find fascinating and immensely useful. 413 illustrations of more than 300 chairs, benches, racks, beds, cupboards, mirrors, shelves, tables, and other furniture will show all the simple beauty and character of early New England furniture. 55 detailed drawings carefully analyze outstanding pieces. "With its rich store of illustrations, this book emphasizes the individuality and varied design of early American pine furniture. It should be welcomed," ANTIQUES. 413 illustrations and 55 working drawings. 475. 8 x 10¾. T145 Clothbound **$10.00**

THE HUMAN FIGURE, J. H. Vanderpoel. Every important artistic element of the human figure is pointed out in minutely detailed word descriptions in this classic text and illustrated as well in 430 pencil and charcoal drawings. Thus the text of this book directs your attention to all the characteristic features and subtle differences of the male and female (adults, children, and aged persons), as though a master artist were telling you what to look for at each stage. 2nd edition, revised and enlarged by George Bridgman. Foreword. 430 illustrations. 143pp. 6⅛ x 9¼. T432 Paperbound **$1.50**

LETTERING AND ALPHABETS, J. A. Cavanagh. This unabridged reissue of LETTERING offers a full discussion, analysis, illustration of 89 basic hand lettering styles — styles derived from Caslons, Bodonis, Garamonds, Gothic, Black Letter, Oriental, and many others. Upper and lower cases, numerals and common signs pictured. Hundreds of technical hints on make-up, construction, artistic validity, strokes, pens, brushes, white areas, etc. May be reproduced without permission! 89 complete alphabets; 72 lettered specimens. 121pp. 9¾ x 8. T53 Paperbound **$1.35**

STICKS AND STONES, Lewis Mumford. A survey of the forces that have conditioned American architecture and altered its forms. The author discusses the medieval tradition in early New England villages; the Renaissance influence which developed with the rise of the merchant class; the classical influence of Jefferson's time; the "Mechanicsvilles" of Poe's generation; the Brown Decades; the philosophy of the Imperial facade; and finally the modern machine age. "A truly remarkable book," SAT. REV. OF LITERATURE. 2nd revised edition. 21 illustrations. xvii + 228pp. 5⅜ x 8. T202 Paperbound **$1.65**

THE STANDARD BOOK OF QUILT MAKING AND COLLECTING, Marguerite Ickis. A complete easy-to-follow guide with all the information you need to make beautiful, useful quilts. How to plan, design, cut, sew, appliqué, avoid sewing problems, use rag bag, make borders, tuft, every other aspect. Over 100 traditional quilts shown, including over 40 full-size patterns. At-home hobby for fun, profit. Index. 483 illus. 1 color plate. 287pp. 6¾ x 9½. T582 Paperbound **$2.00**

THE BOOK OF SIGNS, Rudolf Koch. Formerly $20 to $25 on the out-of-print market, now only $1.00 in this unabridged new edition! 493 symbols from ancient manuscripts, medieval cathedrals, coins, catacombs, pottery, etc. Crosses, monograms of Roman emperors, astrological, chemical, botanical, runes, housemarks, and 7 other categories. Invaluable for handicraft workers, illustrators, scholars, etc., this material may be reproduced without permission. 493 illustrations by Fritz Kredel. 104pp. 6½ x 9¼. T162 Paperbound **$1.00**

PRIMITIVE ART, Franz Boas. This authoritative and exhaustive work by a great American anthropologist covers the entire gamut of primitive art. Pottery, leatherwork, metal work, stone work, wood, basketry, are treated in detail. Theories of primitive art, historical depth in art history, technical virtuosity, unconscious levels of patterning, symbolism, styles, literature, music, dance, etc. A must book for the interested layman, the anthropologist, artist, handicrafter (hundreds of unusual motifs), and the historian. Over 900 illustrations (50 ceramic vessels, 12 totem poles, etc.). 376pp. 5⅜ x 8. T25 Paperbound **$2.00**

Fiction

THE LAND THAT TIME FORGOT and THE MOON MAID, Edgar Rice Burroughs. In the opinion of many, Burroughs' best work. The first concerns a strange island where evolution is individual rather than phylogenetic. Speechless anthropoids develop into intelligent human beings within a single generation. The second projects the reader far into the future and describes the first voyage to the Moon (in the year 2025), the conquest of the Earth by the Moon, and years of violence and adventure as the enslaved Earthmen try to regain possession of their planet. "An imaginative tour de force that keeps the reader keyed up and expectant," NEW YORK TIMES. Complete, unabridged text of the original two novels (three parts in each). 5 illustrations by J. Allen St. John. vi + 552pp. 5⅜ x 8½.

T1020 Clothbound **$3.75**
T358 Paperbound **$2.00**

AT THE EARTH'S CORE, PELLUCIDAR, TANAR OF PELLUCIDAR: THREE SCIENCE FICTION NOVELS BY EDGAR RICE BURROUGHS. Complete, unabridged texts of the first three Pellucidar novels. Tales of derring-do by the famous master of science fiction. The locale for these three related stories is the inner surface of the hollow Earth where we discover the world of Pellucidar, complete with all types of bizarre, menacing creatures, strange peoples, and alluring maidens—guaranteed to delight all Burroughs fans and a wide circle of adventure lovers. Illustrated by J. Allen St. John and P. F. Berdanier. vi + 433pp. 5⅜ x 8½.

T1051 Paperbound **$2.00**

THREE MARTIAN NOVELS, Edgar Rice Burroughs. Contains: Thuvia, Maid of Mars; The Chessmen of Mars; and The Master Mind of Mars. High adventure set in an imaginative and intricate conception of the Red Planet. Mars is peopled with an intelligent, heroic human race which lives in densely populated cities and with fierce barbarians who inhabit dead sea bottoms. Other exciting creatures abound amidst an inventive framework of Martian history and geography. Complete unabridged reprintings of the first edition. 16 illustrations by J. Allen St. John. vi + 499pp. 5⅜ x 8½.

T39 Paperbound **$1.85**

TO THE SUN? and OFF ON A COMET!, Jules Verne. Complete texts of two of the most imaginative flights into fancy in world literature display the high adventure that have kept Verne's novels read for nearly a century. Only unabridged edition of the best translation, by Edward Roth. Large, easily readable type. 50 illustrations selected from first editions. 462pp. 5⅜ x 8.

T634 Paperbound **$1.75**

FROM THE EARTH TO THE MOON and ALL AROUND THE MOON, Jules Verne. Complete editions of two of Verne's most successful novels, in finest Edward Roth translations, now available after many years out of print. Verne's visions of submarines, airplanes, television, rockets, interplanetary travel; of scientific and not-so-scientific beliefs; of peculiarities of Americans; all delight and engross us today as much as when they first appeared. Large, easily readable type. 42 illus. from first French edition. 476pp. 5⅜ x 8.

T633 Paperbound **$1.75**

THREE PROPHETIC NOVELS BY H. G. WELLS, edited by E. F. Bleiler. Complete texts of "When the Sleeper Wakes" (1st book printing in 50 years), "A Story of the Days to Come," "The Time Machine" (1st complete printing in book form). Exciting adventures in the future are as enjoyable today as 50 years ago when first printed. Predict TV, movies, intercontinental airplanes, prefabricated houses, air-conditioned cities, etc. First important author to foresee problems of mind control, technological dictatorships. "Absolute best of imaginative fiction," N. Y. Times. Introduction. 335pp. 5⅜ x 8.

T605 Paperbound **$1.50**

SEVEN SCIENCE FICTION NOVELS, H. G. Wells. Full unabridged texts of 7 science-fiction novels of the master. Ranging from biology, physics, chemistry, astronomy to sociology and other studies, Mr. Wells extrapolates whole worlds of strange and intriguing character. "One will have to go far to match this for entertainment, excitement, and sheer pleasure . . . ," NEW YORK TIMES. Contents: The Time Machine, The Island of Dr. Moreau, First Men in the Moon, The Invisible Man, The War of the Worlds, The Food of the Gods, In the Days of the Comet. 1015pp. 5⅜ x 8.

T264 Clothbound **$4.50**

28 SCIENCE FICTION STORIES OF H. G. WELLS. Two full unabridged novels, MEN LIKE GODS and STAR BEGOTTEN, plus 26 short stories by the master science-fiction writer of all time. Stories of space, time, invention, exploration, future adventure—an indispensable part of the library of everyone interested in science and adventure. PARTIAL CONTENTS: Men Like Gods, The Country of the Blind, In the Abyss, The Crystal Egg, The Man Who Could Work Miracles, A Story of the Days to Come, The Valley of Spiders, and 21 more! 928pp. 5⅜ x 8.

T265 Clothbound **$4.50**

THE WAR IN THE AIR, IN THE DAYS OF THE COMET, THE FOOD OF THE GODS: THREE SCIENCE FICTION NOVELS BY H. G. WELLS. Three exciting Wells offerings bearing on vital social and philosophical issues of his and our own day. Here are tales of air power, strategic bombing, East vs. West, the potential miracles of science, the potential disasters from outer space, the relationship between scientific advancement and moral progress, etc. First reprinting of "War in the Air" in almost 50 years. An excellent sampling of Wells at his storytelling best. Complete, unabridged reprintings. 16 illustrations. 645pp. 5⅜ x 8½.

T1135 Paperbound **$2.00**

Music

A GENERAL HISTORY OF MUSIC, Charles Burney. A detailed coverage of music from the Greeks up to 1789, with full information on all types of music: sacred and secular, vocal and instrumental, operatic and symphonic. Theory, notation, forms, instruments, innovators, composers, performers, typical and important works, and much more in an easy, entertaining style. Burney covered much of Europe and spoke with hundreds of authorities and composers so that this work is more than a compilation of records . . . it is a living work of careful and first-hand scholarship. Its account of thoroughbass (18th century) Italian music is probably still the best introduction on the subject. A recent NEW YORK TIMES review said, "Surprisingly few of Burney's statements have been invalidated by modern research . . . still of great value." Edited and corrected by Frank Mercer. 35 figures. Indices. 1915pp. 5⅜ x 8. 2 volumes. T36 The Set, Clothbound **$12.50**

A DICTIONARY OF HYMNOLOGY, John Julian. This exhaustive and scholarly work has become known as an invaluable source of hundreds of thousands of important and often difficult to obtain facts on the history and use of hymns in the western world. Everyone interested in hymns will be fascinated by the accounts of famous hymns and hymn writers and amazed by the amount of practical information he will find. More than 30,000 entries on individual hymns, giving authorship, date and circumstances of composition, publication, textual variations, translations, denominational and ritual usage, etc. Biographies of more than 9,000 hymn writers, and essays on important topics such as Christmas carols and children's hymns, and much other unusual and valuable information. A 200 page double-columned index of first lines — the largest in print. Total of 1786 pages in two reinforced clothbound volumes. 6¼ x 9¼. The set, T333 Clothbound **$17.50**

MUSIC IN MEDIEVAL BRITAIN, F. Ll. Harrison. The most thorough, up-to-date, and accurate treatment of the subject ever published, beautifully illustrated. Complete account of institutions and choirs; carols, masses, and motets; liturgy and plainsong; and polyphonic music from the Norman Conquest to the Reformation. Discusses the various schools of music and their reciprocal influences; the origin and development of new ritual forms; development and use of instruments; and new evidence on many problems of the period. Reproductions of scores, over 200 excerpts from medieval melodies. Rules of harmony and dissonance; influence of Continental styles; great composers (Dunstable, Cornysh, Fairfax, etc.); and much more. Register and index of more than 400 musicians. Index of titles. General Index. 225-item bibliography. 6 Appendices. xix + 491pp. 5⅝ x 8¾. T705 Clothbound **$10.00**

THE MUSIC OF SPAIN, Gilbert Chase. Only book in English to give concise, comprehensive account of Iberian music; new Chapter covers music since 1941. Victoria, Albéniz, Cabezón, Pedrell, Turina, hundreds of other composers; popular and folk music; the Gypsies; the guitar; dance, theatre, opera, with only extensive discussion in English of the Zarzuela; virtuosi such as Casals; much more. "Distinguished . . . readable," Saturday Review. 400-item bibliography. Index. 27 photos. 383pp. 5⅜ x 8. T549 Paperbound **$2.00**

ON STUDYING SINGING, Sergius Kagen. An intelligent method of voice-training, which leads you around pitfalls that waste your time, money, and effort. Exposes rigid, mechanical systems, baseless theories, deleterious exercises. "Logical, clear, convincing . . . dead right," Virgil Thomson, N.Y. Herald Tribune. "I recommend this volume highly," Maggie Teyte, Saturday Review. 119pp. 5⅜ x 8. T622 Paperbound **$1.25**

Prices subject to change without notice.

Dover publishes books on art, music, philosophy, literature, languages, history, social sciences, psychology, handcrafts, orientalia, puzzles and entertainments, chess, pets and gardens, books explaining science, intermediate and higher mathematics, mathematical physics, engineering, biological sciences, earth sciences, classics of science, etc. Write to:

Dept. catrr.
Dover Publications, Inc.
180 Varick Street, N.Y. 14, N.Y.